Apache Solr Beginner's Guide

Configure your own search engine experience with
real-world data with this practical guide to Apache Solr

Alfredo Serafini

[PACKT] open source *
PUBLISHING   community experience distilled

BIRMINGHAM - MUMBAI

Apache Solr Beginner's Guide

First published: December 2013

Production Reference: 1181213

Published by Packt Publishing Ltd.
Livery Place
35 Livery Street
Birmingham B3 2PB, UK.

ISBN 978-1-78216-252-0

www.packtpub.com

Cover Image by Gorkee Bhardwaj (afterglowpictures@gmail.com)

Credits

Author

Alfredo Serafini

Reviewers

John Fiala

Jeevanandam M.

Greg Rundlett

Param Sethi

Acquisition Editor

Sam Birch

Andrew Duckworth

Lead Technical Editor

Balaji Naidu

Copy Editors

Roshni Banerjee

Janbal Dharmaraj

Dipti Kapadia

Kirti Pai

Alfida Paiva

Laxmi Subramanian

Technical Editors

Krishnaveni Haridas

Aman Preet Singh

Project Coordinator

Suraj Bist

Proofreaders

Lawrence A. Herman

Clyde Jenkins

Indexer

Hemangini Bari

Graphics

Ronak Dhruv

Production Coordinator

Aparna Bhagat

Cover Work

Aparna Bhagat

About the Author

Alfredo Serafini is a freelance software consultant, currently living in Rome, Italy.

He has a mixed background. He has a bachelor's degree in Computer Science Engineering (2003, with a thesis on Music Information Retrieval), and he has completed a professional master's course in Sound Engineering (2007, with a thesis on gestural interface to MAX/MSP platform).

From 2003 to 2006, he had been involved as a consultant and developer at Artificial Intelligence Research at Tor Vergata (ART) group. During this experience, he got his first chance to play with the Lucene library. Since then he has been working as a freelancer, alternating between working as a teacher of programming languages, a mentor for small companies on topics like Information Retrieval and Linked Data, and (not surprisingly) as a software engineer.

He is currently a Linked Open Data enthusiast. He has also had a lot of interaction with the Scala language as well as graph and network databases.

You can find more information about his activities on his website, titled *designed to be unfinished,* at `http://www.seralf.it/`.

Acknowledgments

This is my first book, and I was out of my mind when I thought about writing an entire book in English, which is not my native language. Now it's done, and I have to thank all the people from Packt Publishing who have worked hard on this project, and for their huge patience in tolerating my bad attitude with schedules, formatting, and weird errors. I am thankful to them for their kindness and for always giving me the best suggestions. All the responsibility for some disjointed phrase, or some errors that survived the revisions, should be attributed only to me.

I also want to thank all the people on the Solr or Lucene mailing list. People who find and share solutions on a day-to-day basis without having the time to write a book. I have tried to cite every idea that comes to me by external, direct, or indirect suggestions, but as you see it's almost impossible. I've found inspiration from the books of David Smiley, Eric Pughs, and Jack Krupansky, and also from the huge contributions by the LucidWorks company, starting with the new reference guide.

I also want to thank professor Roberto Basili, who introduced me to this field some years ago.

I know I have probably oversimplified some of the more advanced topics, in order to expose readers to a broader vision of the context in which this technology exists. But when conducting technical courses I have learned that people often need to share ideas in order to construct their own path into a practical knowledge. So I thank you in advance for every time you'll want to share this read with your teammates, integrating different knowledge and points of view, exploring these topics outside an approach oriented merely to the technical features.

I want to give all my gratitude to my beloved father, who taught me to respect other's people work, and to my mother and sister for their constant trust in me. Also, I want to thank my friends for their support. However, this is only the first step, and I am supposed to do better in future with a little help from my friends.

About the Reviewers

Jeevanandam M. is a software architect and programmer living in India. He realized his passion for programming in the ninth grade and loves computers. Ever since, he has been enjoying every moment he spent with computers, programming and designing. In April 2011, he began blogging at `http://myjeeva.com` and actively contributing to open source communities, sometimes personally through `http://github.com/jeevatkm`.

He works for HCL Technologies as a Technical Architect; he was a campus recruit from SRM University, Chennai, India. He is a technology enthusiast and has expertise in Enterprise Search Platform (ESP), Web Content Management and Digital Asset Management, CDN, Cloud Enablement, BigData, Application Modelling and Proof of Concepts & Prototype space; he also has industry knowledge on publishing, education, Local Marketing Solutions, e-learning and LMS, and the editorial domain.

Greg Rundlett is the founder of eQuality Technology, a company that offers enterprise grade solutions to small and medium-sized companies. He is a long time free software advocate. He is active in the local community, and he participates in groups such as the Boston Linux User Group and Greater New Hampshire Linux User Group. Greg has also written for the Linux Pro magazine. He lives with his two sons in Salisbury, MA.

> I'd like to thank my friends and family for their love and inspiration that keeps me grounded, but always inspires me to reach for the stars.

Param Sethi is a software developer with more than eight years of experience in designing, architecture, and developing highly scalable Web applications with a user base of more than half a billion. She has worked in backend and middle layer technologies for most of her career. She has worked on Core Java, J2EE, MySQL, Oracle, Apache Solr, Tomcat, XML, and JSON, and she recently started working on C#, ASP.net, JavaScript, and IIS. She is enthusiastic about working in Research and Development and the latest technologies. Apart from professional contributions, she is a passionate blogger and keeps a technical blog at `http://params.me` for sharing her experience in the tech space. She also provides professional guidance to budding engineers. Outside of her professional interests, she travels widely, reads, writes, snorkels, and enjoys living in California with her family. In her own words, "I feel the journey is what makes you feel the importance of the destination."

Param moved to northern California a couple of years ago for a new gig in Silicon Valley, working for a major tech company. Prior to sunny California, she was working in Virginia on Big Data Analytics. Her work involved examining large amounts of data of various types to uncover hidden patterns, unknown correlations, and other useful information, which provided competitive advantages over rival organizations and resulted in business benefits. Earlier, she worked on designing REST APIs for various web applications, and these were used across many teams in the company for providing secure data information. She was a cultural ambassador at her previous company and received the Star Performer and Star Performer Team awards for her technical contributions.

www.PacktPub.com

Support files, eBooks, discount offers and more

You might want to visit www.PacktPub.com for support files and downloads related to your book.

Did you know that Packt offers eBook versions of every book published, with PDF and ePub files available? You can upgrade to the eBook version at www.PacktPub.com and as a print book customer, you are entitled to a discount on the eBook copy. Get in touch with us at service@packtpub.com for more details.

At www.PacktPub.com, you can also read a collection of free technical articles, sign up for a range of free newsletters and receive exclusive discounts and offers on Packt books and eBooks.

PACKTLiB™

http://PacktLib.PacktPub.com

Do you need instant solutions to your IT questions? PacktLib is Packt's online digital book library. Here, you can access, read and search across Packt's entire library of books.

Why Subscribe?

- Fully searchable across every book published by Packt
- Copy and paste, print and bookmark content
- On demand and accessible via web browser

Free Access for Packt account holders

If you have an account with Packt at www.PacktPub.com, you can use this to access PacktLib today and view nine entirely free books. Simply use your login credentials for immediate access.

Table of Contents

Preface

If you need to add search capabilities to your server or application, you probably need Apache Solr. This is an enterprise search server, which is designed to develop good search experiences for the users. A search experience should include common full-text keyword-based search, spellchecking, autosuggestion, and recommendations and highlighting. But Solr does even more. It provides faceted search, and it can help us shape a user experience that is centered on faceted navigation. The evolution of the platform is open to integration, ranging from Named Entity Recognition to document clustering based on the topic similarities between different documents in a collection.

However, this book is not a comprehensive guide to all its technical features, instead, it is designed to introduce you to very simple, practical, easy-to-follow examples of the essential features. You can follow the examples step-by-step and discuss them with your team if you want. The chapters follow a narrative path, from the basics to the introduction of more complex topics, in order to give you a wide view of the context and suggest to you where to move next.

The examples will then use real data about paintings collected from DBpedia, data from the Web Gallery of Arts site, and the recently released free dataset from the Tate gallery. These examples are a good playground for experimentation because they contain lots of information, intuitive metadata, and even errors and noises that can be used for realistic testing. I hope you will have fun working with those, but you will also see how to index your own rich document (PDF, Word, or others). So, you will also be able to use your own data for the examples, if you want.

What this book covers

Chapter 1, *Getting Ready with the Essentials*, introduces Solr. We'll cite some well-known sites that are already using features and patterns we'd like to be able to manage with Solr. You'll also see how to install Java, Solr, and cURL and verify that everything is working fine with the first simple query.

Chapter 2, Indexing with Local PDF Files, explains briefly how a Lucene index is made. The core concepts such as inverted index, document, field, and tokenization will be introduced. You'll see how to write a basic configuration and test it over real data, indexing the PDF files directly. At the end, there is a small list of useful commands that can be used during the development and the maintenance of a Solr index.

Chapter 3, Indexing Example Data from DBpedia – Paintings, explains how to design an entity, and introduces the core types and concepts useful for writing a schema. You will write a basic text analysis, see how to post a new document using JSON, and acquire practical knowledge on how the update process works. Finally, you'll have the chance to create an index on real data collected from DBpedia.

Chapter 4, Searching the Example Data, covers the basic and most important Solr query parameters. You'll also see how to use the HTTP query parameter by simulating remote queries with cURL. You'll see some basic type of queries, analyze the structure of the results, and see how to handle results in some commonly used ways.

Chapter 5, Extending Search, introduces different and more flexible query parsers, which can be used with the default Lucene one. You will see how to debug the different parsers. Also, you'll start using more advanced query components, for example, highlighting, spellchecking, and spatial search.

Chapter 6, Using Faceted Search – from Searching to Finding, introduces faceted search with different practical examples. You'll see how facets can be used to support the user experience for searches, as well as for exposing the suggestions useful for raw data analysis. Very common concepts such as matching and similarity will be introduced and will be used for practical examples on recommendation. You'll also work with filtering and grouping terms, and see how a query is actually parsed.

Chapter 7, Working with Multiple Entities, Multicores, and Distributed Search, explains how to work with a distributed search. We will focus not only on how to use multiple cores on a local machine, but also on the pros and cons of using multiple entities on a single denormalized index. Eventually, we will be performing data analysis on that. You will also analyze different strategies from a single index to a SolrCloud distributed search.

Chapter 8, Indexing External Data Sources, covers different practical examples of using the DataImportHandler components for indexing different data sources. You'll work with data from a relational database, and from the data collected before, as well as from remote sources on the Web by combining multiple sources in a single example.

Chapter 9, Introducing Customizations, explains how to customize text analysis for a specific language, and how to start writing new components using a language supported on the JVM. In particular, we'll see how how it is simple to write a very basic Named Entity Recognizer for adding annotations into the text, and how to adopt an HTML5-compliant template directly as an alternate response writer. The examples will be presented using Java and Scala, and they will be tested using JUnit and Maven.

Appendix, *Solr Clients and Integrations*, introduces a short list of technologies that are currently using Solr, from CMS to external applications. You'll also see how Solr can be embedded inside a Java (or JVM) application, and how it's also possible to write a custom client combining SolrJ and one of the languages supported on the JVM.

What you need for this book

The prerequisites are as follows:

- A working Java installation, JDK release. A Java 1.5+ should be good. I suggest using the Oracle Java 1.7, which is the current one at the time of writing this book.

- Apache Solr 4.5.

- The examples are available at `https://bitbucket.org/seralf/ solrstarterbook`.

- The cURL tool, which will be used for most of the examples.

- A working installation of Maven if you want to use the projects containing the code examples for customizations that are exposed in *Chapter 9*, *Introducing Customizations*. This is optional.

- A Scala installation if you want to reproduce some of the scripts for downloading data from DBpedia. This is optional.

Who this book is for

This book is for anyone who wants to explore Solr from its basic concepts and operations to acquire a practical knowledge of how to use its features. Every example is designed to focus on a single argument. I suggest that you read this book with your team if possible, and create your own examples using your data—following and combining the configurations proposed.

The book contains very small and simple code scripts. It is designed to be used as an introduction even for people who have little or even no specific experience in programming. Thus, the only chapter that contains extensive programming examples is *Chapter 9*, *Introducing Customizations*. If you are not interested in customization or you are not a programmer, you can easily skip this part. However, I hope you'll want to share it with some of your colleagues.

Conventions

In this book, you will find several headings appearing frequently.

To give clear instructions on how to complete a procedure or task, we use:

Time for action – heading

1. Action 1
2. Action 2
3. Action 3

Instructions often need some extra explanation so that they make sense, so they are followed with:

What just happened?

This heading explains the working of tasks or instructions that you have just completed.

You will also find some other learning aids in the book, including:

Pop quiz – heading

These are short multiple choice questions intended to help you test your own understanding.

Code words in text, database table names, folder names, filenames, file extensions, pathnames, dummy URLs, user input, and Twitter handles are shown as follows: "We can include other contexts through the use of the include directive."

A block of code is set as follows:

```
<?xml version="1.0" encoding="UTF-8" ?>
<config>
  <luceneMatchVersion>LUCENE_45</luceneMatchVersion>
  <requestHandler name="standard" class="solr.StandardRequestHandler"
default="true" />
  <requestHandler name="/update" class="solr.UpdateRequestHandler" />
  <requestHandler name="/admin/" class="org.apache.solr.handler.admin.
AdminHandlers" />
  <admin>
    <defaultQuery>*:*</defaultQuery>
  </admin>
</config>
```

When we wish to draw your attention to a particular part of a code block, the relevant lines or items are set in bold:

```
<?xml version="1.0" encoding="UTF-8" ?>
<config>
  <luceneMatchVersion>LUCENE_45</luceneMatchVersion>
  <requestHandler name="standard" class="solr.StandardRequestHandler"
default="true" />
  <requestHandler name="/update" class="solr.UpdateRequestHandler" />
   <requestHandler name="/admin/" class="org.apache.solr.handler.
admin.AdminHandlers" />
  <admin>
    <defaultQuery>*:*</defaultQuery>
  </admin>
</config>
```

Any command-line input or output is written as follows:

```
cd %SOLR_DIST%\example
java -Dsolr.solr.home=path/to/your/core -jar start.jar
```

New terms and **important words** are shown in bold. Words that you see on the screen, in menus or dialog boxes for example, appear in the text like this: "On the **Select Destination Location** screen, click on **Next** to accept the default destination."

> Warnings or important notes appear in a box like this.

> Tips and tricks appear like this.

Reader feedback

Feedback from our readers is always welcome. Let us know what you think about this book—what you liked or may have disliked. Reader feedback is important for us to develop titles that you really get the most out of.

To send us general feedback, simply send an e-mail to feedback@packtpub.com, and mention the book title through the subject of your message.

If there is a topic that you have expertise in and you are interested in either writing or contributing to a book, see our author guide on www.packtpub.com/authors.

Customer support

Now that you are the proud owner of a Packt book, we have a number of things to help you to get the most from your purchase.

Downloading the example code

You can download the example code files for all Packt books you have purchased from your account at `http://www.packtpub.com`. If you purchased this book elsewhere, you can visit `http://www.packtpub.com/support` and register to have the files e-mailed directly to you.

Errata

Although we have taken every care to ensure the accuracy of our content, mistakes do happen. If you find a mistake in one of our books—maybe a mistake in the text or the code—we would be grateful if you would report this to us. By doing so, you can save other readers from frustration and help us improve subsequent versions of this book. If you find any errata, please report them by visiting `http://www.packtpub.com/submit-errata`, selecting your book, clicking on the **errata submission form** link, and entering the details of your errata. Once your errata are verified, your submission will be accepted and the errata will be uploaded to our website, or added to any list of existing errata, under the Errata section of that title.

Piracy

Piracy of copyright material on the Internet is an ongoing problem across all media. At Packt, we take the protection of our copyright and licenses very seriously. If you come across any illegal copies of our works, in any form, on the Internet, please provide us with the location address or website name immediately so that we can pursue a remedy.

Please contact us at `copyright@packtpub.com` with a link to the suspected pirated material.

We appreciate your help in protecting our authors, and our ability to bring you valuable content.

Questions

You can contact us at `questions@packtpub.com` if you are having a problem with any aspect of the book, and we will do our best to address it.

1
Getting Ready with the Essentials

In this chapter we will introduce Apache Solr. We will start by giving an idea about what it is and when the project began.

We will prepare our local Solr installation, using the standard distribution to run our examples; we will also see how to start/stop Solr from the command line in a simple way, how to index some example data, and how to perform the first query on the web interface.

We will also introduce some convenient tools such as cURL, which we will use later in the book. This is a simple and effective way to play with our examples, which we will use in the next chapters too.

Understanding Solr

Apache Solr is an open source Enterprise Java full-text search server. It was initially started in 2004 at CNET (at that time, one of the most well-known site for news and reviews on technology), then it became an Apache project in 2007, and since then it has been used for many projects and websites. It was initially conceived to be a web application for providing a wide range of full-text search capabilities, using and extending the power of the well-known Apache Lucene library. The two projects have been merged into a single development effort since 2010, with improved modularity.

Solr is designed to be a standalone web server, exposing full-text and other functionalities via its own REST-like services, which can be consumed in many different ways from nearly any platform or language. This is the most common use case, and we will focus on it.

It can be also used as an embedded framework if needed, adding some of its functionalities into our Java application by a direct call to its internal API. This is a special case: useful if you need it, for example, for using its features inside a desktop application. We will only give some suggestions on how to start programming using an embedded Solr instance, at the end of the book.

Moreover Solr is not a database; it is very different from the relational ones, as it is designed to manage indexes of the actual data (let's say, metadata useful for searching over the actual data) and not the data itself or the relations between them. However, this distinction can be very blurry in some contexts, and Solr itself is becoming a good NoSQL solution for some specific use cases. You can also see Solr as an open and evolving platform, with integrations to external third-party libraries: for data acquisitions, language processing, document clustering, and more. We will have the chance to cite some of those advanced topics when needed though the book, to have a broader idea of the possible scenarios, looking for interesting readings.

Learning the powerful aspects of Solr

Solr is a very powerful, flexible, mature technology, and it offers not only powerful full-text search capabilities but also autosuggestion, advanced filtering, geocoded search, highlighting in text, faceted search, and much more. The following are the most interesting ones from our perspective:

◆ **Advanced full-text search**: This is the most obvious option. If we need to create some kind of an internal search engine on our site or application, or if we want to have more flexibility than the internal search capabilities of our database, Solr is the best choice. Solr is designed to perform fast searches and also to give us some flexibility on terms that are useful to intercept a natural user search, as we will see later. We can also combine our search with out of the box functionalities to perform searches over value intervals (imagine a search for a certain period in time), or by using geocoding functions.

◆ **Suggestions**: Solr has components for creating autosuggestion results using internal similarity algorithms. This is useful because autosuggestion is one of the most intuitive user interface patterns; for example, think about the well-known Google search box that is shown in the following screenshot:

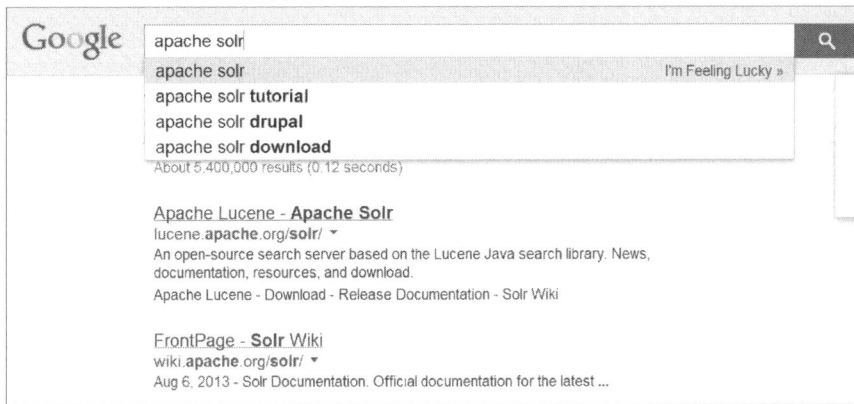

This simple Google search box performs queries on a remote server while we are typing, and automatically shows us some alternative term sequence that can be used for a query and has a chance to be relevant for us; it uses recurring terms and similarity algorithms over the data for this purpose. In the example, the `tutorial` keyword is suggested before the `drupal` one as it is judged more relevant from the system. With Solr, we can provide the backend service for developing our own autosuggestion component, inspired by this example.

◆ **Language analysis**: Solr permits us to configure different types of language analysis even on a per-field basis, with the possibility to configure them specifically for a certain language. Moreover, integrations with tools such as Apache UIMA for metadata extraction already exist; and in general, you might have more new components so that you will be able to plug in to the architecture in the future, covering advanced language processing, information extraction capabilities, and other specific tasks.

♦ **Faceted search**: This is a particular type of search based on classification. With Solr, we can perform faceted search automatically over our fields to gain information such as how many documents have the value `London` for the `city` field. This is useful to construct some kind of faceted navigation. This is another very familiar pattern in user experience that you probably know from having used it on e-commerce site such as Amazon. To see an example of faceted navigation, imagine a search on the Amazon site where we are typing `apache  s`, as shown in the following screenshot:

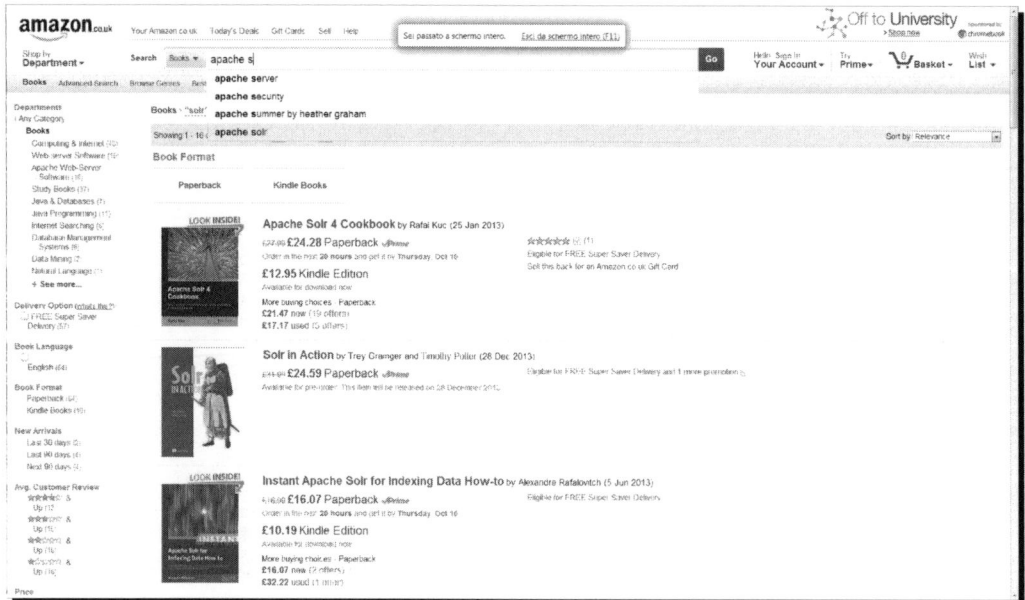

♦ In the previous screenshot you can clearly recognize some facets on the top-left corner, which is suggesting that we will find a certain number of items under a certain specific "book category". For example, we know in advance that we will find 11 items for the facet "Books: Java Programming". Then, we can decide from this information whether to narrow our search or not. In case we click on the facet, a new query will be performed, adding a filter based on the choice we implicitly made. This is exactly the way a Solr faceted search will perform a similar query. The term category here is somewhat misleading, as it seems to suggest a predefined taxonomy. But with Solr we can also obtain facets on our fields without explicitly classifying the document under a certain category. It's indeed Solr that automatically returns the faceted result using the current search keywords and criteria and shows us how many documents have the same value for a certain field. You may note that we have used an example of a user interface to give an introductory explanation for the service behind. This is true, and we can use faceted results in many different ways, as we will see later in the book. But I feel the example should help you to fix the first idea; we will explore this in *Chapter 6, Using Faceted Search – from Searching to Finding*.

It's easy to index data using Solr: for example, we can send data using a POST over HTTP, or we can index the text and metadata over a collection of rich documents (such as PDF, Word, or HTML) without too much effort, using the Apache Tika component. We can also read data from a database or another external data source, and configure an internal workflow to directly index them if needed—using the `DataImportHandler` components.

Solr also exposes its own search services that are REST-like on standard open formats such as JSON and XML, and it's then very simple to consume the data from JavaScript on HTTP.

> **Representational State Transfer (REST)** is a software architecture style that is largely used nowadays for exposing web services.
>
> Refer to: `http://en.wikipedia.org/wiki/Representational_state_transfer`

- The services are designed to be paginated, and to expose parameters for sorting and filtering results; so it's easy to consume the results from the frontend.

- Note that other serialization formats can be used; which are designed for specific languages, such as Ruby or PHP, or to directly return the serialization of a Java object. There are already some third-party wrappers developed over these services to provide integration on existing applications, from **Content Management Systems (CMS)** such as Drupal, WordPress, to e-commerce platforms such as Magento. In a similar way, there are integrations that use the Java APIs, such as Alfresco and Broadleaf, directly (if you prefer you can see this as a type of "embedded" example).

It's possible to start Solr with a very small configuration, adopting an almost schemaless approach; but the internal schema is written in XML, and it is simple to read and write. The Solr application gives us a default web interface for administration, simple monitoring of the used resources, and direct testing of our queries.

This list is far from being exhaustive, and it had the purpose of only introducing you to some of the topics that we will see in the next chapters. If you visit the official site at `http://lucene.apache.org/solr/features.html`, you will find the complete list of features.

Working with Java installation

The first thing we need to start exploring Solr is a working Java installation. If you already have one (for example, if you are a Java programmer you will probably have it), you can skip to the *Installing and testing Solr* section directly.

Downloading and installing Java

If you don't have Java installed, please download the most appropriate version for your operating system from `http://www.java.com/it/download/manual.jsp`, paying attention to the appropriate architecture choice (32 or 64 bit) as well. Since it's impossible to provide a detailed step-by-step description on how to install Java for every platform, I'll ask you to follow the steps described on the Oracle site: `http://www.java.com/en/download/help/download_options.xml`. The described procedure is not complex; it would require only a few minutes.

> The **Java Virtual Machine** (**JVM**) has been open sourced since some years, so it's possible to use some alternative implementation of the JVM specification. For example, there is an OpenJDK implementation for the *nix users (`http://openjdk.java.net/`), or the IBM one (`http://www.ibm.com/developerworks/java/jdk/`); these are largely adopted, but we will use the official Java distribution from Oracle. The official documentation warns about GNU's GCJ, which is not supported and does not work with Solr.

Configuring CLASSPATH and PATH variables for Java

When Java is installed, we need to configure two environment variables: `PATH` and `CLASSPATH`. These are described again at the Oracle website: `http://docs.oracle.com/javase/tutorial/essential/environment/paths.html`.

The `PATH` variable is generally used to make a command available on the terminal, without having to prepend the full path to call it; basically we will be able to call the Java interpreter from within every folder. For example, the simplest way to verify that this variable is correctly configured is to ask for the Java version installed, which is done as follows:

```
>> java -version
```

The `CLASSPATH` variable is needed to load the core Java libraries instead and makes them available to Solr components.

Installing and testing Solr

Once Java is correctly installed, it's time to install Solr and make some initial tests. To simplify things, we will adopt the default distribution that you can download from the official page: `http://lucene.apache.org/solr/` (the current version at the time of writing is Version 4.5). The zipped package can be extracted and copied to a folder of choice.

Once extracted, the Solr standard distribution will contain the folders shown in the following screenshot:

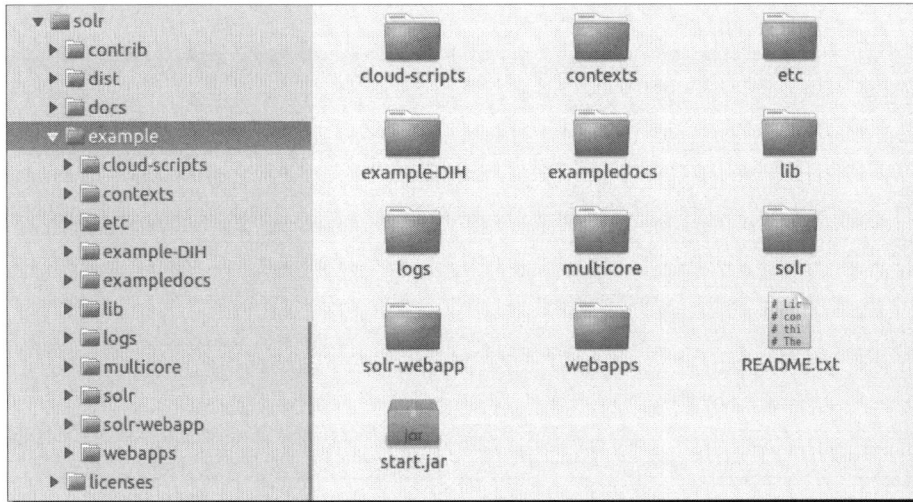

We will start Solr from here; even if we don't need to use all the libraries and examples obtained with the distribution, you can continue exploring the folders with your own examples after reading this book. Some of the folders are as follows:

- `/solr`: This represents a simple single core configuration
- `/multicore`: This represents a multiple core (multicore) configuration example
- `/example-DIH`: This provides examples for the data import handler capabilities
- `/exampledocs`: This contains some toy data to play with

For the moment, we will ignore the folders external to `/`. These folders will be useful later when we will need to use third-party libraries.

The simplest way to run the Solr instance will be by using the `solr.jar` launcher, which we can find in the `/example` folder. For our convenience, it's useful to define a new environment variable `SOLR_DIST` that will point to the absolute path: `/the-path-of-solr-distribution/example`. In order to use the example, in the most simplest way, I suggest you to put the unzipped Solr distribution at the location `/SolrStarterBook/solr`, where `SolrStarterBook` is the folder where you have the complete code examples for this book. We can easily create this new environment variable in the same way we created the `CLASSPATH` one.

Time for action – starting Solr for the first time

Ok, now it's time to start Solr for the first time.

1. If we execute the following command from the terminal (from Windows, Linux, or Mac):

```
>> cd %SOLR_DIST% (windows)

>> cd $SOLR_DIST (mac, linux)
```

2. We change the directory to /example, and then we finally start Solr using the following command:

```
>> java -jar start.jar
```

3. We should obtain an output similar to the one seen in the following screenshot:

```
3480 [main] INFO  org.apache.solr.servlet.SolrDispatchFilter   - user.dir=/home/seralf/SolrStarterBook/sol
r/example
3481 [main] INFO  org.apache.solr.servlet.SolrDispatchFilter   - SolrDispatchFilter.init() done
3520 [main] INFO  org.eclipse.jetty.server.AbstractConnector   - Started SocketConnector@0.0.0.0:8983
3533 [searcherExecutor-4-thread-1] INFO  org.apache.solr.core.SolrCore   - [collection1] webapp=null path=
null params={event=firstSearcher&q=static+firstSearcher+warming+in+solrconfig.xml&distrib=false} hits=0 s
tatus=0 QTime=54
3533 [searcherExecutor-4-thread-1] INFO  org.apache.solr.core.SolrCore   - QuerySenderListener done.
3534 [searcherExecutor-4-thread-1] INFO  org.apache.solr.handler.component.SpellCheckComponent   - Loading
 spell index for spellchecker: default
```

4. You will quickly become familiar with the line highlighted in this output as it is easily recognizable (it ends in 0.0.0.0:8983). If we have not noticed any errors before it in the output, our Solr instance is running correctly. When Solr is running, you can leave the terminal window open and minimized in order to be able to see what happened when you need, in particular if there were errors as and when you need. This can be avoided on production systems where we will have scripts to automate start and stop Solr, but it's useful for our testing.

5. When you wish to stop Solr, simply press the *Ctrl + C* combination in the terminal window.

What just happened?

The solr.jar launcher is a small Java library that starts an embedded Jetty container to run the Solr application. By default, this application will be running on port 8983. Jetty is a lightweight container that has been adopted for distributing Solr for its simplicity and small memory footprint. While Solr is distributed as a standard Java web application (you can find a solr.war under the /example/webapps folder), and then its WAR file can be deployed to any application server (such as Tomcat, JBoss, and others), the standard preferable way to use it is with the embedded Jetty instance. Then, we will start with the local Jetty instance bundled with Solr in order to let you familiarize yourself with the platform and its services, using a standard installation where you can also follow the tutorials on your own.

Note that in our example we need to change the current directory to /
`example`, which is included in the folder that is unzipped from the standard
distribution archive. The `start.jar` tool is designed to start the local jetty
instance by accepting parameters for changing the Solr configurations. If it
does not receive any particular option (as in our case), it searches the Solr
configurations from the default examples. So, it needs to be started from that
specific directory. In a similar way, the `post.jar` tool can be started from
every directory containing the data to be sent to Solr.

If you want to change the default port value for Jetty (for example, if the default port results
is occupied by other programs), you should look at the `jetty.xml` file in the [SOLR_
DIST]/examples/etc directory where I wrote [SOLR_DIST] in place of the Windows,
Mac, and Linux versions of the same environment variable. If you also want some control
over the logging inside the terminal (sometimes it could become very annoying to find errors
inside a huge quantity of lines running fast), please look for the `logging.properties` file
in the same directory.

Taking a glance at the Solr interface

Now that the server is running, we are curious about how the Solr web application
will look in our browser, so let's copy and paste this URL into the browser: `http://
localhost:8983/solr/#/`. We will obtain the default home screen for the Solr web
application, as shown in the following screenshot:

Note that since the default installation does not provide automatic redirection from the base root to the path seen before, a very common error is pointing to `http://localhost:8983/` and obtaining the error shown in the following screenshot:

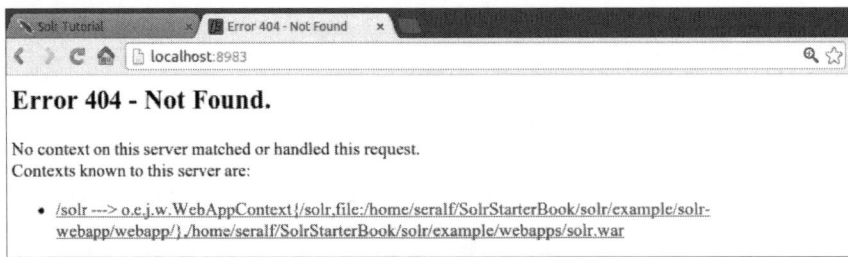

We can easily ignore this error for our purposes; so remember to check if you are using the correct address when you obtain this type of error.

We can execute our first query in the default admin screen on the default `collection1` core: `http://localhost:8983/solr/#/collection1/query`. (In the next chapter, we will introduce the concept of core. So please be patient if there are things not well documented.)

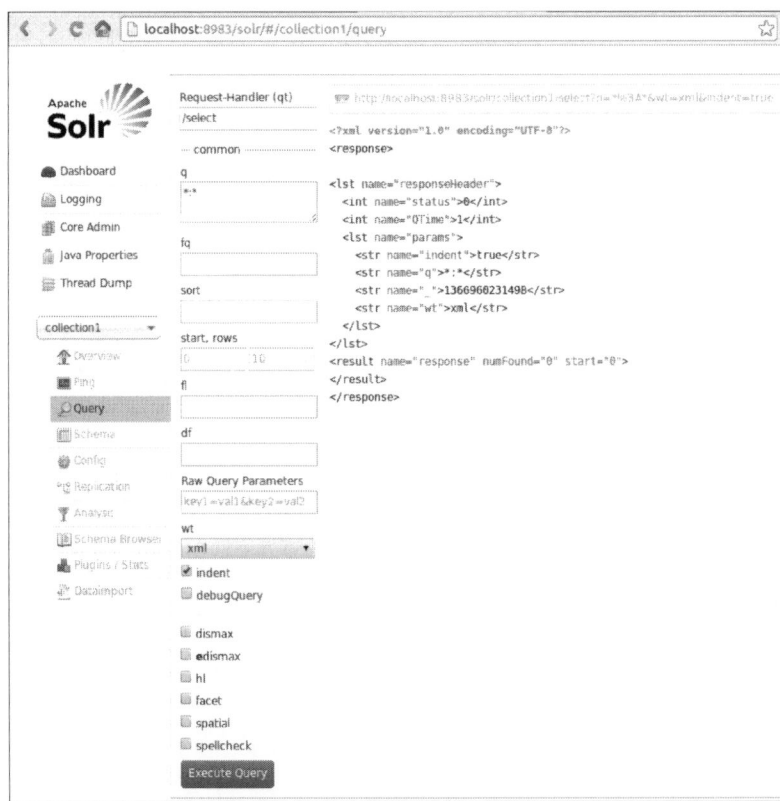

We will obtain some XML results that clearly contain no data, as expected. In fact, we have not yet indexed any data.

Time for action – posting some example data

Now that we have prepared the system and installed Solr, we are ready to post some example data as suggested by the default tutorial. In order to check if our installation is working as expected, we need to perform the following steps:

1. We can easily post some of the example data contained in the /example/ exampledocs folder of our Solr installation. First of all, we move to that directory using the following command:

    ```
    >> cd %SOLR_DIST% (windows)

    >> cd $SOLR_DIST (linux, mac)
    ```

2. Then we will index some data using the post.jar library provided, using the following command:

    ```
    >> java -jar post.jar .
    ```

3. In the /example/exampledocs subfolder, you can find some documents written using the XML, CSV, or JSON format that Solr recognizes to index the data. The post.jar Java library is designed to send every file contained in a directory (in this case, the current directory). This library is written in one of these formats to a running Solr instance, in this case the default one. The data is sent by an HTTP POST request, and this should explain the name.

4. Once the example data is indexed, we can again run a query with simple parameters, as shown in the following screenshot:

5. Here, we are able to see some results exposed by default using the `json` format. The example data describes items in a hypothetical catalog of electronic devices.

What just happened?

As you can see in the screenshot, the results are recognizable as items inside a docs collection; we can see the first, which has both fields containing a single value or multiple values (these are easily recognizable by the [,] JSON syntax for lists). The header section of the results contains some general information. For example, the query sent (q=* : *, which basically means "I want to obtain all the documents") and the format chosen for the output (in our case JSON). Moreover, you should note that the number of results is 32, which is bigger than the number of files in that directory. This should suggest to us that we send more than one single document in a single post (we will see this in the later chapters).

Lastly, you can see in the address that we are actually querying over a subpath called `collection1`. This is the name of the default collection where we have indexed our example data. In the next chapter, we will start using our first collection instead of this example one.

Time for action – testing Solr with cURL

If you look at the top of the previous screenshot containing results, you would recognize the address `http://localhost:8983/solr/collection1/query?q=*:*&wt=json&i` `ndent=true`. It represents a specific query with its parameters. You can copy this address and paste it directly into the browser to obtain the same results as seen before, without necessarily passing it from the web interface. Note that the browser will encode some character when sending the query via HTTP. For example, the character `:` will be encoded as `%3A`. This will be one of our methods for directly testing queries. But while the browser can be more comfortable in many cases, a command-line approach is surprisingly clearer on many others; and I want to you to be familiar with both ones.

This can be easily done by running the same query on the browser interface and also with the cURL tool. You will become familiar with this process after executing it a few times, and it's useful to focus on how the data are actually transferred over HTTP, giving us the best start to understanding how we can write a direct access to the HTTP services. This will be useful for writing frontends with JavaScript or other languages.

> You can download the latest cURL version for your platform/architecture from here: `http://curl.haxx.se/download.html`.
>
> Please remember that it is better for Linux systems to use the package manager of your distribution (yum, apt, and similar ones). For Windows users, it's important to add the cURL executable into the environment variable PATH as we have done previously for Java. This is done in order to have it usable from the command line, without having to prepend the absolute path every time.

We can execute the following query with cURL on the command line in the same way we ran it before:

```
>> curl -X  GET "http://localhost:8983/solr/collection1/query?q=*:*&wt=js
on&indent=true"
```

Next chapter onwards, we will use the browser and cURL interchangeably; adopting from time to time the clearest method for each specific case.

What just happened?

When cURL is configured, the result of the query will be the same seen in the browser. We generally use cURL by putting the HTTP request address containing its parameters in double quotes; and we will explicitly adopt the `-X GET` parameter to make the requests more clear: saving in some `.txt` files the cURL requests made permits us, for example, to fully reconstruct the exact queries sent. We can also send POST queries with cURL, and this is very useful to perform indexing and administrative tasks (for example, a delete action) from the command line.

Who uses Solr?

Solr is widely used in many different scenarios: from the well-known, big, new sites such as The Guardian (`http://www.guardian.co.uk/`) to an application as popular as Instagram (`http://instagr.am/`). It has also been adopted by big companies such as Apple, Disney, or Goldman Sachs; and there have been some very specific adoptions such as the search over `http://citeseerx.ist.psu.edu/network` for scientific citations.

Two very widely adopted use cases are aggregators and metasearch engines and **Open Catalog Access** (**OPAC**). The first type requires continuous indexing over sparse data and makes a business out of being able to capture users by its indexes, and the second generally needs a read-only exposition of metadata with powerful search. Good examples of online catalogs that have used Solr for a long time are Internet Archive (`http://www.archive.org/`), the well-known open digital library, and VuFind (`http://www.vufind.org/`), an open source discovery portal for libraries.

Other very common use cases include news sites, institutional sites such as USA government sites, a publisher site, and others. Even if every site will not necessarily require full-text and the other features of Solr, the use cases can fill a very long list.

For a more extended and yet incomplete list of projects and sites that are using Solr in the world, please refer to the following page in the official documentation:

`http://wiki.apache.org/solr/PublicServers`

Resources on Solr

A good place to play with some more queries is the official tutorial on the site `http://lucene.apache.org/solr/4_5_0/tutorial.html`, where you'll see some functionality that we will see in action in *Chapter 3, Indexing Example Data from DBpedia – Paintings*.

For a better understanding while you are reading the book and playing with our examples, you can refer to the excellent reference guide at this link: `https://cwiki.apache.org/confluence/display/solr/Apache+Solr+Reference+Guide`. I strongly suggest that you read this once you have finished reading this book. It will help you move a step further.

We will introduce faceted search in detail in *Chapter 6 Using Faceted Search – from Searching to Finding*. Since this is one of the main features of Solr, you can be interested to start reading about the topic since the beginning. For an introduction to faceted classification, faceted search, and faceted navigation, there are two good books: *Design Patterns: Faceted Navigation, Jeffery Callender* and *Peter Morville*, on the **A List Apart** blog at `http://alistapart.com/article/design-patterns-faceted-navigation`, and *Usability Studies of Faceted Browsing: A Literature Review*, by *Jody Condit Fagan* at `http://napoleon.bc.edu/ojs/index.php/ital/article/download/3144/2758`.

How will we use Solr?

The main focus of this book will be a gradual introduction to Solr that can be used by a beginner without too much code at the beginning, even if we will introduce some coding near the end. In this approach, I hope that you'll find the chance to share what you read and your ideas with your teammates also if you want, and hopefully you'll have the freedom to find your own way of adopting this technology.

I would also like to suggest the adoption of Solr at an earlier stage of development, as a prototype tool. We will see that indexing data is easy; it doesn't matter if we do not have a final design for our data model yet. Hence, providing filters and faceting capabilities that can be adopted at the beginning of the user experience design. A Solr configuration can be improved at every stage of an incremental development (not necessarily when all the actual data already exists, as you might think), without "breaking" functionalities and giving us a fast view of the data that is near to the user perspective. This can be useful to construct a working preview for our customers, which is flexible enough to be improved fast later.

In order to use the scripts available in the repository for the book examples that we will use in the next chapters, we have defined a SOLR_DIST environment variable that will be available for some useful scripts you will find in the repository. The code can be downloaded as a zipped package from https://bitbucket.org/seralf/solrstarterbook. If you are familiar with Mercurial, you can download it directly as the source. We will use some of the scripts used to download the toy data for our indexing tests that are written using the Scala language. So, you can directly add the Scala library to the system CLASSPATH variable for you convenience, although it's not needed. We will discuss our scripts and example later in *Chapter 3*, *Indexing Example Data from DBpedia – Paintings*.

Pop quiz

Q1. Which of the following are the features of Solr?

1. Full-text and faceted search

2. Web crawling and site indexing

3. Spellchecking and autosuggestion

Q2. From which of these options can we obtain a list of all the documents in the example?

1. Using the query q=*:*

2. Using the query q=documents:*

3. Using the query q=*:all

Q3. Why does the standard Solr distribution include a working Jetty instance?

    1.   Because Solr can't be run without Jetty

    2.   Because we can't deploy the Solr war (web application) into other containers/application servers, such as Tomcat or Jboss

    3.   Because Solr war needs to be run inside a web container, such as Jetty

Q4. What is cURL?

    1.   cURL is a program used for parsing data from a remote URL, using the HTTP protocol

    2.   cURL is a command line tool for transferring data with URL syntax, using the HTTP protocol

    3.   cURL is a command line tool for sending queries to Solr, using the HTTP protocol

Q5. Which of the following statements are not true?

    1.   Solr application exposes full-text and faceting search capabilities

    2.   Solr application can be used for adding full-text search capabilities to a database systems

    3.   Solr can be used as an embedded framework in Java application

Summary

In this first chapter, we have introduced Apache Solr; we have explained what it is and what it is not, cited its history, and explained the main role of the Apache Lucene library. We cited a list of features that are the most interesting ones from our perspective. Then we saw how to set up a simple Solr instance, how to have it running using the default distribution, and its examples. Using these examples we performed our first query by using the web interface, the direct call to Solr REST services, and the cURL command-line tool, which will be useful in the next chapters.

We end the chapter citing how Solr is widely adopted by players who have been using Solr for some years. Then we resume the perspective we will adopt through the book, which will be based on prototypes and writing as little code as possible.

2
Indexing with Local PDF Files

In this chapter we will have the chance to index and query some local PDFs (some examples are provided for your tests) as first use cases, even if you do not yet have any knowledge of Solr.

We will have a hands on with both cURL and the browser. We will see how an index is made and how to interact with it in various ways, introducing the web user interface. We will describe the main concepts behind what is an index and a core, which will be useful for the examples covered in the subsequent chapters.

Understanding and using an index

The main component in Solr is the Lucene library, a full-text search library written in Java. Since Solr hides the Lucene layer from us, we don't have to study how Lucene works in detail now; you can study it in depth later. Yet it is important to have an idea of what a Lucene index is, and how it's made. Lucene's core concepts are as follows:

◆ **Document**: This is the main structure used both for searches and indexes. A document is an in-memory representation of the data values we need to use for our searches. In order for this to work, every document resource consists of a collection of fields, which is the most simple data structure.

◆ **Field**: This has its own name and value and consists of at least one *term*. So every document can be seen as nothing more than a list of very simple (field name and term value) pairs. If a field is designed to be multivalued, we can save as many values as we want within the same key; otherwise, if we enter new values, the last one will simply overwrite the previous.

◆ **Term**: This is a basic unit for indexing. For simplicity let's imagine a single word, but the word can consist of a string of words, depending on configuration details.

◆ **Index**: This is the in-memory structure where Lucene (and Solr) perform the searches. We can then think about a document to be a single record in the Index. From an abstract logical point of view, we can easily imagine a data structure as shown in the following figure:

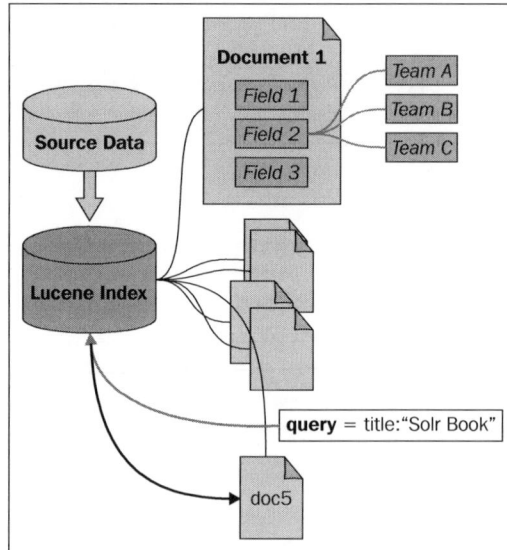

The best way to understand how a generic query works is by focusing on documents and trying to imagine how to search for them. While searching for the string `Solr Book` in the field `title`, if the index has been created and the fields in our query exist, we expect Lucene to search correspondences for the name-value pair `title: 'Solr Book'` iterating over all the existing documents currently added to the index.

These kind of document-oriented representations are often useful, as it is a common way of representing data used by many people. However, the real internal structure adopted for storing index data (and the actual process to search over the index data) is less intuitive, and we will cover it later in this chapter.

Posting example documents to the first Solr core

First, we will cover how to write a generic, simple, and useful configuration for **Solr core** and become familiar with the number of binary files saved to the disk.

We will write our new configuration from the beginning, using as few elements as we can, reducing them to essential parts in order to focus on the main concepts.

Analyzing the elements we need in Solr core

In order to use Solr we have to create a small set of files that define what we usually call a configuration for a *core*. Solr core is simply a working Lucene index with Solr configuration files, which we need to learn to write.

A typical Solr core directory looks like the one shown in the following figure, which is a structure for the `basic` example I have put on the disk under the `/SolrStarterBook/solr-app/chp01/` directory, after posting some documents:

```
/home/seralf/SolrStarterBook/solr-app/chp01
├── basic
│   ├── conf
│   │   ├── schema.xml
│   │   └── solrconfig.xml
│   └── data
│       └── index
│           ├── _4.fdt
│           ├── _4.fdx
│           ├── _4.fnm
│           ├── _4_Lucene41_0.doc
│           ├── _4_Lucene41_0.pos
│           ├── _4_Lucene41_0.tim
│           ├── _4_Lucene41_0.tip
│           ├── _4.si
│           ├── segments_6
│           └── segments.gen
├── README.txt
├── solr.xml
└── zoo.cfg
```

We call the **Solr Home** folder on the filesystem, where a running Solr instance reads the configuration to start with. This should not be confused with the installation of Solr, as that can be on a different path. Solr Home contains one or more Solr cores, each containing a special `/conf` directory that holds its configurations and a `/data` directory for storing the index on the disk.

> You can obtain a copy of the resources for this book at `https://bitbucket.org/seralf/solrstarterbook`. It contains the instructions to download the correct resource files.
>
> We will refer to the resources path as `/SolrStarterBook`, so please remember where you copy the provided examples! To simplify things a bit more, I suggest you download the latest Solr distribution and put it under the directory `/SolrStarterBook/solr`; this would make it easier to adapt a relative path to the library when needed for our configurations.

If you look at the /SolrStarterBook/solr-app directory in the sources provided for the book, you will find that it contains different examples of core configuration, organized according to the chapters in which they are explained. Every folder of a chapter can be used as a Solr Home directory. Even for *Chapter 1*, *Getting Ready with the Essentials*, I created an example (named basic, in the /chp01 directory), with the smallest set of configurations derived from the default example. Feel free to use them in your first tests as a sort of template for your own experimentation.

After posting some data, you should find some files in the other /data/index directory. These are the binary files to save the state of the index on a disk, split into optimized segments.

Time for action – configuring Solr Home and Solr core discovery

The first file we need to define is solr.xml. This file defines the general configuration of a particular **Solr Home**, containing one or more cores (*multicore*). This turns out to be useful if we want to apply different configurations over the same example, or to play with different examples. This will help us in becoming familiar with multicore from the beginning. Steps for configuring Solr Home are as follows:

1. All we have to do is to create the solr.xml file under the path /SolrStarterBook/solr-app/chp02/:

```xml
<?xml version='1.0' encoding='UTF-8' ?>
<solr>
  <solrcloud />
</solr>
```

2. The essential configuration seen will enable core discovery on all the folders containing a special file named core.properties. We can, for example, create a subfolder named simple under chp02 and put our simple core.properties file in it:

```
name=simple
config=solrconfig.xml
schema=schema.xml
loadOnStartup=true
```

3. This way the simple core will be automatically loaded with its own configurations, which we will write in a while.

What just happened?

In this default example, all we had to do to enable automatic discovery of cores was add the `<solrcloud />` XML tag, omitting other configurations that can be added later when we need them. When Solr finds this tag, it will search all the subfolders for a `core.properties` file. If a file with that name exists in a directory, Solr will try to load the corresponding core. Note that this file can even be empty, and in that case the values used are the default ones that we have used here, explicitly to fix ideas. In fact the only nondefault value is the name. If the name is not defined, it will be assumed that the name of the folder containing the file is the core name.

Note that if you want to hide a core from the discovery mechanism, you can simply rename the `core.properties` file (for example, rename it to something like `core.properties.skip`).

Knowing the legacy solr.xml format

Before Solr 4.4, the `solr.xml` file syntax was completely different, and this will be *deprecated from Solr 5*. You can still use the syntax of both the versions in the current version, but you have to expect that the legacy format will be dropped in the near future. However, many examples on the internet and books are still based on this legacy format. So it's important to be able to recognize at least the basic elements for it.

We can reproduce the configuration using the legacy format:

```
<?xml version='1.0' encoding='UTF-8' ?>
<solr persistent='false'>
  <cores adminPath='/admin/cores' >
    <core name='simple' instanceDir='simple'
      config='solrconfig.xml' schema='schema.xml' />
  </cores>
</solr>
```

Note how in this case the presence of the `core.properties` file is ignored, and every core that we want to load must have an entry in the XML file, as shown in the preceding code example.

As you can imagine, the legacy and current syntax are mutually exclusive. If both are used on the same configuration, an exception is thrown in order to avoid problems from the start.

You can find some more detailed information about legacy parameters on the reference guide at

`https://cwiki.apache.org/confluence/display/solr/Legacy+solr.xml+Configuration`

Time for action – writing a simple solrconfig.xml file

In the `solrconfig.xml` file we can define how to manage requests and data manipulation for the user. This file can contain a number of different configurations. Here we can plug-in specific components and define how they are integrated within the default workflow of the data. Their typical uses include helping API with suggestions to expose, and to customize them for different language localizations.

The basic structure will more or less include the following elements:

```
<config>
  <requestHandler name='standard' … />
  <requestHandler name='/update' ... />
  <requestHandler name='/admin/' … />
  <updateHandler class='solr.DirectUpdateHandler2' … />
  ...
</config>
```

Steps for writing a simple `solrconfig.xml` file are as follows:

1. Using this structure as a reference, let's write a basic `sorlconfig.xml` file, and save it, for example, save it under the path `/SolrStarterBook/solr-app/chp02/simple/conf/`.

> While you follow the instruction to reproduce a full example in the repository, I suggest you create your own parallel version of the same example from scratch and simply adopt a different name for it (for example, something like `simple_ex`), so that you can still look at the working example if you have problems.

2. The created `solrconfig.xml` file will look as shown in the following code:

```
<?xml version='1.0' encoding='UTF-8' ?>
<config>
  <luceneMatchVersion>LUCENE_45</luceneMatchVersion>

  <requestHandler name='standard' class=
    'solr.StandardRequestHandler' default='true' />
  <requestHandler name='/update' class=
    'solr.UpdateRequestHandler' />

  <requestHandler name='/admin/' class=
    'org.apache.solr.handler.admin.AdminHandlers' />
  <admin>
    <defaultQuery>*:*</defaultQuery>
  </admin>
</config>
```

3. In a standard configuration there are a few more tags, but I have omitted them here as we don't need them at the moment.

What just happened?

Solr exposes various components as services, in order to provide a different kind of functionality. These components are managed with the `RequestHandler` components:

♦ **Query handler**: this is a standard handler implicitly mapped on the path `/select`, unless we decide to explicitly use another name. We have already seen this handler in action, as it was the one that received our first test query.

♦ **Update handler**: This is explicitly mapped to the path `/update`. This is used to receive new data to be indexed. Please note that the data to be indexed in Solr are generally called *documents*, and it's important to distinguish them from the original data we want to search over. A Solr document is indeed a flat, unstructured sequence of the indexed metadata we want to use to represent a specific resource in our search domain.

♦ **Admin handler**: This is explicitly mapped to the path `/admin`. This is essential for using the admin web interface and having access to statistics, debug, and so on. Somewhat related to this definition is the definition of the default query to use in the admin interface.

In a common configuration there can be other exposed services such as `/ping` (used for checking if a core is still correctly running), but for now I decided to omit them to keep things simple and focus on understanding how the various sections are designed.

Time for action – writing a simple schema.xml file

We can define the structure of a Solr document by writing the `schema.xml` file (by defining its fields); we can also define some data manipulation strategy such as tokenizing texts in order to take care of single words instead of full phrases. The steps for writing a simple `schema.xml` file are as follows:

1. The focus here is on *how to model the data* on which we will do the searches and navigation for our specific domain of interest. We are only shaping metadata or let's say a 'projection' of data useful for our searches. A typical structure for the `schema.xml` file will involve the following elements:

```
<schema name='simple' version='1.1'>
  <types> … </types>
  <fields> … </fields>
  <uniqueKey> … </uniqueKey>

    …
</schema>
```

2. We can write a simple schema and save it as `/SolrStarterbook/solr-app/chp02/conf/schema.xml`:

```xml
<?xml version='1.0' ?>
<schema name='simple' version='1.1'>
  <types>
    <fieldtype name='string' class='solr.StrField' />
    <fieldType name='long' class='solr.TrieLongField' />
  </types>

  <fields>
    <field name='id' type='long' required='true' />
    <field name='author' type='string' multiValued='true' />
    <field name='title' type='string' />
    <field name='text' type='string' />
    <dynamicField name='*_string' type='string'
      multiValued='true' indexed='true' stored='true' />
    <copyField source='*' dest='fullText' />
    <field name='fullText' type='string'
      multiValued='true' indexed='true' />
  </fields>

  <uniqueKey>id</uniqueKey>
  <defaultSearchField>fullText</defaultSearchField>
  <solrQueryParser defaultOperator='OR' />

</schema>
```

Note how we have defined different fields for handling different types of data.

What just happened?

It is important to underlay the difference between storing the actual data and creating an indexing process over the *metadata manipulated and derived* (extracted, projected, filtered, and so on) from them. With Solr we usually take care of the second case, even in a special case where we can also be interested in storing the actual data, using Solr as a NoSQL database, as we will see later.

We may not necessarily be interested in describing all the data we have (for example, what we have in our databases), but only what can be relevant in the search and navigation context.

At the beginning it can look like a duplication of functionality between Solr and a relational database technology, but it is not. Solr is not designed to replace traditional relational databases. In most cases Solr is used in parallel with the relational database, to expose a simple and efficient full-text API over the DBMS data. As we will see later, the data can not only be indexed but also stored in Solr so that it's even possible to adopt it as a NoSQL store in certain cases.

You should easily recognize the essential parts of this file as follows:

- **Types**: This is used for defining a list of different data types for values. We can define strings, numeric types, or new types as we like. It's very common to have two or three different data types for handling text values shaped for different purposes, but for the moment we need to focus on the main concepts.

> If you are not a programmer or you are not familiar with data types, I suggest you start by using the basic `string` type. When you have something working, you can move to using more advanced features, specific for a certain data type. For example, dates. If dates are saved using the required specific data type, it allows optimization for range queries over a certain period of time.

- **Fields**: These are an essential part of this file. Every field should declare a unique name and associate it with one of the types defined previously. It's important to understand that not every instance of a Solr document must have a value for every field; when mandatory, a field can be simply marked as required. This approach is very flexible; we index only the actual data values without introducing dummy empty fields when a value is not present.

- **copyfield**: This is used when the content of a source field needs to be added and indexed on some other destination field (usually as a melting pot for very general searches). The idea behind it is that we want to be able to search in all the fields of a document at the same time (the source will be defined by the wildcard *). The most simple way to do this is by copying the values into a default field where we will perform the actual searches. This field will also have its own type and analysis defined.

- **dynamicfield**: By using this type we can start indexing some data without having to define the name of the field. The name will be defined by the wildcard, and it's possible to use prefixes and postfixes so that the actual name of a field is accepted at runtime, while the type should be defined. For example, when writing `<dynamicField name='*_s'  type='string' />` we can post new documents containing string values such as `firstName_s='Alfredo'` and `surname_s='Serafini'`. This is an ideal case for prototypes, as we can work with the Solr API without defining a final schema for our data.

- **uniqueKey**: This is used to give a unique identity to a specific Solr document. It is a concept similar to a *primary key* for DBMS.

- **defaultSearchField**: This field is used when there is no request for a specific field. The best configuration for this is generally the field containing all the full-text tokens (for example, the destination in the copyfield definition seen earlier).

- **defaultOperator**: This is used to choose a default behavior when handling multiple tokens in the search. A *query* that uses and between the various words used for a search is intuitively narrowed to a small set of documents. So in most cases you will use the or operator instead, which is less restrictive and more natural for common queries. The and approach is generally useful, for example, when working with *navigation filters* or conducting an advanced search on large datasets.

Every field can define the following three important *attributes*:

- **multiValued**: If the value of this attribute is true, a Solr document can contain more than one instance of values for the field. The default value is false.

- **indexed**: If it is true, the field is used in index. Generally we will use only indexed fields, but it can be interesting to have them not indexed in certain instances, for example, if we want to save a value without using it for searches.

- **stored**: This is used to permanently save the original data value for a field, whether indexed (and used for searches) or not. Moreover during the indexing phase, a field is analyzed as defined by its type in the schema.xml file to update the index; however, it is not explicitly saved unless we decide to store it.

Imagine indexing several different synonyms of the same word using a word_synonim multivalued field, but storing only this specific word in a word_original field. When the user searches for the word or one of its synonyms, all the documents produced as output will only contain the field word_synonim, which is the only one stored.

Time for action – starting the new core

After writing our first core definition, we are ready to check if everything is working as expected, starting Solr with this core and trying to index some data. At the moment we are using Solr from the default distribution, so the simplest way we have is to start it from there. Steps for starting the new core are as follows:

1. If we have defined an environment variable called SOLR_DIST (pointed to the absolute path where you unzipped the standard Solr distribution on your system), we can easily move to the SOLR_DIST/example/ directory:

```
>> cd $SOLR_DIST/example
```

2. If you are on a Unix system (Linux or Mac) or on Windows:

    ```
    >> cd %SOLR_DIST%\example
    ```

3. Then start Solr with a command-line like the following:

    ```
    >> java -Dsolr.solr.home=path/to/your/core -jar start.jar
    ```

4. For example, on my system this will be as shown in the following command:

    ```
    >> java -Dsolr.solr.home=/home/seralf/SolrStarterBook/solr-app/
    chp02 -jar start.jar
    ```

5. To stop the Solr instance, simply use *Ctrl + C* on the terminal where you started, or close the active terminal window opened by double-clicking the start scripts (if you used them).

What just happened?

This command-line start is really simple, but if you have problems with it, put small start scripts such as `start.sh` or `start.bat`, depending on your system under the path `/SolrStarterBook/test/`. This adds some more parameters and can be used to easily start a specific multicore home. For example:

```
>> ./start.sh chp02
```

The command is used to load the cores in the `/chp02/` folder, used for this chapter.

The `-Dsolr.solr.home=/solr/home/path` attribute is used for passing it to the Java interpreter context, an environment variable containing the path to our Solr Home.

Another way of starting Solr is defining it as a service in order to have it always running and available on your machine. This is generally used for server installations in real-world scenarios, but we don't need to see it at this time as it does not change our configurations.

If everything goes fine you should navigate to your core with the browser at `http://localhost:8983/solr/#/simple`. There you will see the following default admin interface:

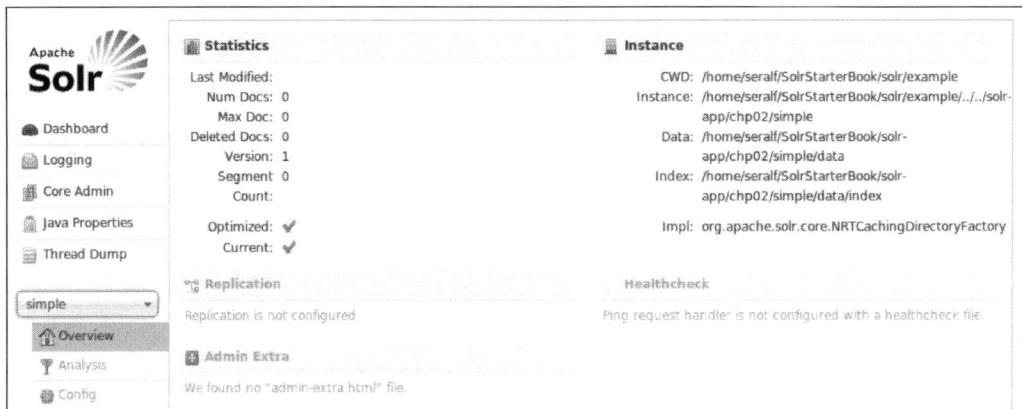

As shown in the preceding screenshot, this page contains some general information and statistics that may prove useful during development.

Time for action – defining an example document

We can now define a new Solr document and post it to the new core to index it with the following steps:

1. Our document will have the following structure:

```
<add>
  <doc>
    <field name='id'>01</field>
    <field name='author'>Erich Gamma</field>
    <field name='author'>Richard Helm</field>
    <field name='author'>Ralph Johnson</field>
    <field name='author'>John Vlissides</field>
    <field name='title'>Design Patterns: Elements of
      Reusable Object-Oriented Software</field>
    <field name='text'>Design Patterns: Elements of
      Reusable Object-Oriented Software is a software
      engineering book describing recurring solutions to
      common problems in software design.
      (Source:http://en.wikipedia.org/wiki/Design_Patterns)
    </field>
    <field name='fullText' type='string'>The most famous
      book about Design Patterns.</field>
    <field name='keyword_string'>Design Patterns</field>
```

```
        <field name='keyword_string'>Software</field>
        <field name='language_string'>C++</field>
        <field name='language_string'>Smalltalk</field>
    </doc>
</add>
```

2. Now, to simplify,save it with the name `docs.xml` under the `/SolrStarterBook/solr-app/test/chp02/` directory.

What just happened?

In this small example we can easily recognize how the different types of fields are used. We write a value for every field representing the document, and multiple lines for multivalued fields (one for each different value to be added). Note that the field with the names `keyword_string` and `language_string` are handled as dynamic fields in our configuration.

Finally we directly added some text for the field `fullText`, even if we have defined it just as a destination for `copyField` and as the default field for searches. We did this to demonstrate two basic facts: the field is just a normal field, and its value will be added twice in the index according to `copyField` we have defined, which takes every field as a source (`source='*'`). The reason for this apparently wrong behavior is that `copyField` concatenates values on the destination field. So if you already have text in the field you use as the destination, you should use another way to select sources. You probably would map sources by an explicit name, and in most real cases you would choose not to post any value to the destination field.

Time for action – indexing an example document with cURL

Now that we have defined our example document, let's index it! Steps for indexing an example document with cURL are as follows:

1. The simplest way to send it for indexing is by using the cURL command-line tool:

   ```
   >> curl -X POST 'http://localhost:8983/solr/simple/
   update?commit=true&wt=json' -H 'Content-Type: text/xml' -d @docs.
   xml
   ```

2. If you have named the file to be posted in a different way, just use your own name in the command. I assume that you are executing cURL from the `/test/chp02` directory; if not, please use the full path name for your file.

3. If everything goes well, you should receive output like the following:

   ```
   >> {'responseHeader':{'status':0,'QTime':901}}
   ```

4. This result will inform us about the time used to process the query, and send us a code representing a status and an error message in case an exception is thrown.

> Note that we don't see any documents here; we will need to process some query to be able to see them.

What just happened?

Request parameters: Note that the output is in JSON, as we requested in the query using the `wt=json` parameter. We also asked Solr to directly add the document, using the `commit=true` parameter. When you have to insert a huge number of documents (for example, using a batch script that sends every document in this way), you probably want to speed up the process by inserting a certain number of documents and asking for a **commit** at the end, as the changes will not be fixed till the next commit.

Response parameters: Here status represents a status code (`0` is ok, as it represents no errors), and `QTime` is for query time (the time internally used to execute a search or, in this case, an insert).

cURL specific parameters: We are using the format as shown in the following command:

```
>> curl -X POST [http://solr?q1=v1&q2=v2] -H [http headers] -d @[path-of-
file].xml
```

When you use cURL, you can send a request to an HTTP address using one of the standard *HTTP methods*. I strongly suggest that you explicitly declare the method you are using with the parameter `-X`, because it makes things more readable, especially if you plan to define your own test scripts, save them, and share with others. The `-H` parameter is used for headers for the same reason. In this case we are sending our file called `docs.xml` (written using the Solr XML syntax) by the POST method. The parameter `-d` (or `-data-binary`) is used to define the binary data to be sent, and the `@` character declares that we use the name of the file and not the actual data.

A good place to read something more about cURL is in the official documentation at `http://curl.haxx.se/docs/manpage.html`, or `http://curl.haxx.se/docs/httpscripting.html`.

If you want to read something more on HTTP, there are several resources on the web. I suggest you start with wikipedia pages at

`http://en.wikipedia.org/wiki/Hypertext_Transfer_Protocol`
`http://en.wikipedia.org/wiki/Query_string`

You can also take a look at the site `http://www.jmarshall.com/easy/http/`

The binary data for the index is saved by default in the `/data` directory, under the Solr Home. This folder will contain an `/index/` folder with the binary files for the index itself, and can contain a directory to store other data for the specific functions we will see later in the book (for example, spellchecking). It's interesting to view the files saved under the `/data` directory. Every index is split into several parts. When an optimization is run, the segments may vary in size, number, and names.

The structure of the XML file we created permits us to add more than one `<doc>` element, so it's up to us to decide if we want to write an XML file for every document, or simply create a unique file for adding a group of documents at the same time.

Executing the first search on the new core

Now that the example document has been added to the index in our `simple` core, let's try returning all the documents with the default query:

```
>> curl -X GET 'http://localhost:8983/solr/simple/select?q=*:*&wt=json&indent=true'
```

This query executed on the command line corresponds to the one automatically generated on the web interface when we move into the **Query** section; now click on the **Execute Query** button:

As expected the `fullText` field contains all the results. Every single value is encapsulated into a `<str>` string element, and there is no explicit mention in the output about a field being dynamic or not.

The response format (in this case, in JSON) includes the parameters we have seen when posting the XML file via cURL in the header. Solr always responds with the same general format.

Adding documents to the index from the web UI

Another option to add documents to an index is to send them directly from a web interface, as shown in the following screenshot:

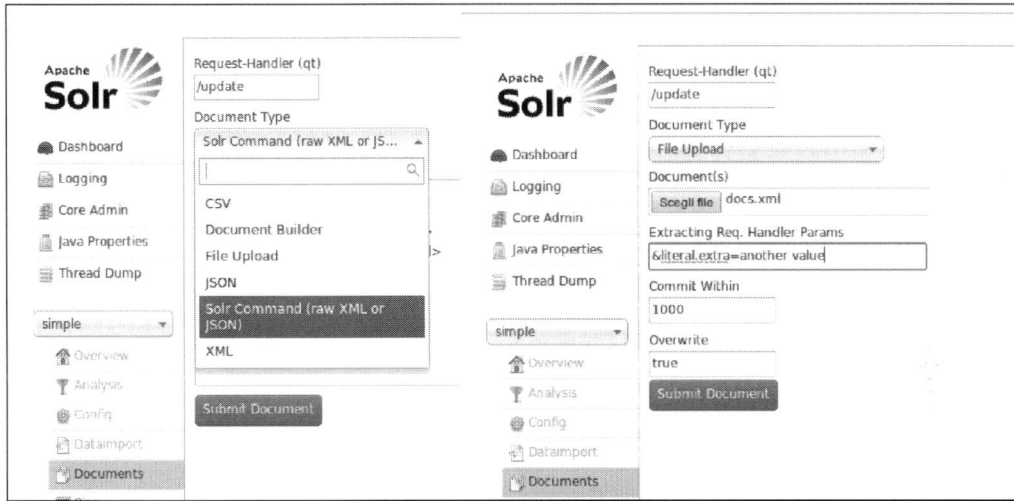

In the screenshot you can recognize two different options for posting the document to be indexed. On the left, we can choose to copy and paste the content of our `docs.xml` file in page form. We can also post the corresponding JSON format that we will see later in the book, and simply push the **Submit Document** button. On the right part of the image, you'll see that we can also upload the `docs.xml` file. In this case we also have the chance to add custom metadata, which is useful if we want to add, for example, administrative metadata (such as provenance or the date of the last update) for maintenance purposes.

The two examples are available in the document section on the left, and you can easily recognize other intuitive options from the screenshot, including a plain CSV format that does not interest us at the moment, but can be very useful in a number of real situations.

From my point of view the most surprising part of this interface is the **Document Builder** option, as shown in the following screenshot:

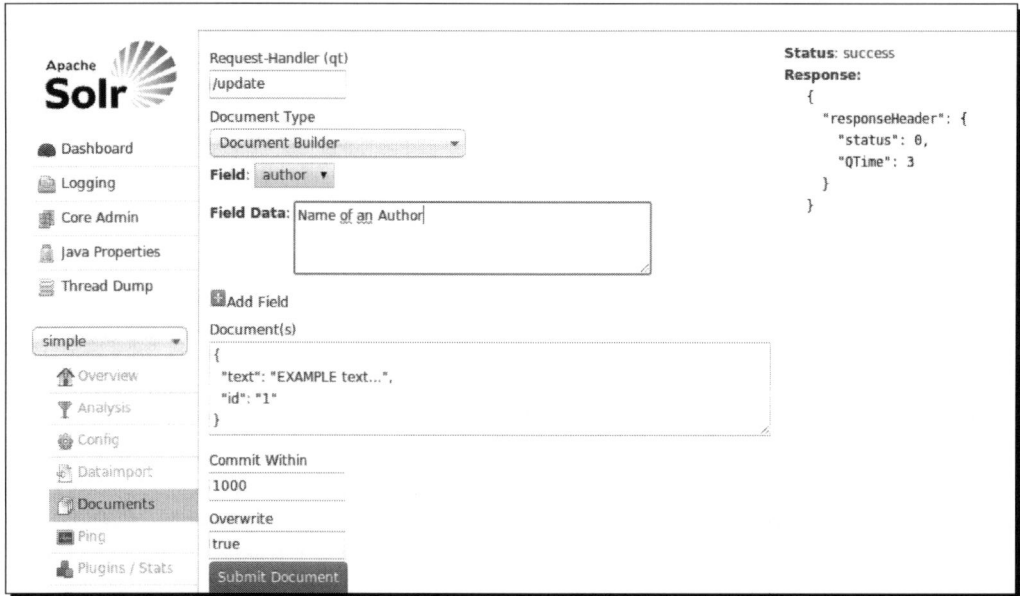

As you can see this interface permits us to 'construct' an example document and post it directly to the index. The sequence of steps is very simple:

1. Select a field.

2. Write some field data.

3. Add the field (with the green button).

At the end of this simple three-step iteration, the current version of the document you are constructing will be presented in the preview text area in a JSON format. You can directly re-edit the document there, and you can also re-iterate the three steps as many times as you want for adding new fields.

As you may imagine, this interface is still evolving (it has been introduced recently, by the way) and probably still lacks some useful functionalities, but it is very good to play with at the beginning, and it can offer us another way to perform our tests. My suggestion is to have at least two different browser windows (or tabs) opened on your Solr instance: one for performing queries, and the other for testing indexing if needed.

We will focus on cURL in the book, in order to better focus on a process that can be easily reproduced later with programming languages; but feel free to make your own experiments with this interface, too.

Time for action – updating an existing document

Sometimes you may want to update an existing document. Suppose we want to add to an existing document before a `uri` field that indicates its provenance:

1. All we have to do is edit the XML file seen before adding a field value like this:

    ```
    <field name='url_string'>http://en.wikipedia.org/wiki/Design_
    Patterns</field>
    ```

2. Then we re-execute the same cURL command:

    ```
    >> curl -X POST 'http://localhost:8983/solr/simple/
    update?commit=true&wt=json' -H 'Content-Type: text/xml' -d @docs.
    xml
    ```

What just happened?

Solr uses `uniqueKey` (in our case, ID) for identifying the document. The default update behavior in Solr is based on a *delete-and-add* strategy. If we execute our example, we will obtain the same document containing a new `uri_string` field. But this returned document is actually the result of a full delete (of the document with that ID) and a full post (of the entire modified document).

Verifying how the update process works is simple; however, we can create a new document containing only the ID and uri field. In this case the update will produce a result in which we will be able to recognize the last posted values. This may sound strange, but it is useful in most contexts as the metadata regarding a specific resource is maintained all at the same time, and deleting and rewriting them can help us maintain optimized indexes.

There can be other cases in which you would probably want to update on a per-field basis. This is quite similar to what normally happens with a database management system, and it introduces us to the context of *atomic updates*, which we will see in *Chapter 3, Indexing Example Data from DBpedia – Paintings*.

Time for action – cleaning an index

One of the most common things you will need to do when you are starting with your own experiments is to clean the index, deleting all the documents in it. This is a very common case when you want a fresh start with the data, to be able to see more clearly what is happening, or just because you are writing a script for updating your index and you want to test it, in order to make its behavior repeatable:

1. Clearing the index corresponds to deleting every document:

    ```
    >> curl -X POST 'http://localhost:8983/solr/simple/
    update?commit=true' -H 'Content-Type: text/xml' --data-binary
    '<delete><query>*:*</query></delete>'
    ```

2. As you see, the request for deletion is made by using a specific XML syntax; in this case we write it all in-line for simplicity, but the XML data can be also saved to a file.

What just happened?

We can easily delete Solr documents by using a query for selecting them. The q=*:* parameter here tells Solr that *we are searching in every field for every term occurrence*, so we are obtaining all the documents, and once selected deleting them (Solr will identify them internally by their id field).

Creating an index prototype from PDF files

Creating a small prototype of searches to test real data is a good way to identify a path for acquiring knowledge for a beginner when starting with new technologies. A prototype is indeed a working example that we can create at the beginning, even when we do not have a final analysis of the data model, or a complete collection of real data. This is useful to fix ideas, to test on 'almost real' data, and to create shared knowledge with the team, while doing tests. While dealing with real-world text, the kind of queries needed and the expected behaviors often appear to be clear by intuition, and we are able to eventually study how to specifically resolve them properly, one at a time. This is probably not that far from what you would discuss with your team and your clients or customers, too, and in this sense Solr can be used as a good tool to get them more involved in your design methodologies, especially if you use some kind of incremental development approach.

The path `/SolrStarterBook/resources/pdfs/` contains a directory of the sources of PDF files exported from free online repositories, which can be used as a source for our experimentations. You can also use your own collection as a simple test case for a new simple index.

Time for action – defining the schema.xml file with only dynamic fields and tokenization

The best way to keep the `schema.xml` file simple is to use only dynamic fields, so that we don't need to decide on the fields used from the beginning.

Our example will then have the following format:

```
<schema name='simple' version='1.1'>
  <types>
    <fieldtype name='string' class='solr.StrField'
postingsFormat='SimpleText' />
  </types>
```

```
<fields>
  <dynamicField name='*' type='string' multiValued='true'
indexed='true' stored='true' />
  <copyField source='*' dest='fulltext' />
  <field name='fullText' type='string' multiValued='true' />
</fields>
<defaultSearchField>fullText</defaultSearchField>
<solrQueryParser defaultOperator='OR' />
</schema>
```

As you can see, the schema.xml file is almost identical to the first example and even simpler; this should be one of the easiest and simplest ways to have a working Solr instance very quickly.

What just happened?

Here we write only a few things, and we are able to index every kind of field (posted to the /update API that we will see in a while) on our new Solr core called pdfs. We can conduct some tests with the XML posting format, but in this case we will anticipate the use of an internal Solr component (*SolrCell/Tika*) capable of doing an automatic extraction of metadata and text from PDF. So it's important to have a schema flexible enough to receive every field emitted from it, without the knowledge of the fields that will be emitted.

Time for action – writing a simple solrconfig.xml file with an update handler

One of the essential parts of the solrconfig, xml file will be the definition of an update handler for posting documents.

1. We can start with a basic example, in order to add some more complicated components later:

```
<config>
  <luceneMatchVersion>LUCENE_45</luceneMatchVersion>
  <directoryFactory name='DirectoryFactory' class='solr.
MMapDirectoryFactory' />

  <requestHandler name='standard' class=
    'solr.StandardRequestHandler' default='true' />
  <requestHandler name='/update' class='solr.UpdateRequestHandler'
/>
  <requestHandler name='/admin/' class='org.apache.solr.handler.
admin.AdminHandlers' />
  <admin>
```

```
        <defaultQuery>*:*</defaultQuery>
    </admin>

</config>
```

2. As you see, this basic configuration will include a standard /update handler, in order to receive the posted documents and index them.

What just happened?

This particular solrconfig.xml file configuration, as you see, only defines the default handler for accepting queries, and it generally will expose the simplest update handler. Using this handler in conjunction with our *schemaless* approach, let us index basically every new field posted to Solr.

Testing the PDF file core with dummy data and an example query

The best way to test if a core is working correctly is to post data to it and verify the results of simple queries. Then, to see if everything is working correctly, we can post some dummy data to our new index:

```
>> curl -X POST 'http://localhost:8983/solr/pdfs/
update?commit=true&wt=json' -H 'Content-Type: application/xml' -d
'<add><doc><field name='title'>Dummy Test Document</field><field
name='text'>Hello World</field></doc></add>'
```

Now we can easily see if the data has been correctly indexed:

```
>> curl -X GET 'http://localhost:8983/solr/pdfs/select?q=*:*&wt=json&inde
nt=true'
```

Once we have added at least two/three documents, repeat this process and change the example values to search for the documents containing the term hello. How do we search for it? Remember that the parameter q=*:* queries all the fields for every term; a basic search for hello can be written as q=fullText:hello or even replace with q=fulltext:'hello', where the double quotation is used for querying on an exact sequence of words (we will see it later with a phrase search), but is unnecessary now:

```
>> curl -X GET 'http://localhost:8983/solr/pdfs/select?q=fullText:hello&w
t=json&indent=true'
```

If we had simply written q=hello, defaultSearchField will be used. Note that searching for the term hello will not work at the moment, since we have adopted a string type for the fields, which indexes the textual values as a unique term. If we want this example to work correctly, we need to split the text into two different terms (to find Hello as a single term), and ignore the case (to be able to recognize Hello as a match for hello). We will add those capabilities in the next section.

Defining a new tokenized field for fulltext

In this section we will introduce a simple analyzer configuration for a fulltext field.

We can now update our `schema.xml` file, defining a new field type that we will call `text`. This internally uses two very common elements for the types, a **tokenizer** and a **filter**:

```
<types>
...
<fieldtype name='text' class='solr.TextField'>
  <analyzer>
    <tokenizer class='solr.WhitespaceTokenizerFactory' />
    <filter class='solr.LowerCaseFilterFactory' />
  </analyzer>
</fieldtype>
...
</types>
```

The **WhitespaceTokenizerFactory** is one of the most common tokenizers. A *tokenizer* is a component that splits an entire text fragment (a *string*) into several terms. This particular tokenizer splits terms by whitespace, for example, the string `Hello World` will be split into the terms `Hello` and `World`.

The **LowerCaseFilterFactory** is a filter that transforms the case of all the terms to lowercase.

Using these two combined and yet simple components, we are able to perform better searches. The best place to use this new field type in our example is probably the `fullText` field itself:

```
<field name='fullText' type='text' multiValued='true' />
```

Now we should have a chance to search for a simple term `hello`:

1. Stop and restart our Solr instance, to load the updated configuration containing the new type definition.
2. Index the example document again, in order to have its values analyzed with the new configuration.
3. Retry the query to obtain our document in the results, as expected.

With this simple addition, we are now able to perform queries searching only a single term.

Time for action – using Tika and cURL to extract text from PDFs

Solr integrates many powerful components, for example, **SolrCell** can be used to extract text from rich text documents and even PDF files, and to help us to automatically index it, as we will see in a while. The **Tika** library is designed to perform the following functions:

◆ Extract text from rich documents such as PDF, doc, and others

◆ Extract metadata for a file

◆ Identify the mime type of a file

◆ Automatically identify the language used in a document

We can play with Tika to extract text from one of the PDFs in the `/SolrStarterBook/resources/pdfs/` directory. We will now see how it's possible to map Tika inside Solr in order to index a PDF with a simple HTTP POST request:

1. First of all it's important to add the SolrCell component to make it executable by a specific Solr handler. All we have to do is to add a specific configuration in `solrconfig.xml`:

```
<config>
  <luceneMatchVersion>LUCENE_45</luceneMatchVersion>
...
  <lib dir='${solr.core.instanceDir}/../lib' />
...
  <requestHandler name='/update' class='solr.UpdateRequestHandler'
/>

  <requestHandler name='/update/extract' class='solr.extraction.
ExtractingRequestHandler'>
    <lst name='defaults'>
      <str name='captureAttr'>true</str>
      <str name='lowernames'>true</str>
      <str name='overwrite'>true</str>
      <str name='literalsOverride'>true</str>
      <str name='fmap.a'>link</str>
    </lst>
  </requestHandler>
...
</config>
```

2. The new request handler will also contain an interesting parameter, used to instruct Tika on how to emit metadata from the binary PDF file.

What just happened?

We have defined imports for the needed Tika libraries; on most of the `solrconfig.xml` files they have to be placed in the first part of the file. In our example we are importing all the jars contained in the same folder in the lib directory as the core folder. This configuration will produce the same result that we would get when we added the library in our configuration of the `solr.xml` file:

```
<str name='sharedLib'>lib</str>
```

The libraries we need to copy and put into the `lib` directory are:

* `SOLR_DIST/dist/`: `solr-cell-4,5,0.jar`
* `SOLR_DIST/extraction/lib/`: `tika-core-1.4.jar`, `tika-parsers-1.4.jar`, `pdfbox-1.8.1.jar`, `fontbox-1.8.1.jar`, `xercesimpl-2.9.2.jar`

Note that we imported some libraries specific to PDF. If we need to parse metadata from different sources, we have to add a specific library for parsing it.

We have defined a new `requestHandler` to the path `/update/extract`. This is the address where we have to post our PDF file to obtain from it the extracted text by Tika.

Navigate to the directory where you have your PDF, for example:

```
>> cd /SolrStarterBook/resources/pdfs/
```

Now we will extract data from the PDF using Tika by the `/update/extract` API:

```
>> curl -X POST 'http://localhost:8983/solr/pdfs/update/extract?extractOn
ly=true&extractFormat=text' -F 'Lucene.pdf=@Lucene.pdf'
```

The output extracted will be a structured text containing metadata parsed by Tika and plain text. We can try different values for `extractFormat`, `XML` and `JSON`. The `extractOnly` parameter is used to call Tika for extraction, without sending the extracted metadata to the update handler.

You can read more specific information on the SolrCell component at `http://wiki.apache.org/solr/ExtractingRequestHandler`.

The Tika component exposes several metadata from rich documents, depending on the type of the document. It is possible to index metadata even for MP3s or images, so we can, for example, search into EXIF values or into an album description in ID3.

Using cURL to index some PDF data

Using cURL we can send every kind of request to Solr core. We can even post files to be indexed using SolrCell. Once we have seen how Tika is able to extract metadata and texts from files, we can finally start indexing them into Solr:

```
>> curl -X POST 'http://localhost:8983/solr/pdfs/update/extract?extractFo
rmat=text&literal.annotation=The+Wikipedia+Page+About+Apache+Lucene&commi
t=true' -F 'Lucene.pdf=@Lucene.pdf'
```

From the preceding example we have started extracting the `extractOnly` parameter (we can write `extractOnly=false`), so that the metadata will not give an output and we can send the metadata directly to the update handler. Then `commit=true` ensures that the indexed data is saved and available for searches. A last note: `literal.annotation` can be used to add custom metadata during the `extract/post` phase.

Time for action – finding copies of the same files with deduplication

What if we added the same file more than once? This is possible, particularly when indexing a large number of files. One interesting case is trying to find if a document has already been added. **Deduplication** is the name we use for the process by which redundant information or duplicated files can be found, so that we can delete the copies and maintain an archive with only a single instance of every document. This can be very important, particularly in the context of a document management system, a shared documentation repository, or similar business cases.

We can easily create a unique key based on the content of the file. This new field can be used to find a document that has been added more than once:

1. We need to add the new field (let's call it `uid`) in our `schema.xml` file:

   ```
   <field name='uid' type='string' indexed='true' stored='true'
   multiValued='false' />
   <uniqueKey>uid</uniqueKey>
   ```

2. We can define a specific `updateRequestProcessorChain` for computing this particular `uid` unique identifier, modifying our `solrconfig.xml` file:

   ```
   <requestHandler name='/update/extract' class='solr.extraction.
   ExtractingRequestHandler'>
     <lst name='defaults'>
       <str name='captureAttr'>true</str>
       <str name='lowernames'>true</str>
       <str name='overwrite'>true</str>
       <str name='literalsOverride'>true</str>
   ```

```xml
            <str name='fmap.a'>link</str>
            <str name='update.chain'>deduplication</str>
         </lst>
      </requestHandler>

      <updateRequestProcessorChain name='deduplication'>
        <processor class='org.apache.solr.update.processor.
          SignatureUpdateProcessorFactory'>
          <bool name='overwriteDupes'>false</bool>
          <str name='signatureField'>uid</str>
          <bool name='enabled'>true</bool>
          <str name='fields'>content</str>
          <str name='minTokenLen'>10</str>
          <str name='quantRate'>.2</str>
          <str name='signatureClass'>solr.update.processor.
            TextProfileSignature</str>
        </processor>
        <processor class='solr.LogUpdateProcessorFactory' />
        <processor class='solr.RunUpdateProcessorFactory' />
      </updateRequestProcessorChain>
```

As you see, we introduce a new deduplication processor chain designed to manage this process, and call it by name inside the path of the /update/extract request handler, so that it will be executed every time we try to index metadata extracted from a source.

What just happened?

The new processor chain needs to be activated. We can do this by concatenating its invocation at the end of the /update/extract result handler:

```xml
    <str name='update.chain'>deduplication</str>
```

Once a uid field is introduced, we can execute the same command multiple times:

```
>> curl -X POST 'http://localhost:8983/solr/pdfs_4/update/extract?extract
Format=text&literal.uid=11111&commit=true' -F 'Lucene.pdf=@Lucene.pdf'
```

Changing the uid value provided, we are indexing the same file a number of times. You can also try to copy the file and index the copied one as well; after some additions, a simple default query will return more than one result. If we execute a simple query given as follows:

```
>> curl -X GET 'http://localhost:8983/solr/pdfs_4/select?q=*:*&start=0&ro
ws=0&wt=json&indent=true
```

We can see from the results that there will be no copies of the metadata indexed from the same file. At the end of the extraction phase, our deduplication processor starts and creates a 'footprint' for the content field in the form of a hash key, saved into the uid field, which will be signatureField. With the parameter fields=content (<str name='fields'>content</str>), we defined the source for calculating the hash. This way every uid represents the connection to a single document value. Indexing the same document several times will produce the same uid, which we also defined as uniqueKey. So the final result will have only a copy of it in memory, regardless of whether it was inserted first or last.

Please note how the tag lst is used to define a collection of parameter values, each of them defined into a tag that reflects theirs type (str for string, bool for boolean, and so on).

If you want to have some fun with data, it's possible to use a specific kind of query to count how many documents indexed from the same file exist. We can run this query to verify that all is going well (we expect a single document with its own UID for every file), and we can also run the same query after disabling the deduplication part, indexing the same resources many times, to see the counter grow:

```
>> curl -X GET 'http://localhost:8983/solr/pdfs_4/select?q=*:*&start=0&ro
ws=0&wt=json&indent=true&facet=true&facet.field=stream_source_info'
```

This is actually a *faceted query* on the field stream_source_info. We will discuss faceted queries in detail and how to use them in *Chapter 6, Using Faceted Search – from Searching to Finding*.

Time for action – looking inside an index with SimpleTextCodec

I would suggest the use of SimpleTextCodec to start looking inside a Solr Index, observing its internal structure saved as structured text.

A **codec** is a particular component that implements a specific policy to handle binary data, so you can consider it as the engine used for internal serialization of an index.

In order to enable it, it's important to add a specific codecFactory codec in the solrconfig.xml file:

```
<codecFactory name='CodecFactory' class='solr.SchemaCodecFactory' />
```

Once the codec is added, we can decide which fields (in schema.xml, as usual) are to be saved using the codec. Every field that we want to serialize by the codec needs to be declared explicitly, as shown in the following piece of code:

```
<fieldtype name='string' class='solr.StrField'
postingsFormat='SimpleText' />
```

If you update the configuration and restart your Solr instance, it's important to clean up the index before indexing example data again. This is done just to avoid potential problems and confusion. When we are done with this, we can easily take a look at the plain textual representation of what our index contains.

What just happened?

The `SimpleTextCodec` codec is a particular codec started as an experimental tool, and has now been added to the official components available in the default installation. It saves **Terms** in plain text files, so it's possible to directly view how the data is saved into the index itself, by simply opening one of the files ending in `.pst`:

```
of sub-projects, such as Lucene.NET, Mahout,Solr and Nutch. Solr has merged into the Lucene
project itself and Mahout, Nutch, and Tika have moved to becomeindependent top-level
projects.  Features and common useWhile suitable for any application which requires full text
indexing and searching capability, Lucene has beenwidely recognized[4][5] for its utility in
the implementation of Internet search engines and local, single-site searching.At the core of
Lucene's logical architecture is the idea of a document containing fields of text. This
flexibility allowsLucene's API to be independent of the file format. Text from PDFs, HTML,
Microsoft Word, and OpenDocumentdocuments, as well as many others (except images), can all be
indexed as long as their textual information can
beextracted.[6]
    doc 0
      freq 1
      pos 0
field content_type
  term application/pdf
    doc 0
      freq 1
      pos 0
field dcterms_created
  term 2013-05-10T17:37:54Z
    doc 0
      freq 1
      pos 0
field fulltext
  term application
    doc 0
      freq 2
      pos 468
      pos 610
  term enterprise
    doc 0
      freq 2
      pos 588
      pos 594
  term example,twitter
    doc 0
      freq 1
      pos 711
```

Be aware that this kind of codec is only useful for testing and learning purposes, as the process of writing to text files is one of the slowest. The performance degrades very quickly and hence it is not the ideal choice for a production environment. But if you want to update your index and save or update some document in it, it can be very interesting to observe how the index changes internally.

Observing the data and having an idea on what an index looks like internally finally introduces us to one of the most important concepts, the *inverted index*.

Understanding the structure of an inverted index

A Lucene index is basically an *Inverted Flat Index*. This means that when Lucene indexes the text for a resource we are interested in, it creates an internal representation where it registers every term found, the number of times it recurs, and in which documents it is found.

So, the real internal structure for an index is somewhat similar to the following diagram:

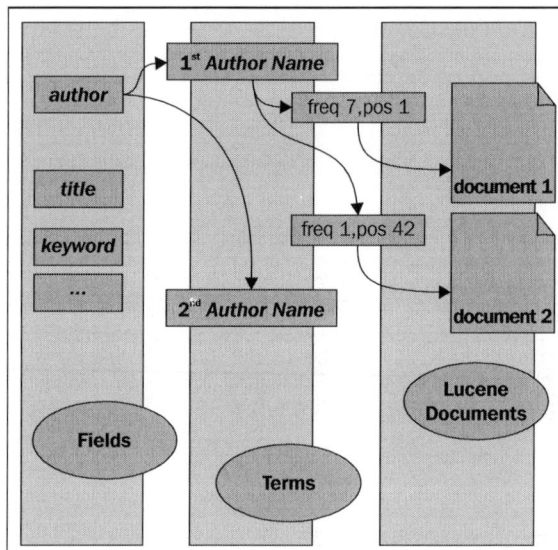

The structure is what is generally called an **inverted index**, and explains why Lucene is so fast at giving results in complex full-text searches and at creating and saving indexes, and generally has a limited memory footprint. This structure suggests that once a textual value has been analyzed and its frequencies and positions are saved, we don't necessarily need to save it while updating a field instance in the index. This is why Lucene generally retrieves documents by searches very quickly, but can require a certain amount of time for a full update of very big indexes.

> You can get a complete introduction to the Lucene syntax at
>
> `http://lucene.apache.org/core/4_5_0/queryparser/org/apache/lucene/queryparser/classic/package-summary.html`
>
> You can get a gradual and clear introduction at
>
> `http://www.lucenetutorial.com/basic-concepts.html`
>
> You can find useful and clear materials to study at `http://www.lucenetutorial.com/lucene-query-syntax.html`.

Understanding how optimization affects the segments of an index

Running an optimization is very common to find out the number of segment file changes. As the result of an optimization process, the segments are usually *merged into fewer files*, obtaining a more compact index. You will have a small recipe to request an optimization in a while, so I suggest you play with these recipes on your data, as an exercise.

Writing the full configuration for our PDF index example

Now let's see how the configuration files looks after all the modifications.

If you look at the provided sources, you'll find the full configuration at the path `/SolrStarterBook/solr-app/chp02/pdfs/conf`, the index data saved at the path `/SolrStarterBook/solr-app/chp02/pdfs/data/index`, and some scripts useful for your testing at the path of the companion directory `/test/chp02/pdfs`. In case you miss something while reading, you will also find the step-by-step version of the updated configurations in the same `/cho02/` folder.

Writing the solrconfig.xml file

Our configuration will now look as shown in the following piece of code:

```
<?xml version='1.0' encoding='UTF-8' ?>
<config>
  <luceneMatchVersion>LUCENE_45</luceneMatchVersion>
  <directoryFactory name='DirectoryFactory'
     class='solr.MMapDirectoryFactory' />
  <codecFactory name='CodecFactory' class=
     'solr.SchemaCodecFactory' />
  <lib dir='${solr.core.instanceDir}/../lib' />
  <requestHandler name='standard' class
    ='solr.StandardRequestHandler' default='true' />
  <requestHandler name='/update' class='solr.UpdateRequestHandler'>
    <lst name='defaults'>
      <str name='update.chain'>deduplication</str>
    </lst>
  </requestHandler>
  <requestHandler name='/update/extract' class=
    'solr.extraction.ExtractingRequestHandler'>
    <lst name='defaults'>
      <str name='captureAttr'>true</str>
      <str name='lowernames'>true</str>
      <str name='overwrite'>true</str>
```

```
            <str name='literalsOverride'>true</str>
            <str name='fmap.a'>link</str>
            <str name='update.chain'>deduplication</str>
        </lst>
    </requestHandler>
    <updateRequestProcessorChain name='deduplication'>
        <processor class='org.apache.solr.update.processor.
          SignatureUpdateProcessorFactory'>
            <bool name='overwriteDupes'>false</bool>
            <str name='signatureField'>uid</str>
            <bool name='enabled'>true</bool>
            <str name='fields'>content</str>
            <str name='minTokenLen'>10</str>
            <str name='quantRate'>.2</str>
            <str name='signatureClass'>solr.update.processor.
              TextProfileSignature</str>
        </processor>
        <processor class='solr.LogUpdateProcessorFactory' />
        <processor class='solr.RunUpdateProcessorFactory' />
    </updateRequestProcessorChain>
    <requestHandler name='/admin/' class=
      'org.apache.solr.handler.admin.AdminHandlers' />

    <admin><defaultQuery>*:*</defaultQuery></admin>
</config>
```

In the following chapters we will avoid transcribing a full configuration file, to make the example more readable. In this chapter we had the first look at a complete file. Though it is very simple, it will become more complex. This will help us to understand the ideas of the whole process more clearly.

Writing the schema.xml file

This file now contains all the types used in the examples, with their analysis (tokenization, case transformation):

```
<?xml version='1.0' encoding='UTF-8' ?>
<schema name='pdfs' version='1.1'>
<types>
<fieldtype name='string' class='solr.StrField'
postingsFormat='SimpleText' />
<fieldtype name='text' class='solr.TextField'
postingsFormat='SimpleText'>
  <analyzer>
```

```
      <tokenizer class='solr.WhitespaceTokenizerFactory' />
      <filter class='solr.LowerCaseFilterFactory' />
    </analyzer>
  </fieldtype>
  </types>
  <fields>
    <field name='uid' type='string' indexed='true'
      stored='true' multiValued='false' />
    <dynamicField name='*' type='string' multiValued=
      'true' indexed='true' stored='true' />
    <copyField source='*' dest='fullText' />
    <field name='fullText' type='text' multiValued='true' />
  </fields>
  <defaultSearchField>fullText</defaultSearchField>
  <solrQueryParser defaultOperator='OR' />
  <uniqueKey>uid</uniqueKey>
  </schema>
```

Dynamic fields have been introduced to include some flexibility, directly indexing every field exposed by Tika as metadata.

Summarizing some easy recipes for the maintenance of an index

There are some actions useful for the ordinary maintenance of an index, essential for testing it while we modify our configurations. Some of these commands should be saved for later reference, as they are commonly used.

Let's try to include some of them in a short list:

- Adding a simple dummy document:

```
>> curl -X POST 'http://localhost:8983/solr/pdfs/
update?commit=true&wt=json' -H 'Content-Type: text/xml' -d
'<add><doc><field name='id'>ID01</field><field name='text'>Test
Content</field></doc></add>'
```

- Deleting a document by criteria:

```
>> curl -X POST 'http://localhost:8983/solr/pdfs/
update?commit=true -H 'Content-Type: text/xml' --data-binary
'<delete><query>uid:00000000</query></delete>'
```

- Extracting text and metadata from a file:

```
>> curl -X POST 'http://localhost:8983/solr/pdfs/update/
extract?extractOnly=true' -F 'Lucene.pdf=@Lucene.pdf'
```

◆ Posting and indexing a file:

```
>> curl -X POST 'http://localhost:8983/solr/pdfs/update/
extract?commit=true' -F 'Lucene.pdf=@Lucene.pdf'
```

◆ Saving the last uncommitted modifications to the index:

```
>> curl -X POST 'http://localhost:8983/solr/pdfs/
update?commit=true' -H 'Content-Type: text/xml' --data-binary
'<commit />'
```

◆ Ignoring the last uncommitted modifications to the index:

```
>> curl -X POST 'http://localhost:8983/solr/pdfs/
update?commit=true' -H 'Content-Type: text/xml' --data-binary
'<rollback />'
```

◆ Optimizing the index:

```
>> curl -X POST 'http://localhost:8983/solr/pdfs/
update?commit=true' -H 'Content-Type: text/xml' --data-binary
'<optimize />'
```

◆ Cleaning the index

```
>> curl -X POST 'http://localhost:8983/solr/pdfs/
update?commit=true' -H 'Content-Type: text/xml' --data-binary
'<delete><query>*:*</query></delete>'
```

This short list can be easily used as a *quick cheat sheet* for the most used operations when testing Solr; I'm sure you will use them many times while reading this book.

In further chapters we will move to more details, step by step, to explore the main parts of the two XML files seen here.

Pop quiz

Q1. Where is the data actually saved?

1. Under the `core/index` folder
2. Under the `core/index/data` folder
3. Under the `core/data/index` folder

Q2. What are the differences between enabling a field to be stored or indexed?

1. A field stored is always indexed
2. A field defined as indexed can be used for searches, while a stored one cannot
3. A field defined as indexed can be used for searches, regardless if is stored or not
4. A field defined as stored can be returned in the output

Q3. How do we remove only the documents with a field `author` containing the term `Alighieri` from the index ?

1. Posting a document containing the text `<delete><query>*:*</query></delete>`

2. Posting a document containing the text `<delete><query><field name='author'>alighieri</field></query></delete>`

3. Posting a document containing the text `<delete><query>author:alighieri</query></delete>`

Q4. What can we see with `SimpleTextCodec`?

1. The codec used for saving binary files

2. The internal structure of an index

3. The text saved in the index for a full-text search

Q5. Disable tokenization, restart and look again at the index, then index some more data again. Take a look at the `SimpleTextCodec` saved file; has the data been saved differently?

1. There are no differences in the file

2. There are more items in the file, one for each word

3. There are more items in the file, one for each term

Q6. After cleaning or optimizing your Index with one of the recipes provided at the end of the Chapter, how does the index change?

1. The number of segments in the `core/data/index` directory changes

2. All the files in the `core/data/index` directory get deleted

3. All the files in the core/index directory get deleted

Q7. How can we index more than one document?

1. Writing a single XML file containing multiple documents for indexing them at once

2. Writing multiple XML files, one for each document to be indexed

3. Changing the configuration for an update handler

Q8. Is it possible to index a PDF file, adding custom metadata to the corresponding generated Solr document?

1. Yes, using a parameter in the request sent to the `/update` handler

2. No, all the metadata is extracted from Tika and we can't control them

3. Yes, but only changing the configuration files for the Tika library

Summary

In this chapter we have introduced some basic components in a simple way, and it's perfectly normal to find that there are a lot of elements to deepen our search.

We have defined two simple Solr cores, to be able to start from them as sort of templates for our next Solr experimentation. We saw how the core discovery feature can help us to manage multiple cores.

In the `simple` core we have focused on the structure of a Solr document to be indexed. The format used here for posting data is the XML default format. Feel free to try the examples again, using other formats such as JSON. We briefly take a look at the new Web interface for adding documents in `docs.xml` file.

The main PDF example helps us to focus on the dynamic field, and the capabilities of Solr to be used for managing rich text documents, a very powerful feature used in platforms such as Alfresco or Liferay.

3
Indexing Example Data from DBpedia – Paintings

In this chapter, we are going to collect some example data from DBpedia, create new indexes for searches, and start familiarizing you with analyzers.

We decided to use a small collection of paintings' data because it offers intuitive metadata and permits us to focus on some different aspects of data, which are open to different improvements seen in the next few chapters.

Harvesting paintings' data from DBpedia

First of all we need to have some example resources. Let's say data describing paintings, collected from real data freely available on the Internet.

A good source for free data available on the Internet is **Wikipedia**, so one of the options is to simply index Wikipedia as an exercise. This can be done as a very good exercise but it requires some resources (Wikipedia dumps have a huge size), and we may need to spend time on setting up a database and the needed Solr internal components. Since this example uses the DataImportHandler component, which we will see later, I suggest you follow it when we will talk about importing data from external sources:

```
http://wiki.apache.org/solr/DataImportHandler#Example:_Indexing_
wikipedia
```

Because we want to start with a simpler process, it's best to focus on a specific domain for our data. First, we retrieve Wikipedia pages on some famous paintings. This will reduce some complexity in understanding how the data is made. The data collection will be big enough to analyze, simulating different use cases, and small enough to use again and again different configuration choices by *completely* cleaning up the indexes every time. To simplify the process more, also using well-structured data, we will use the **DBpedia** project as our data source, because it contains data collected from Wikipedia and is exposed in a more structured and easy-to-query way.

> From day-to-day processes, such as *web scraping* of interesting external data or *Named Entity Recognition*, processes to annotate the content in some CMS are beginning to be very common. Solr also gives us the possibility to index some content we might not be interested in saving anywhere; we may only want to use it for some kind of *query expansion*, designed to make our search experience more accurate or wide.
>
> Suppose, as an example, we are a small publisher, and want to produce e-books for schools, we would want to add an extended search system on our platform. We want the users to be able to find the information they need and expand them with free resources on the web. For example, the History of Art book could cite the *Mona Lisa*, and we would want the users to find the book in the catalog even when they digit the original Italian name *Gioconda*. If we index our own data and also the alternative names of the painting in other languages without storing them, we will be able to guarantee this kind of flexibility in the user searches.

Nowadays, Solr is used in several projects involved in the so-called "web of data" movement. You will probably expect to have multiple sources for your data in the future—not only your central database—as some of them will be used to "augment" your data—or to expand their metadata descriptions—as well as your own queries, as a common user.

Just to give you an example of what data is available on DBpedia, let's look at the metadata page for the resource `Mona Lisa` at `http://dbpedia.org/page/Mona_Lisa`, as shown in the following screenshot:

dbpprop:artist	• dbpedia:Leonardo_da_Vinci
dbpprop:city	• Paris
dbpprop:hasPhotoCollection	• http://www4.wiwiss.fu-berlin.de/flickrwrappr/photos/Mona_Lisa
dbpprop:height	• 77 (xsd:integer)
dbpprop:heightInch	• 30 (xsd:integer)
dbpprop:imageFile	• Mona Lisa, by Leonardo da Vinci, from C2RMF retouched.jpg
dbpprop:imageSize	• 250 (xsd:integer)
dbpprop:museum	• dbpedia:Musée_du_Louvre
dbpprop:otherLanguage	• Italian • French
dbpprop:otherTitle	• La Joconde • La Gioconda
dbpprop:title	• Mona Lisa
dbpprop:type	• Oil on poplar
dbpprop:video	• Leonardo's "Mona Lisa", Smarthistory
dbpprop:width	• 53 (xsd:integer) • 210 (xsd:integer)
dbpprop:widthInch	• 21 (xsd:integer)
dbpprop:wikiPageUsesTemplate	• dbpedia:Template:Infobox_artwork • dbpedia:Template:External_media • dbpedia:Template:Infobox_Painting
dbpprop:year	• c. 1503–1519
dcterms:subject	• category:Mona_Lisa
rdf:type	• yago:LeonardoDaVinciPaintings • yago:1500sPaintings • yago:PaintingsOfTheLouvre
rdfs:comment	• La Gioconda o Mona Lisa és una pintura de Leonardo da Vinci, el retrat més famós d... mira directament l'espectador amb una expressió que sovint ha estat descrita com a e... per l'autor. La tècnica usada va ser l'esfumat (sfumato), procediment molt característic... • Mona Lisa, též označovaná Gioconda, je patrně nejslavnější portrét všech dob, na po... Autor si toto své dílo přibalil mezi svá zavazadla, když v roce 1516 nuceně opouštěl F... na jehož pozvání do Francie přijel, za poměrně vysokou částku 4000 zlatých dukátů.

We will see later how to collect a list of paintings from DBpedia, and then download the metadata describing every resource, `Mona Lisa` included. For the moment, let's simply start by analyzing the description page in the previous screenshot to gain suggestions for designing a simple schema for our example index.

Analyzing the entities that we want to index

In this section, we will start analyzing our data, and define the basic fields for a logical entity, which will be used for writing the documents to be indexed.

Looking at the structures of the RDF/XML downloaded files (they are represented using an XML serialization for RDF descriptions), we don't need to think too much about the RDF in itself for our purpose. On opening them with a text editor, you will find that they contain the same metadata for every resource, so you can easily find its corresponding DBpedia page. As seen before, most of them are based on best practices and standard vocabularies, such as *dublin core*, which are designed to share the representation of resources, and can be indexed almost directly. Starting from that, we can decide how to describe our paintings for our searches, and then what are the basic elements we need to select to construct our basic example core.

You can look at the sketch schema shown in the following diagram. It's simple to start thinking about a `painting` entity, which you can think of like a box for some fields:

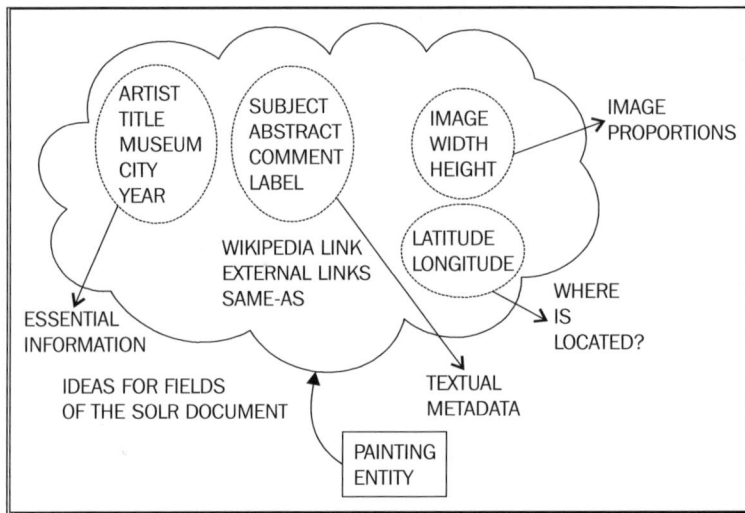

The elements cited are inspired by some of the usual metadata we intuitively expect and are able to find in most cases in the downloaded files.

I strongly suggest you to make a schema like the previous image when you are about to start writing your own configuration. This makes things more clearer than when you start coding directly, and also helps us to speak with each other, sharing, and understanding an emergent design.

In this collection of ideas for important elements, we can then start isolating some essential fields (let's see things directly from the Solr perspective), and when the new Solr core first runs, we could then add new specific fields and configurations.

Analyzing the first entity – Painting

To represent our `Painting` entity, define a simple Solr document with the following fields:

Field	Example
uri	`http://dbpedia.org/page/Mona_lisa`
title	Mona Lisa
artist	Leonardo Da Vinci
museum	Louvre
city	Paris

Field	Example
year	~1500
wikipedia_link	http://en.wikipedia.org/wiki/Mona_Lisa

We have adopted only a few fields, but there could be several; in this particular case we have selected those which seem to be the most easy and recognizable for us to explore.

Writing Solr core configurations for the first tests

We want to shape a simple Solr core configuration to be able to post some data to it, and experiment on the schema we are planning to define without playing with too much data.

If you are writing your own example from scratch while reading this book, remember to add the `solr.xml` file in the `/SolrStarterBook/solr-app/chp03/` directory, where we also create the new `/paintings_start/` folder, that will contain the new `core.properties` file. For the new core to work, we first have to define the usual `schema.xml` and `solrconfig.xml` configuration files.

Time for action – defining the basic solrconfig.xml file

In this paragraph, we will define a basic configuration file and add a handler to trigger commits when a certain amount of data has been posted to the core.

1. Let's start with a very basic `solrconfig.xml` file that will have the following structure:

```
<config>
  <luceneMatchVersion>LUCENE_45</luceneMatchVersion>
  <directoryFactory name="DirectoryFactory" class="solr.
MMapDirectoryFactory" />
  <codecFactory name="CodecFactory" class=
    "solr.SchemaCodecFactory" />

  <requestHandler name="standard"
    class="solr.StandardRequestHandler"default="true" />
  <requestHandler name="/update" class="solr.
UpdateRequestHandler"/>

  <requestHandler name="/admin/" class=
    "org.apache.solr.handler.admin.AdminHandlers" />
  <admin>
```

```
        <defaultQuery>*:*</defaultQuery>
    </admin>
    <requestHandler name="/analysis/field"
        class="solr.FieldAnalysisRequestHandler" />

    <updateHandler class="solr.DirectUpdateHandler2">
        <updateLog>
            <str name="dir">${solr.ulog.dir:}</str>
        </updateLog>
        <autoCommit>
            <maxTime>60000</maxTime>
            <maxDocs>100</maxDocs>
        </autoCommit>
    </updateHandler>

</config>
```

The only notable difference from the previous examples seen in *Chapter 2, Indexing with Local PDF Files*, is in the addition of the update handler `solr.DirectUpdateHandler2`, which is needed by Solr for handling internal calls to the update process, and a different choice for the codec used to save the binary data.

2. In this case, we are using a standard, but you can easily adopt the `SimpleTextCodec` seen before if you want to use it for your tests. If you change codec during your tests, remember to clean and rebuild the index.

What just happened?

Most of the configuration is identical to the previous examples, and will be used again for the next, so we will focus on the elements introduced that are new to us.

> **solr.* alias**
>
> When writing Solr configuration files, we can use short names alias for the fully qualified Java class name. For example, we wrote `solr.DirectUpdateHandler2`, which is a short alias for the full name: `org.apache.solr.update.DirectUpdateHandler2`.
>
> This alias works for Solr's internal types and components defined in the main packages:.`org.apache.solr.` (schema/core/analysis/search/update/request/response).

This example introduced the `DirectUpdateHandler2` component that is used to perform commits automatically depending on certain conditions.

With `<autoCommit>`, we can trigger a new automatic commit action when a certain amount of milliseconds have passed (`maxTime`) or after a certain amount of documents have been posted (`maxDocs`) and are waiting to be indexed.

The `<updateLog/>` tag is used for enabling the *Atomic Update* feature (for more details on the Atomic Update feature, see `http://wiki.apache.org/solr/Atomic_Updates`) introduced in the recent versions. This feature permits us to perform an *update on a per field basis* instead of using the default delete-and-add mechanism for *an entire document*. We also have to add a specific stored field for tracking versions, as we see in the `schema.xml` configuration details.

Looking at the differences between commits and soft commits

We always refer to the standard commit mechanism; a document will not be found on an index until it has been included in a commit, which *fixes* the modifications in updating an index. This way we are obtaining an almost stable version of the binary data for index storage, but reconstructing the index every time a new document is added can be very expensive and does not help when we need features such as atomic updates, distributed indexes, and near real-time searches (`http://wiki.apache.org/solr/NearRealtimeSearch`). From this point of view, you'll also find references to a *soft commit*. This is intended to make modifications to a document available for search even if a complete (hard) commit has not been performed yet. Because a commit can consume time and resources on big indexes, this is useful to fix a list of operations on the document while waiting to update the entire index with its new values. These small temporary updates can be triggered too with a corresponding, similar `<autoSoftCommit>` configuration.

Time for action – defining the simple schema.xml file

In this section, we will introduce lowercase and character normalization during text analysis. Steps for defining he simple `schema.xml` file are as follows:

1. We can now write a basic Solr `schema.xml` file, introducing a field for tracking versions, and a new `fieldType` with basic analysis:

```
<schema name="dbpedia_start" version="1.1">
  <types>
    <fieldtype name="string" class="solr.StrField" />
    <fieldType name="long" class="solr.TrieLongField" />

    <fieldType name="text_general" class=
      "solr.TextField" positionIncrementGap="100">
      <analyzer>
```

```
            <charFilter class="solr.MappingCharFilterFactory"
                mapping="mapping-ISOLatin1Accent.txt"/>
            <tokenizer class="solr.StandardTokenizerFactory" />
            <filter class="solr.LowerCaseFilterFactory" />
        </analyzer>
    </fieldType>
</types>

<fields>
    <field name="uri" type="string" indexed="true"
        stored="true" multiValued="false" required="true" />
    <field name="_version_" type="long" indexed=
        "true" stored="true" multiValued="false" />
    <dynamicField name="*" type="string" multiValued
        ="true" indexed="true" stored="true" />
    <field name="fullText" type="text_general" indexed
        ="true" stored="false" multiValued="true" />
    <copyField source="*" dest="fullText" />
</fields>

<defaultSearchField>fullText</defaultSearchField>
<solrQueryParser defaultOperator="OR" />
<uniqueKey>uri</uniqueKey>

</schema>
```

2. Even though this may seem complicated to read at the start, it is a simple schema that simply accepts every field we post to the core using the *dynamic fields* feature already seen before (http://wiki.apache.org/solr/SchemaXml#Dynamic_fields). We also copy every value into a fullText field, where we have defined a basic text analysis with our new type text_general.

What just happened?

The only field "statically" defined in this schema is the uri field, which is used to represent the original uri of the resource as a uniqueKey, and the _version_ fields, that we will analyze in a while. Note that in our particular case, every resource will have a specific unique uri, so we can avoid using a numeric id identifier without loosing consistency. For the moment, uri will be a textual value (string), and _version_ should be a numeric one (long) useful for tracking changes (also needed for the real-time get feature).

We have decided to define all the fields as indexed and stored for simplicity; we have explicitly decided that our dynamic fields should be multiValued and fullText, because they will receive all the values from every other field.

For the `fullText` field, we have defined a new specific type named `text_general`. Every user will perform searches using a combination of words, and our queries on the `fullText` field should be able to capture results using a single word or combination of words, and ignoring case for more flexibility. In short, the terms written by a user in the query will generally not be an exact match of the content in our fields, and we must start taking care of this in our `fullText` field.

If we want to define a customized `fieldType`, we should define a couple of analyzers in it: one for the *indexing* phase and the other for the *querying* phase. However, if we want them to act in the same way, we can simply define a single analyzer, as in our example.

Introducing analyzers, tokenizers, and filters

An analyzer can be defined for a type using a specific custom component (such as `<analyzer class="my.package.CustomAnalyzer"/>`) or by assembling some more fine-grained components into an *analyze chain*, which is composed using three types of components, generally in the following order:

- **Character Filter**: There can be one or more character filters, and they are optional. This component is designed to preprocess input characters by adding, changing, or removing characters in their original text position. In our example, we use `MappingCharFilterFactory`, which can be used to normalize characters with accents. An equivalent map for characters should be provided by a UTF-8 text file (in our case, `mapping-ISOLatin1Accent.txt`).

- **Tokenizer**: It is mandatory, and there can be only one. This kind of component is used to split the original text content into several chunks, or **tokens**, according to a specific strategy. Because every analyze chain must define a tokenizer, the simplest tokenizer that can be used is `KeywordTokenizerFactory`, it simply doesn't split the content, and produces only one token containing the original text value. We decided to use `StandardTokenizerFactory` that is designed for a wider general use case and is able to produce tokens by splitting text using whitespaces and periods with whitespaces, and it's able to recognize (and not split) URL, email, and so on.

- **Token Filter**: It can be one or more and is optional. Every `TokenFilter` will be applied to the token sequence generated by the preceding `Tokenizer`. In our case, we use a filter designed to ignore the case on tokens. Note that most of the token filters have a corresponding `Tokenizer` with a similar behavior. The difference is only in where to perform tokenizations; that is, on the complete text value or on a single token. So the choice between choosing a `Tokenizer` or a `TokenFilter` mostly depends on the other filters to be used in order to obtain the results we imagined for the searches we design.

There are many components that we could use; a nonexhaustive list of components can be consulted when configuring a new field at `http://wiki.apache.org/solr/AnalyzersTokenizersTokenFilters`.

Thinking fields for atomic updates

We have defined a `_version_` field, which can also take only a single value. This field is used to track changes in our data, adding version information. A version number for a modified document will be unique and greater than an old version. This field will be actually written by Solr itself when `<updateLog/>` is activated in the `solrconfig.xml` file. Because we need to obtain the last version values, we also need to have our version field to be stored.

I suggest you start using stored fields for your tests; this way, it's easy to examine them with alternative codecs, such as `SimpletextCodec`. Even if this will cost you some more space on disk, you can eventually evaluate whether a field needs to be stored during later stages of the incremental development.

Indexing a test entity with JSON

Once we have defined the first version of our configuration files, we can index the example `Mona Lisa` entity we used earlier to think about the fields in our schema. First of all, we will play with the first version of the schema then later we will introduce other field definitions substituting the dynamic ones.

In the following examples, we will use the json format for simplicity. There are some minor changes in the structure between json and XML posts. Note that every cURL command should be written in one line even though I have formatted the json part as multiline for more readability.

> **SON** (`http://www.json.org/`) is a lightweight format designed for data interchange. The format was initially conceived for JavaScript applications, but it became widely used in substitution of the more verbose XML in several contexts for web applications. Solr supports json not only as the format for the response, but also performs operations such as adding new documents, deleting them, or optimizing the index.

Both XML and json are widely used on Internet applications and mashups, so I suggest you become familiar with both of them. XML is, in most cases, used for rigorous syntactic checks and validation over a schema in case of data exchange. Json is not a real metalanguage as XML, but it is used more, and more often for exposing data from simple web services (think about typical geo search or autocomplete widgets that interact with remote services) as well as for lightweight, fast-linked approach on the data.

Using JSON with cURL in these example can give you a good idea on how to interact with these services from your platform/languages. As an exercise, I suggest you play the same query using XML as the result format, because there are minor differences in the structure that you can easily study yourself:

1. Clean the index. It's good, when possible, to have the ability to perform tests on a clear index.

```
>> curl 'http://localhost:8983/solr/paintings_start/
update?commit=true' -H 'Content-type:application/json' -d '
{
   "delete" : {
      "query" : "*:*"
   }
}'
```

2. Add the example entity describing a painting.

```
>> curl 'http://localhost:8983/solr/paintings_start/
update?commit=true&wt=json' -H 'Content-type:application/json' -d
'
[
   {
      "uri" : "http://en.wikipedia.org/wiki/Mona_Lisa",
      "title" : "Mona Lisa",
      "museum" : "unknown"
   }
]'
```

3. Add the same painting with more fields.

```
>>curl 'http://localhost:8983/solr/paintings_start/
update?commit=true&wt=json' -H 'Content-type:application/json' -d
'
[
   {
      "uri" : "http://en.wikipedia.org/wiki/Mona_Lisa",
      "title" : "Mona Lisa",
      "artist" : "Leonardo Da Vinci",
      "museum" : "Louvre"
   }
]'
```

4. Find out what is on the index.

```
>>curl 'http://localhost:8983/solr/paintings_start/select?q=*:*&co
mmit=true&wt=json' -H 'Content-type:application/json'
```

5. Please observe how the _version_ value changes while you play with the examples.

Understanding the update chain

When Solr performs an update, generally the following steps are followed:

1. Identifying the document by its unique key.
2. Delete the unique key.
3. Add the new version of the full document.

As you may expect, this process could produce a lot of fragmentation on the index structure ("holes" in the index structure) derived from the delete, and the delete and add operations over a very big index could take some time. It's then important to optimize indexes when possible, because an optimized index reduces the redundancy of segments on disk so that the queries on it should perform better.

Generally speaking, the time spent for adding a new document to an index is more than the time taken for its retrieval by a query, and this is especially true for very big indexes.

In particular context, when we want to perform a commit only after a certain number of documents have been added in the index, in order to reduce time for the rewriting or optimization process, we could look at the soft autocommit and near-realtime features. But for the moment, we don't need them.

Using the atomic update

The **atomic update** is a particular kind of update introduced since Solr 4. The basic idea is to be able to perform the modification of a document without necessarily having to rewrite it. For this to be accomplished, we need the addition of a _version_ field, as we have seen before.

When using atomic updates, we need to define our fields to be stored, because the values are explicitly needed for the updates, but with the default update process we don't need this because the full document is deleted and readded with the new values. The copy-field destination, on the other hand, should not necessarily be defined as stored.

If you need some more information and examples, you can look in the official wiki documentation at http://wiki.apache.org/solr/Atomic_Updates.

The following simple schema, however, can help us visualize the process:

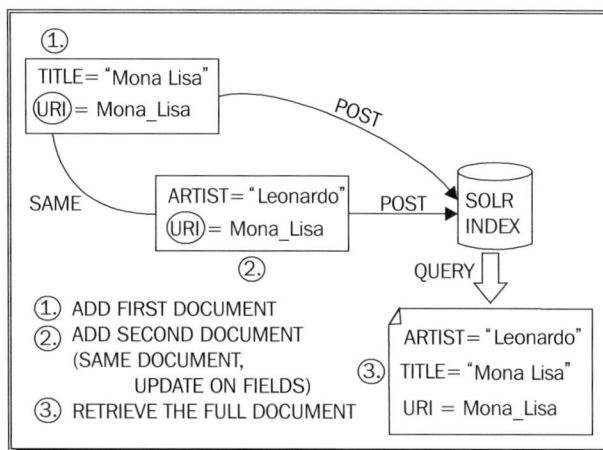

When performing an atomic update, we can also use the special attribute `update` on a per field basis. For example, in the XML format:

```
<add overwrite="true">
  <doc>
    <field name="uri">http://en.wikipedia.org/wiki/Mona_Lisa</field>
    <field name="title" update="set">Mona Lisa (modified)</field>
    <field name="revision" update="inc">1</field>
    <field name="museum" update="set">Another Museum</field>
    <field name="_version_" >1</field>
  </doc>
</add>
```

The corresponding json format has a slightly different structure:

```
[
  {
    "uri" : "http://en.wikipedia.org/wiki/Mona_Lisa",
    "title" : {"set":"Mona Lisa (modified)"},
    "revision"  : {"inc":1},
    "museum" : {"set":"Another Museum"},
    "_version_" : 1
  }
]
```

The values for this attribute define the different actions to be performed over the document:

- **set**: It is used to set or replace a particular value or remove the value if null is specified as the new value. This is useful when updating a single value field.

- **add**: It adds an additional value to a list. This is useful for adding a new value to a multivalue field.

- **inc**: It increments a numeric value by a specific amount. This is a particular attribute useful for some fields defined to act as counters. For example, if we have defined a field for counting the number of times a specific document has been updated.

> If you want to try posting these examples in the usual way (as seen in the previous examples), remember to add a `revision` field in the schema with the `long` type. When you have done this, you have to stop and restart the Solr instance; then, I suggest you take some time to play with the examples, changing data and posting it multiple times to Solr in order to see what happens.

The `_version_` value is handled by Solr itself and when passed, it generates a different behavior for managing updates, as we will see in the next section.

Understanding how optimistic concurrency works

Another interesting approach to use when updating a document is **optimistic concurrency**, which is basically an atomic update in which we provide the `_version_` value for a field. For this to work, we first need to retrieve the `_version_` value for the document we want to update, then if we pass the retrieved version value to the update process, the document will be updated as it exists. For more info please refer:

http://wiki.apache.org/solr/Atomic_Updates

If we provide a nonexistent value, it will be used with the following semantics:

version value	Semantics
>1	The document version must match exactly
1	The document exists
<0	The document does not exist

If we guess the current `_version_` value for performing updates on a certain specific document, we only have to make a query for the document (for example, by `uri`):

```
>> curl -X GET 'http://localhost:8983/solr/paintings_start/
select?q=uri:http\://en.wikipedia.org/wiki/Mona_Lisa&fl=_
version_&wt=json&indent=true'
```

Retrieve the _version_, and then construct the data to be posted. In this example, we have also anticipated the fl (fields list) parameter, which we will see in the next chapter.

Time for action – listing all the fields with the CSV output

We need a simple method to *retrieve a list of all the possible fields*. This could be useful in most situations. For example, when we have to manage several fields, it will be important to be able to check if they are in the index and how to remap them with copyField when needed:

```
>> curl -X GET 'http://localhost:8983/solr/paintings_start/
select?q=*:*&rows=0&wt=csv'
```

This simple combination of parameters permits us to retrieve the list of fields currently available.

What just happened?

In this simple case, we introduced two basic parameters, **write type (wt)** and **number of rows (rows)**. There are cases when we don't need to retrieve the documents explicitly, because we only want some other metadata (rows=0), and we want the results in several formats. For the CSV format, the output will contain a list of headers with the name of the fields to be used as column names, so we have a simple list on combining the two options.

In *Chapter 4, Searching the Example Data*, we will see the response format in more detail.

Defining a new Solr core for our Painting entity

Finally, it's time for refactoring our schema and indexing all the downloaded documents.

First of all, we have to rewrite the configurations. In particular, we will define a new Solr core with the name paintings, having the same solrconfig.xml and a slightly modified schema.xml. When we have defined the new Solr core, we have to simply copy the configurations from paintings_start core to a new paintings core, and then we modify the schema.xml file by adding the basic fields we need for our entity.

Time for action – refactoring the schema.xml file for the paintings core by introducing tokenization and stop words

We will rewrite the configuration in order to make it adaptable to real-world text, introducing stop words and a common tokenization of words:

1. Starting from a copy of the schema designed before, we added two new field types in the `<types>` section:

```
<fieldType name="text_general" class="solr.TextField">
  <analyzer>
    <charFilter class="solr.MappingCharFilterFactory"
      mapping="mapping-ISOLatin1Accent.txt" />
    <tokenizer class="solr.StandardTokenizerFactory" />
    <filter class="solr.StopFilterFactory" ignoreCase=
      "true" words="stopwords.txt"
      enablePositionIncrements="true" />
    <filter class="solr.LowerCaseFilterFactory" />
  </analyzer>
</fieldType>

<fieldType name="url_text" class="solr.TextField">
  <analyzer>
    <charFilter class="solr.MappingCharFilterFactory"
      mapping="mapping-ISOLatin1Accent.txt" />
    <tokenizer class="solr.WhitespaceTokenizerFactory" />
    <filter class="solr.WordDelimiterFilterFactory"
      generateWordParts
      ="1" generateNumberParts="1" catenateWords="0"
      catenateNumbers="0" catenateAll="0"
      splitOnCaseChange="0" preserveOriginal="0" />
    <filter class="solr.LowerCaseFilterFactory" />
  </analyzer>
</fieldType>
```

2. We can then simply add some fields to the default ones using the new fields we have defined:

```
<field name="artist" type="url_text" indexed="true" stored="true"
multiValued="false" />
<field name="title" type="text_general" indexed=
  "true" stored="true" multiValued="false" />
<field name="museum" type="url_text" indexed="true"
  stored="true" multiValued="false" />
<field name="city" type="url_text" indexed=
  "true" stored="true" multiValued="false" />
```

```
<field name="year" type="string" indexed=
  "true" stored="true" multiValued="false" />
<field name="abstract" type="text_general" indexed=
  "true" stored="true" multiValued="true" />
<field name="wikipedia_link" type="url_text" indexed=
  "true" stored="true" multiValued="true" />
```

We have basically introduced a filter for filtering out certain recurring words for improving searches on the `text_general` field, and a new `url_text` designed specifically for handling URL strings.

What just happened?

The `string` type is intended to be used for representing a unique textual token or term that we don't want to split into smaller terms, so we use it for representing only the `year` and `uri` fields. We didn't use the date format provided by Solr because it is intended to be used for range/period queries over dates and uses a specific format. We will see these kind of queries later. On analyzing our dates, we found that in some cases, the year field contains values that describe an uncertain period such as `1502-1509` or `~1500`, so we have to use the `string` value for this type.

On the other hand, for the fields containing normal text, we used the type `text_general` that we had defined and analyzed it for the first version of the schema. We also introduced `StopFilterFactory` into the analyzer chain. This token filter is designed to exclude some terms that are not interesting for a search from the token list. The typical examples are articles such as `the` or offensive words. In order to intercept and ignore these terms, we can define a list of these in an apposite text file called `stopwords.txt`, line by line. By ignoring case, it is possible to have more flexibility, and `enablePositionIncrements=true` is used for ignoring certain terms, maintaining a trace of their position between other words. This is useful to perform queries such as `author of Mona Lisa`, which we will see when we talk about *phrase query*.

Lastly, there are several values in our data that are `uri`, but we need to treat them as values for our searches. Think about, for example, the `museum` field of our first example entity, `http://dbpedia.org/resource/Louvre`. The `uri_text` field can work because we defined an analyzer that first normalizes all the accented characters (for example in French terms) using a particular character filter called **MappingCharFilter**. It's important to provide queries that are robust enough to find terms with digitization and without the right accents, especially when dealing with foreign languages, so the normalization process replaces the accented letter with the corresponding one without accent. This filter needs a text file to define explicit mappings for the `mapping-ISOLatin1Accent.txt` character substitution, which should be written with a UTF-8 encoding to avoid problems.

The field type analyzer uses a **WhitespaceTokenizer** (we probably could have used a **KeywordTorkenizer** here obtaining the same result), and then two token filters, **WordDelimiterFilterFactory** that splits the part of an uri, and the usual **LowerCaseFilterFactory** for handling terms ignoring cases. The WordDelimiterFactory filter is used to index every part of the uri since the filter splits on the / character into multiple parts, and we decided not to concatenate them but to generate a new part for every token.

Using common field attributes for different use cases

A combination of the true and false values for the attributes of a field typically has an impact on different functionalities. The following schema suggests common values to adopt for a certain functionality to work properly:

Use Case	Indexed	Stored	Multi Valued
searching within field	true		
retrieving contents		true	
using as unique key	true		false
adding multiple values and maintaining order			true
sorting on field	true		false
highlighting	true	true	
faceting	true		

In the schema you will also find some of the features that we will see in further chapters; it is just to give you an idea in advance on how to manage the predefined values for fields that are designed to be used in specific contexts.

For an exhaustive list of the possible configurations, you can read the following page from the original wiki: http://wiki.apache.org/solr/FieldOptionsByUseCase.

Testing the paintings schema

Using the command seen before, we can add a test document:

```
>> curl -X POST 'http://localhost:8983/solr/paintings/
update?commit=true&wt=json' -H 'Content-type:application/json' -d '
[
  {
    "uri" : "http://dbpedia.org/resource/Mona_Lisa",
    "title" : "Mona Lisa",
    "artist" : "http://dbpedia.org/resource/Leonardo_Da_Vinci",
```

```
    "museum" : "http://dbpedia.org/resource/Louvre"
  }
]'
```

Then, we would like to search for something using the term `lisa` and be able to retrieve the `Mona Lisa` document:

```
>> curl -X GET 'http://localhost:8983/solr/paintings/select?q=museum:Louv
re&wt=json&indent=true' -H 'Content-type:application/json'
```

Now that we have a working schema, it's finally time to collect the data we need for our examples.

Collecting the paintings data from DBpedia

It's now time to collect metadata from DBpedia. This part is not strictly related to Solr in itself, but they are useful for creating more realistic examples. So, I have prepared, in the repository, both the scripts to download the files and some Solr document already created for you from the downloaded files. If you are not interested in retrieving the files by yourself, you can directly skip to the *Indexing example data* section.

In the `/SolrStarterBook/test/chp03/` directory, you will also find the `INSTRUCTIONS.txt` file that describes the full process step-by-step from the beginning to a simple query.

Downloading data using the DBpedia SPARQL endpoint

DBpedia is a project aiming to construct a structured and *semantic* version of Wikipedia data represented in **RDF (Resource Description Framework)**. Most of the data in which we are interested is described using the **Yago** ontology, which is one well-known knowledge base and can be queried by a specific language called **SPARQL**.

> The **Resource Description Framework** is widely used for conceptual data modeling and conceptual description. It is used in many contexts on the Web and can be used to describe the "semantics" of data. If you want to know more, the best way is to start from the Wikipedia page, `http://en.wikipedia.org/wiki/Resource_Description_Framework`, which also contains links the most recent RDF specifications by W3C.

Just to give you an idea for obtaining a list of pages, we could, use SPARQL queries similar to the following (I omit the details here) against the DBpedia endpoint found at `http://dbpedia.org/sparql`:

```
SELECT DISTINCT ?uri
WHERE {
```

```
    ?uri rdf:type ?type.
    {?type rdf:type <http://dbpedia.org/class/yago/Painting...>}
}
```

When the list is complete (we can ask the results directly as a CSV list of uris), we can then download every item from it in order to extract the metadata we are interested in.

> The **Scala** language is a very good option for writing scripts and combines the capabilities of the standard Java libraries with a powerful, synthetic, and (in most cases) easy-to-read syntax, so the scripts are written using this language. You can download and install Scala following the official instructions from http://www.scala-lang.org/download/, and add the Scala interpreter and compiler to the PATH environment variable as we have done with Java.

We can directly execute the SCALA sources in /SolrStarterBook/test/chp03/paintings/. (Let's say you want to customize the script.) For example we can start the download process calling the downloadFromDBPedia script (if you are on a Windows platform, simply use the bat version instead):

>> ./downloadFromDBPedia.sh

If you don't want to install Scala, you can simply run the already compiled downloadFromDBPedia.jar file with Java, including the Scala library, with the alternative script:

>> ./downloadFromDBPedia_java.sh

Note that these two methods are equivalent as when the first is running, it creates the executable jar if the jar does not exist.

> When playing with the **Wikipedia api**, it is simple to obtain a single page. If you look for examples at http://en.wikipedia.org/w/api.php?action=parse&format=xml&page=Mona_Lisa, you will see what we are able to retrieve directly from the Wikipedia API—the resource page describing the well know painting *La Giaconda*. If you are interested in using the existing *webcrawlers'* libraries to automate these processes without have to write an ad hoc code every time, you should probably take a look at *Apache Nutch* at http://nutch.apache.org/ and how to integrate it with Solr.

Once the download terminates (it could take a while depending on your system and network speed), we will finally have collected several RDF/XML files in /SolrStarterBook/resources/dbpedia_paintings/downloaded/. These files are our first source of information, but we need to create Solr XML documents to post them to our index.

Creating Solr documents for example data

The XML format used for posting is the one that is usually seen by default. Due to the number of resources that have to be added, I prefer to create a single XML file for posting every resource. In a real system, this process could have been handled differently but in our case, this permits us to easily skip problematic documents.

To create the Solr XML document, we have two options. Again, it's up to you to decide if you want to use the Scala script directly or call the compiled jar using one of the following two command statements:

```
>> ./createSolrDocs.sh
>> ./createSolrDocs_java.sh
```

This process internally uses an XSLT transformation (dbpediaToPost.xslt) to create a Solr document with the fields in which we are interested for every resource. You may notice some errors on the console since some of the resources can have issues regarding data format, encoding, and others. These will not be a problem for us, and also could be used as a realistic example to see how to manage character normalization or data manipulation in general.

Indexing example data

The first thing we need to index data is to have a running Solr instance for our current configuration. For your convenience you can use the script provided in /SolrStarterBook/test:

```
>> ./start.sh chp03
```

In the directory /SolrStarterBook/resources/dbpedia_paintings/solr_docs/, we have the Solr documents (in XML format) that can be posted to Solr in order to construct the index. To simplify this task, we will use a copy of the post.jar tool that you'll find on every Solr standard installation:

```
>> java -Dcommit=yes -Durl=http://localhost:8983/solr/paintings/update
-jar post.jar ../../../resources/dbpedia_paintings/solr_docs/*.xml
```

Note how the path used is relative to the current /SolrStarterBook/test/chp03/paintings/ folder.

Testing our paintings core

Once the data has been posted to the paintings core, we can finally play with our paintings core using the web interface to verify whether everything is working fine.

Time for action - looking at a field using the Schema browser in the web interface

Here, we can play with the web interface, select our core, and choose **Schema browser** in order to have a visual summary of the different elements of a field in our schema. For example, the field artist shown in the following screenshot:

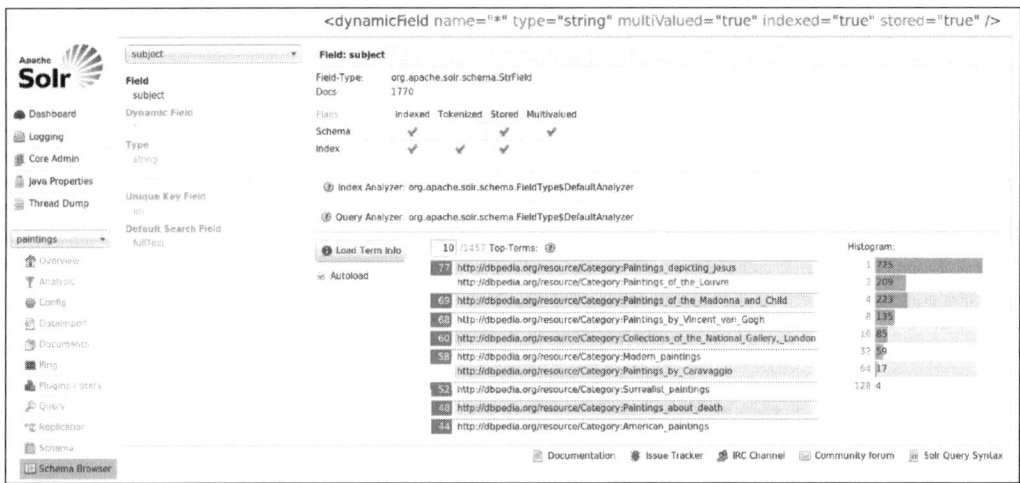

What just happened?

In the previous screenshot, it is simple to recognize the options we entered for the field in the file `schema.xml` and a list of the most used terms. For example, we find that in our example data there are at the moment a number of paintings about religious subjects.

Time for action – searching the new data in the paintings core

One of the first things to think when configuring a Solr core are the kind of searches we are interested in. It could seem trivial, but is not since every field in our schema definition typically needs a good and specific configuration.

The basic searches we want to perform are probably as follows (consider this just as a start):

1. Search for a specific artist.

2. Search for titles of the works by the artist `caravaggio`.

3. Search a term or a name in the full text or abstract field.

Request-Handler (qt)	
/select	🔲 http://localhost:8983/solr/paintings/select?q=lionardo~0.5&rows=1

```
--- common ---
q
lionardo~0.5

fq

sort

start, rows
0            10

fl
title

df

Raw Query Parameters
key1=val1&key2=val2

wt
CSV
```

```
title
Portrait of a Musician
"The Battle of Anghiari,The Battle of Anghiari"
"St. John the Baptist,St. John the Baptist"
"Bacchus,Bacchus"
Lady with an Ermine
The Battle of Anghiari
St. John the Baptist
Bacchus
"The Last Supper,The Last Supper"
"Christ Crowned with Thorns,Christ Crowned with Thorns"
```

What just happened?

The first search is the most simple one. We only search in the artist field for an artist with a name containing the term picasso. The result format chosen is XML.

In the second search, we want to use the CSV response format seen before and yet we play with the fields list (fl) parameter, which is designed to choose which fields' projection to include in the results. In our example, we want only a list of titles in plain text, so we use wt="CSV" and fl="title".

In the last search, we play with a simple anticipation of *fuzzy search*, which we will see in *Chapter 4, Searching the Example Data*. The query for artist:lionardo~0.5 permits us to search for a misspelled name, which is a typical case when searching for a name in a foreign language.

Using the Solr web interface for simple maintenance tasks

At last, it's important to remember that the web interface could be used to have a visual outline of the Solr instances that are now running. In our examples, we are often trying to use some basic command line tool because it permits us to pay attention on what is happening during a particular task. In the web interface, on the other hand, it's quite useful to have a general view of the overall system. For example, the dashboard gives us a visual overview of the memory used, version installed, and so on as shown in the following screenshot:

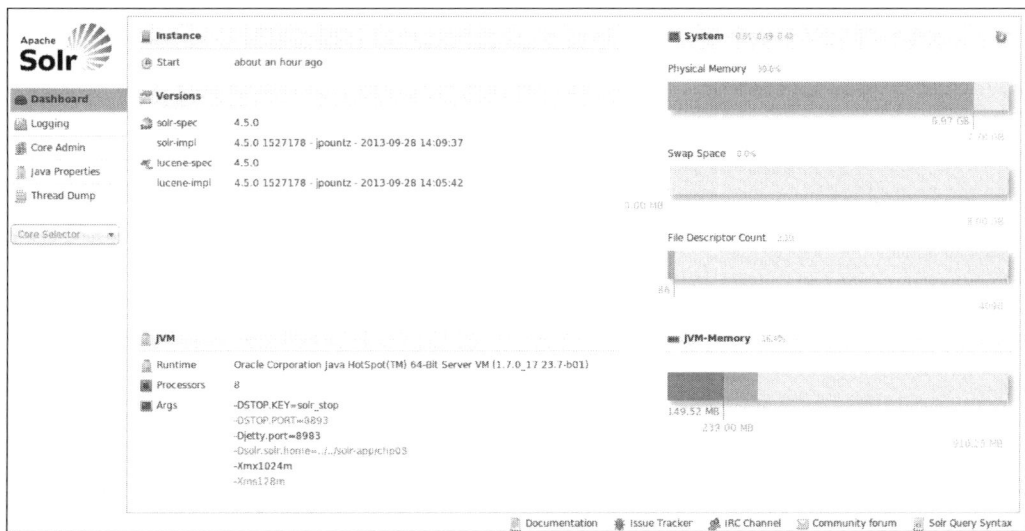

The web interface has greatly evolved from the previous versions. Now, it is much more like a frontend to the services provided by the server; we can use the same directly from our language or tool of choice, for example, with cURL, again.

For example, we could easily perform an optimization by selecting a core on the left, and then just clicking the **optimize now** button. You can see that there are two icons informing us about the state of the index and whether it needs to be optimized or not.

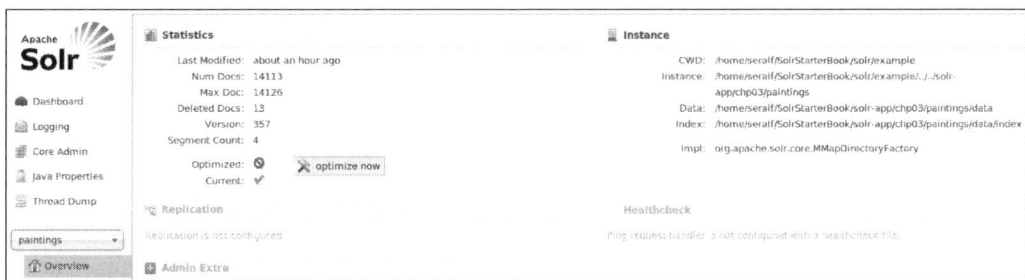

Just to give you an idea, the *optimization process* is very important when we need to upgrade from the previous Solr index constructed before the version 4.x. This is because Solr 3 indexes are different from the Solr 4 branch but can be loaded from the last distribution if updated with a Solr 3.6 version and, obviously, if the fields defined are compatible. That said, a little trick for such an update process is to update the old Solr instance to the last of the Solr 3 branch, perform an optimization on the indexes (so that they are overwritten with a compatible structure for Solr 4), and then move to Solr 4.

Using the **Core Admin** menu item on the left in the web interface, we can also see an *overview page for every core* as shown in the following screenshot:

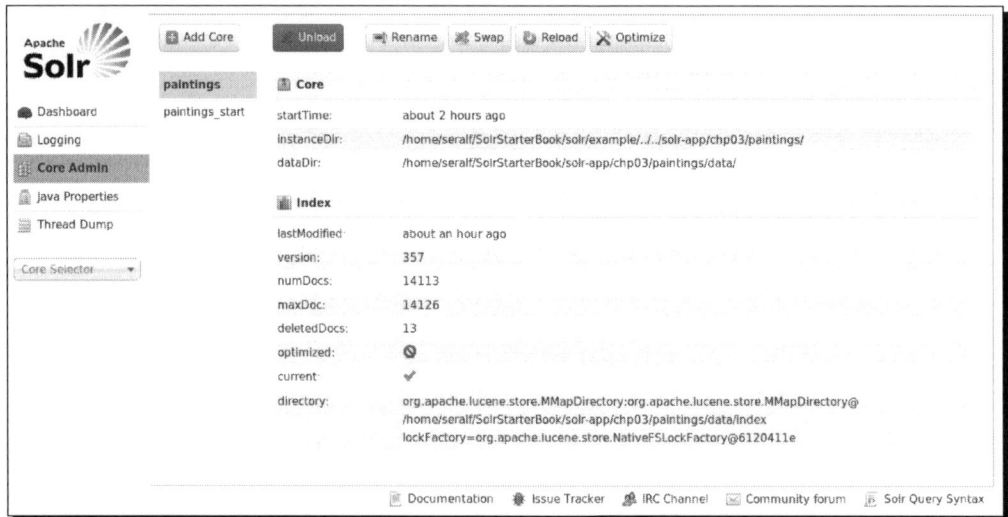

In this case, we could not only request for an optimization, but also for loading/unloading cores or swapping them to perform administration tasks.

We can expect the interface to add more functionality and flexibility in the next version, responding to the requests of the community, so the best option is to follow the updates from version to version.

Pop quiz

Q1. What is the purpose of an `autoCommit` configuration?

1. It can be used to post a large amount of documents to a Solr index.
2. It can be used to automatically commit the change to a certain amount of documents.
3. It can be used to automatically commit changes to documents after a certain amount of time.

Q2. What is the main difference between a char filter and a token filter?

1. Using a char filter is mandatory, while using a token filter is not.
2. A token filter is used on an entire token (a chunk of text), while a char filter is used on every character.
3. There can be more than a single char filter but only a single token filter can be used.

Q3. What does a tokenizer do?

1. A tokenizer is used to split text into a sequence of characters.
2. A tokenizer is used to split text into a sequence of words.
3. A tokenizer is used to split text into a sequence of chunks (tokens).

Q4. In what contexts will an atomic update be useful?

1. When we want to perform a single update.
2. When we want to update a single document.
3. When we want to update a single field for a document.

Summary

In this chapter we used a couple of scripts to collect RDF resources from DBpedia, which contains structured paintings' metadata that we will use in our examples.

We saw how to define a simple core configuration and did tests, indexing, and updating of a single document to start with.

The next step was to analyze the data collected and extend our schema in order to add fields in which we are interested, focusing on natural searches.

Finally, we played with the admin web interface to familiarize with it a little more, play simple searches, and find out how to use it to request for an optimization of the core.

4
Searching the Example Data

In this chapter, we will proceed with short examples and cover the essential syntax, which can be expanded later in several ways.

Starting from a core configuration, which is more or less identical to the one seen in Chapter 3, Indexing Example Data from DBpedia – Paintings, we will focus on the standard basic parameters. We will see how to pass a simple query with multiple terms, assembling them by various type of Boolean conditions, including the adoption of incomplete or misspelled terms. We will also see how to shape results projecting fields, and pagination, introducing the possibility of rearranging and sorting results.

We will continue with some more complex and specific requests in the further chapters.

Looking at Solr's standard query parameters

The basic engine of Solr is **Lucene**. So, Solr accepts a query syntax based on Lucene. Even if there are some minor differences, they should not affect our experiments, because they involve more advanced behavior. You can find an explanation of the Solr Query syntax on wiki at: `http://wiki.apache.org/solr/SolrQuerySyntax`.

Let's see some example of a query using the basic parameters. Before starting our tests, we need to configure a new core again in the usual way.

Adding a timestamp field for tracking the last modified time

We can define a new core using the the same configuration seen in *Chapter 3, Indexing Example Data from DBpedia – Paintings*, for the `paintings` core, we can copy and paste both the `schema.xml` and `solrconfig.xml` files and start from those.

Once the new core is created at the location `/SolrStarterBook/chp04/solr-app/paintings/`, we can add a new administrative metadata field in the `schema.xml` file, which describes the date and time of last modification of a document:

```
<fieldType name="date" class="solr.TrieDateField"  />
<field name="timestamp" type="date" indexed="true" stored="true" />
```

We will use this field later in this chapter.

The field is defined with a specific datatype that uses a canonical representation of the date and time (ISO 8601 standard). We could add current time while indexing a new document by simply posting the value NOW, which is used as a placeholder for the current time calculation:

```
<field name="timestamp">NOW</field>
```

This method is good for local Solr, but it can cause some problems to the distributed instances of SolrCloud, because it can produce unexpected difference in time. A good practice is to modify the default update handler in `solrconfig.xml`, introducing a specific update chain for generating timestamps:

```
<requestHandler name="/update" class="solr.UpdateRequestHandler">
  <lst name="defaults">
  <str name="update.chain">timestamp</str>
  </lst>
</requestHandler>
<updateRequestProcessorChain name="timestamp" default="true">
  <processor class="solr.TimestampUpdateProcessorFactory">
    <str name="fieldName">timestamp</str>
  </processor>
  <processor class="solr.LogUpdateProcessorFactory" />
  <processor class="solr.RunUpdateProcessorFactory" />
</updateRequestProcessorChain>
```

This example is useful to get an anticipation of how a custom *update chain* works (we will see this in detail later). It is interesting to notice how a specific component will be used to compute the current time (`TimeStampUpdateProcessor`). Moreover, when using distributed instances of Solr, every local update process (`RunUpdateProcess`) will have its own update chain executed and then a distributed update (`DistributingUpdateProcessor`) will be attached in the end by default.

Sending Solr's query parameters over HTTP

It is important to take care of the fact that our queries to Solr are sent over the HTTP protocol, unless we are using Solr in embedded mode (we will see this later). With cURL, we can handle the HTTP encoding of parameters. For example, we can write the following command:

```
>> curl -X POST 'http://localhost:8983/solr/paintings/select?start=3&r
ows=2&fq=painting&wt=json&indent=true' --data-urlencode 'q=leonardo da
vinci&fl=artist title'
```

This previous command is used in place of the following command:

```
>> curl -X GET "http://localhost:8983/solr/paintings/
select?q=leonardo%20da%20vinci&fq=painting&start=3&row=2&fl=artist%20
title&wt=json&indent=true"
```

In the example, notice how we can write the parameter's values, including characters that need to be encoded over HTTP by using the `--data-urlencode` parameter.

Testing HTTP parameters on browsers

On modern browsers such as Firefox or Chrome, you can look at the parameters directly into the provided console. For example, using Chrome you can open the console (the keyboard shortcut for opening the console in Chrome is *F12*):

In the previous image, you can see under this **Query String Parameters** section on the right that the parameters are shown on a list, We can easily switch between the encoded and the more readable un-encoded value's version.

If you don't like using Chrome or Firefox and want a similar tool, you can try the *Firebug lite* (`http://getfirebug.com/firebuglite`). This is a JavaScript library conceived to port Firebug plugin functionality to every browser, but at the cost of adding this library to your HTML page during the test process.

Choosing a format for the output

When sending a query to Solr directly (using the browser or cURL), we can ask for results in multiple formats. This includes, for example, JSON:

```
>> curl -X GET 'http://localhost:8983/solr/paintings/select?q=*:*&wt=json
&indent=true'
```

Here, the `indent=true` parameter can be used to improve readability. We will see different options for `wt` (response writer) in the next chapter.

Time for action – searching for all documents with pagination

When performing a query, we need to remember we are potentially asking for a huge number of documents. Let's observe how to manage partial results using *pagination*:

1. For example, think about the `q=*:*` query that we saw in previous examples. it was used for asking *all the documents, without a specific criteria*. In a case like this, in order to avoid problems with resources, Solr will actually send us only the first results, as defined by a parameter in the configuration. The default number of returned results will be `10`. So, we need to be able to ask for a second group of results, a third, and so on and on. This is what is generally called a pagination of results, similarly as for scenarios involving SQL.

2. The command is executed as follows:

```
>> curl -X GET "http://localhost:8983/solr/paintings/select?q=*:*&
start=0&rows=0&wt=json&indent=true"
```

3. We should obtain a result similar to the following screenshot. The number of documents `numFound` and the time spent for processing query `QTime` could vary, depending on your data and the system you are using:

```
{
  - responseHeader: {
      status: 0,
      QTime: 1
    },
  - response: {
      numFound: 12484,
      start: 0,
      docs: [ ]
    }
}
```

```
>>curl -X GET "http://localhost:8983/solr/paintings/select?
q=*:*&start=0&rows=0&wt=json&indent=true"
{
  "responseHeader":{
    "status":0,
    "QTime":1},
  "response":{"numFound":12484,"start":0,"docs":[]
  }}
>>
```

In the previous screenshot, we see the same results in two different ways: on the right-hand side you'll recognize the output from cURL, and on the left-hand side of the browser you see how the results appear in the browser window.

> In the first example, we had the *Json View plugin* installed in the browser. This gave a very helpful visualization of json with indentation and colors.
> You can install it for *Chrome* if you want by using the following link:
>
> https://chrome.google.com/webstore/detail/jsonview/
> chklaanhfefbnpoihckbnefhakgolnmc
>
> For *Firefox*, the plugin can be installed from:
>
> https://addons.mozilla.org/it/firefox/addon/jsonview/

Notice how even if we have found 12,484 documents, we are currently seeing none of them in the results!

What just happened?

In the previous example, we already use two very useful parameters: `start` and `rows`. We should always think of them as a couple, even if we may be using only one of them explicitly. We could change the default values for these parameters from the `solrconfig.xml` file, but this is generally not needed. The following takes place in the previous example:

◆ From the documents matching our search criteria, the **start** value defines the original index of the first document returned in the response, starting from the value 0. The default value will again start at 0.

◆ The **rows** parameter is used to define how many documents we want in the results. The default value will be 10 for rows.

So, for example, if we only want the second and third document from the results, we can obtain them using the query:

```
>> curl -X GET "http://localhost:8983/solr/paintings/select?q=*:*&start=1
&rows=2&wt=json&indent=true'
```

In order to obtain the second document in the results, we need to remember that the enumeration starts from 0 (so the second will be at 1); while to see the next group of documents (if present), we will send a new query with values such as start=10 and rows=10. We are still using wt and indent parameters only to have results formatted in a clear way.

> The start/rows parameters play roles in this context which are quite similar to the OFFSET/LIMIT clause in SQL.

This process of segmenting the output to be able to read it in group or *pages* of results is usually named **pagination**, and it is generally handled by some programming code. You should know this mechanism so that you can play with your test even on a small segment of data, without any loss of generalization. I strongly suggest you always add these two parameters explicitly in your examples.

Time for action – projecting fields with fl

Another important parameter to consider is fl, that can be used for fields projection, obtaining *only certain fields* in the results:

If we are interested on obtaining the titles and artist reference for all the documents, we can use the following command:

```
>>curl -X GET 'http://localhost:8983/solr/paintings/select?q=artist:*&wt=
json&indent=true&omitHeader=true&fl=title,artist'
```

The output for the command is similar to the one shown in the following screenshot:

```
>>curl -X GET 'http://localhost:8983/solr/paintings/select?q=artist:*&wt=json&indent=true&omitHeader=true&
fl=title,artist'
{
  "response":{"numFound":686,"start":0,"docs":[
      {
        "artist":["http://dbpedia.org/resource/Abanindranath_Tagore"],
        "title":["Bharat Mata"]},
      {
        "artist":["http://dbpedia.org/resource/Henri_Matisse"],
        "title":["Black Leaf on Green Background"]},
```

4. Notice that the results will be indented as requested, and they will not contain any header to be more readable. Moreover, the parameters list does not need to be written in a specific order.

5. The previous query can also be rewritten:

```
>>curl -X GET 'http://localhost:8983/solr/paintings/select?q=artis
t:*&wt=json&indent=true&omitHeader=true&fl=title&fl=artist'
```

Here we ask for field projection one by one, if needed. For example, when using HTML and JavaScript widget to compose the query following user's choices.

What just happened?

The `fl` parameter stands for the fields list. Using this parameter, we can define a comma-separated list of fields names that explicitly define what fields are projected in the results. We can also use a space to separate fields; but in this case we should use the URL encoding for the space, writing `fl=title+artist` or `fl=title%20artist`.

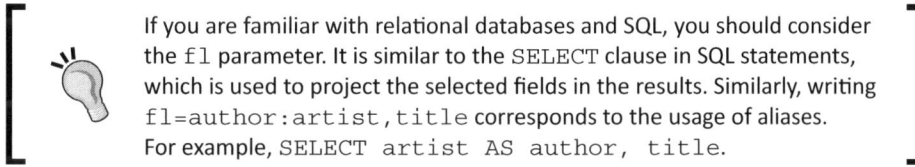

> If you are familiar with relational databases and SQL, you should consider the `fl` parameter. It is similar to the `SELECT` clause in SQL statements, which is used to project the selected fields in the results. Similarly, writing `fl=author:artist,title` corresponds to the usage of aliases. For example, `SELECT artist AS author, title`.

Let's see the full list of parameters in details:

◆ The parameter `q=artist:*` is used in this case in place of a more generic `q=*:*` to select only the fields that have a value for the field artist. The special character `*` is used again for indicating all the values.

◆ The `wt=json`, `indent=true` parameters are used for asking an indented json format.

◆ The `omitHeader=true` parameter is used for omitting the header from the response.

◆ The `fl=title,artist` parameter represents the list of the fields to be projected for the results.

Notice how the fields are projected in the results without using the order asked in `fl`, as this has no particular sense for json output. This order will be used for the CSV response writer (we will see this later) where changing the columns order could be mandatory.

In addition to the existing field, which can be added by using the `*` special character, we could also ask for the projection of the implicit score field. A composition of these two options can be seen in the following query:

```
>>curl -X GET 'http://localhost:8983/solr/paintings/select?q=artist:*&wt=
json&indent=true&omitHeader=true&fl=*,score'
```

This will return every field for every document, including the score field explicitly, which is sometimes called a **pseudo-field** to distinguish it from the field defined by a schema.

Introducing pseudo-fields and DocTransformers

When using fields list, we can also use *transformers* to manipulate a document while returning it. In this way, we can implement and use a custom transformer or use some of the predefined ones, for example, [docid], [explain], and [shard]. Each of these should be considered as a pseudo-field. For example, [docid] can be used to return the explicit value of the internal ID of a document; and [shard] is used for knowing where to find it(in which shard inside a distributed system). We will see this later in *Chapter 8, Indexing External Data Sources*.

In this short list, we can use [explain] in particular to obtain detailed information about how the matching of a document has been calculated:

```
>> curl -X GET 'http://localhost:8983/solr/paintings/select?q=abstract:da
li+vermeer&wt=json&indent=true&fl=[explain+style=nl]'
```

It helps in obtaining the result shown in the following snippet:

```
- [explain]: {
    match: true,
    value: 14.941403,
    description: "sum of:",
  - details: [
    - {
        match: true,
        value: 0.4575712,
        description: "weight(abstract:dali in 9677) [DefaultSimilarity], result of:",
      - details: [
        - {
            match: true,
            value: 0.4575712,
            description: "score(doc=9677,freq=1.0 = termFreq=1.0 ), product of:",
          - details: [
```

This example will contain structured information in the details field, which helps us to see how the final match is assembled, and a description field that exposes the internal parsed query.

We will again see the [explain] pseudo-field in action with the debug parameter, which we will use in the *Chapter 5, Extending Search*.

Adding a constant field using transformers

Sometimes we need to add a constant field value in every document returned, without changing the original data. Think about adding, for example, the request time, or some copyright note.

This can be easily done using the following command:

```
>> curl -X GET 'http://localhost:8983/solr/paintings_transformers/
select?q=*:*&fl=*,[noempty],[source_transformer%20v=dbpedia.
org]&wt=json&indent=true'
```

It can also be done with a specific configuration in `solrconfig.xml`:

```
<transformer name="source_transformer" class="org.apache.solr.
response.transform.ValueAugmenterFactory" >
  <str name="value">dbpedia.org</int>
</transformer>
```

This little addition in our configuration can be also useful when we need to add custom code. For a list of available transformers, you can refer to the official wiki page at `http://wiki.apache.org/solr/DocTransformers`.

Time for action – adding a custom DocTransformer to hide empty fields in the results

Since `DocTransformers` can manipulate the data we are going to return for a given document, they can be very useful for adding custom normalizations or simple data manipulations. Looking briefly at how to design a new transformer can add some clarity.

Imagine we had a transformer designed to avoid returning the empty values in our results (in our case there will be several empty fields):

```
>> curl -X GET 'http://localhost:8983/solr/paintings_transformers/select?
q=*:*&fl=*,[noempty]&wt=json&indent=true'
```

The previous request works if we have added two lines like these in our `solrconfig.xml`:

```
<lib dir="${solr.core.instanceDir}/lib/" regex="solr-plugins-java.jar"
/>

<transformer name="noempty" class="it.seralf.solrbook.doctransformers.
RemoveEmptyFieldsTransformerFactory" />
```

Here, the factory class is used to create an instance of `RemoveEmptyFieldsTransformer`, which has an outline as shown in the following code:

```
class RemoveEmptyFieldsTransformer extends DocTransformer {
  final String name = "noempty";
  @Override
  public String getName() {
    return this.name;
  }
```

```java
    private void removeEmpty(final List<?> list){
      // TODO: remove empty fields in a list
    }
    @Override
    public void transform(final SolrDocument doc, final int docid) {
        final Iterator<Entry<String, Object>> it
          = doc.entrySet().iterator();
      while(it.hasNext()){
        final Entry<String, Object> entry = it.next();
        if(entry.getValue() == null) {
          it.remove();
        }else if(entry.getValue() instanceof List<?>){
          final List<?> list = (List<?>)entry.getValue();
          removeEmpty(list);
          if(list.size()==0) it.remove(); // if the list is empty
        }
      }
    }
  }
}
```

The compiled jar containing the class will be under the `/lib` directory under the core folder. I've omitted the details here, you can find the complete runnable example under the path `/SolrStarterBook/solr-app/chp04/paintings_transformers/`, and the source in the project `/SolrStarterBook/projects/solr-maven/solr-plugins-java`.

What just happened?

The Java class structure is really simple. Every new transformer must extend an abstract, general `DocTransformer` class. There exists a single `transform()` method that contains all the logic, and we expect to receive inside it a `SolrDocument` object to transform its values. We will again see this behavior when we introduce customizations inside the update chain.

The `getName()` method is used to correctly recognize this object. This allows us to call its execution from requests by the name `noempty`. The same name has been used in the configuration file to bind the name to the Java class. Also, notice that a very similar approach can be used to introduce *custom functions*.

Looking at core parameters for queries

At this point, you are probably curious about what are all the parameters that we can use within the Solr request. A complete list will be tedious and difficult to read, because there are many specialized parameters and sometimes fields-specific parameters!. I would suggest you to start reading carefully on how to use the main and basic ones that you can find in the following table:

Parameter	Meaning	Default value
q	This is the query.	* : *
defType	This is the query parser that will be used.	Lucene query parser
q.op	The Boolean query operator used: AND/OR.	OR
df	This is the default field that will be deprecated soon.	defined in schema. xml
start	The ordinal number of the first document to be returned in the results.	0
rows	The number of document to be returned in the results.	10
fl	The list of the fields to be exposed in the results.	all
fq	This is a filter query for filtering the results.	N/A
pageDoc and pageScore	These parameters are useful to request document with a score greater than a certain value. Notice that they need the implicit score field.	N/A
omitHeader	This produces a response without the header part.	false
qt	This is the type of the query handler.	Lucene standard
wt	This is the writer for the response formatting.	XML
debug	This adds debugging info to the output.	false
timeAllowed	This is the maximum time allowed (in milliseconds) for executing a query.	N/A

As usual, this should be considered as a list from which to start. If you want more details, you should check the wiki page for the list:

http://wiki.apache.org/solr/CommonQueryParameters

You can also look at the following wiki pages:

http://wiki.apache.org/solr/SearchHandler

http://wiki.apache.org/solr/SearchComponent

In these pages, you will find that there are actually some different search components that can extend this list. We will cover the most interesting ones for our purposes in *Chapter 5, Extending Search*, and *Chapter 6, Using Faceted Search – from Searching to Finding*. Although they can be used in combination with the ones showed in the table, at the moment we will remain focused on the most essential parts of a Solr query.

Using the Lucene query parser with defType

We can explicitly decide to use the Lucene query parser, which is the default, or a custom parser that uses some different equivalent combination for the `defType` parameter:

- `q={!query defType=lucene}museum:louvre`

- `q={!lucene}museum:louvre`

- `q=museum:louvre&defType=lucene`

- `q=museum:louvre`

For the moment, we choose to use the last case, which uses the most simple syntax. The others will be used in a more advanced search, when you need to choose a specific alternative parser for queries or for handling sub-queries.

Notice that the default field parameter `df` can be used for specifying a default field in which to search, but will be deprecated in the next versions. So, I suggest not to use it.

Time for action – searching for terms with a Boolean query

When performing queries, most simple examples can be created by assembling collections of terms. If we only create a collection of terms separated by white spaces, we will use the default `q.op` operator, as described further in this section.

The most simple way to start is to start with an explicit adoption of operators, creating different combinations:

1. Searching for `lisa` and not `mona` in the abstract field:

   ```
   >> curl -X GET 'http://localhost:8983/solr/paintings/
   select?q=abstract:(lisa AND !mona)'
   ```

2. Searching `lisa` in abstract, including documents with `leonardo` in `artist`:

   ```
   >> curl -X GET 'http://localhost:8983/solr/paintings/
   select?q=abstract:lisa AND +artist:leonardo'
   ```

3. Searching `lisa` in abstract, excluding documents with `leonardo` as artist:

   ```
   >> curl -X GET http://localhost:8983/solr/paintings/
   select?q=abstract:lisa AND -artist:leonardo'
   ```

4. Searching documents not containing painting in the abstract field:

   ```
   >> curl -X GET 'http://localhost:8983/solr/paintings/
   select?q=abstract:NOT painting'
   ```

These examples use simple Boolean operators and combine them to obtain different results, which we can analyze later. Please substitute all the spaces with the correct `%20` encoding.

What just happened?

The first query in the previous example will search the abstract field for documents that match the two contemporary conditions. The conditions will contain the term lisa and will not contain the term mona. The character ! here stands for the Boolean unary operator NOT.

The second query is used for including documents matching the artist:leonardo condition, on the results we got by using the term lisa.

The third query is used for expanding documents matching the artist:leonardo condition, on the selection we got by the lisa term.

The last example introduces a sort of inverted search. We are currently searching for a document which doesn't match the defined condition.

The + and - operators are used to explicitly mark the need for inclusion or exclusion of a document in the results. If you are familiar with popular search engines, such as Google or Yahoo!, you should probably recognize these parameters as they are very similar to some of the ones used by these platforms.

The last example is to find a list of documents not citing the term painting in their abstract. Notice the use of an escaped NOT word abstract:\NOT%20painting.

Time for action – using q.op for the default Boolean operator

The q.op parameter gives us the opportunity to choose what kind of boolean operator should be used in the query. It is generally preferable to choose an OR behavior, because it is more intuitive to reflect user expectations, and AND will act as a filter:

1. We can use the default value for q.op in an explicit way.

   ```
   >> curl -G 'http://localhost:8983/solr/paintings/
   select?rows=0&wt=json' --data-urlencode 'q={!lucene q.op=OR}
   dali christ'
   ```

   The command gives the following output:

   ```
   {"responseHeader":{"status":0,"QTime":5},"response" {"numFound":15
   5,"start":0,"docs":[]}}
   ```

2. We can even override the default choice, adopting a behavior based on AND operator instead.

   ```
   >> curl -G 'http://localhost:8983/solr/paintings/
   select?rows=0&wt=json' --data-urlencode 'q={!lucene q.op=AND}dali
   christ'
   ```

The output obtained is as follows:

```
{"responseHeader":{"status":0,"QTime":5},"response":{"numFound":4,
"start":0,"docs":[]}}
```

As expected, it returns less results. Notice that in this case we deliberately omit the documents returned with value of rows as 0.

What just happened?

In these examples, we saw how simple it is to use different values for the q.op parameter. Since these parameters control the default way in which a collection of terms are combined for a search, this should be used carefully. Also, you should not expect it to change its default value unless you have a very particular case. For example, if we had a request for using *restrictive search keywords* since the AND operator allows the addition of a filter for every term.

Time for action – selecting documents with the filter query

Sometimes, it's useful to be able to narrow the collection of documents on which we are currently performing our search. It is useful to add some kind of explicit linked condition on the logical side for navigation on data, and this will also have a good impact on performance too.

It is shown in the following example:

```
>>curl -G 'http://localhost:8983/solr/paintings/select?q=*:*&wt=json&indent=true&fq=annunciation'
{
  "responseHeader":{
    "status":0,
    "QTime":4},
  "response":{"numFound":23,"start":0,"docs":[
      {
        "uri":"http://dbpedia.org/resource/Bartolini_Salimbeni_Annunciation",
        "timestamp":"2013-10-27T02:38:19.976Z",
        "sameAs":["http://dbpedia.org/resource/Bartolini_Salimbeni_Annunciation",
```

It shows how the default search is restricted by the introduction of a fq=annunciation condition.

What just happened?

The first result in this simple example shows that we obtain results similar to what we could have obtained by a simple q=annunciation search. We will have the chance to see the differences between the two options with more detail in *Chapter 5*, *Extending Search*. Filtered query can be cached (just like facets, which we will see later), improving the performance by reducing the overhead of performing the same query many times and accessing documents from large datasets to the same group many times.

> In this case, the analogy with SQL seems less convincing; but `q=dali` and `fq=abstract:painting` can be seen corresponding to `WHERE` conditions in SQL. The `fq` parameters will then be a *fixed* condition.

For example, in our scenario, we could define specific endpoints with a predefined filter query by author to create specific channels. In this case, instead of passing the parameters every time we could set them on `solrconfig.xml`, as we will see later in the chapter.

Time for action – searching for incomplete terms with the wildcard query

Now that we have some basic idea of the Lucene query syntax, we can extend our syntax with some more useful tricks. One of the most recurring use-case is about partial or incomplete term searches. For example, we could try to intercept a *partial term* written by the user and return a list of documents, including some expansion with documents containing a term that contains the query term as a substring.

For example, let's search for a partial match over `real`, `realism` or `surrealism`, using only the term `real` in the following combinations:

```
>> curl -X GET 'http://localhost:8983/solr/paintings/
select?q=abstract:real*&wt=xml'
```

```
>> curl -X GET 'http://localhost:8983/solr/paintings/select?q=abstract:re
alis&wt=xml'
```

```
>> curl -X GET 'http://localhost:8983/solr/paintings/
select?q=abstract:*real&wt=xml'
```

```
>> curl -X GET 'http://localhost:8983/solr/paintings/select?q=abstract:*r
eal*&wt=xml'
```

What just happened?

In the first example, we are asking for documents containing the terms that start with the `real` substring, as denoted by the use of the `*` wildcard. So, we can expect to find documents with the terms `real`, `realism`, or `reality`. Notice that the `*` wildcard could also intercept no characters following the `real` term.

The second example query should give us no results. This is because without the wildcard, the exact match for term `realis` will be searched. This term is obviously not present, so we will find no results. Notice that if we had used the term "`real`" in this example, all the documents containing the word `real` itself will be returned. So, please be careful in your evaluations.

The next two tests are only for symmetry. We want to check if it's possible to search for match over the last part of a word, or even for a term that is a generic substring of a word.

Notice that this test is not so trivial. This is because in the old version of Solr, the only way to achieve this was to implement a reversed version of the same field values.

If you are able to create your queries programmatically by JavaScript, you can use the *wildcard search* to create a very simple *auto-completion* service. In this case, remember to add a simple timeout for avoid sending request for every char pressed.

Time for action – using the Boost options

It is interesting to pay attention to the results, because you will find that the first document for the last two examples contain only the words *real* or *realistic*, and once we will introduce the parameter `start=10`, we will start seeing some presence of *surrealist* in the documents. The reason for this is the difference in the *ranking* of the documents returned. This will be explained later, but we can also give more importance to some terms over others using the boost options:

```
>> curl -X GET 'http://localhost:8983/solr/paintings/
select?q=abstract:(*real* AND surrealist^2)&wt=json'
```

Again, I have omitted the encoding for spaces. So, please rewrite the appropriate part of the query as `*real*%20AND%20surrealist^2`.

What just happened?

Imagine we want to give more importance to the documents containing the term `surrealist` in the results. In our case, this could be achieved by simply adding the boosted search condition with the AND operator. The boost condition is expressed by the `surrealist^2` syntax, which tells the query parser to consider the occurrence of the term `surrealist` to be two times more interesting than the other. Notice that Solr uses an implicit hidden `score` parameter behind the scene, and we can project it explicitly if we add it to the fields list with `fl`, as seen before.

Understanding the basic Lucene score

A Lucene score is calculated using factors like *term frequency*, *inverse document frequency*, and *normalization of terms over the documents*. It's not important to go into the details now, but you should consider some basic rules:

- A rare word is preferable for giving a high score. For example, if a term recurs on every document, it gives us no additional information useful for retrieval.

- Matching a term inside a short text gives better scoring than on long ones.

◆ If a term is cited more than once, the score will be better. It will be considered as an important term.

◆ A document containing all the search terms and phrases is preferable if we searching with many terms.

Given a certain score, the boost operation acts as a multiplier over the existing score for a term. The same mechanism could be used in the indexing phase too when needed, but we will not go into these details now.

Time for action – searching for similar terms with fuzzy search

Even if the wildcard queries are very flexible, sometimes they simply cannot give us a good result. There could be some weird typo in the term, but we still want to obtain good results wherever it is possible under certain confidence conditions:

1. If we want to write `painting` and I actually search for `plainthing`, use the following command:

```
>> curl - X GET 'http://localhost:8983/solr/paintings/select?q=abs
tract:plainthing~0.5&wt=json'
```

2. And if we have a person using a different language who searched for `leonardo` by misspelling the name we use the following command:

```
>> curl -X GET 'http://localhost:8983/solr/paintings/select?q=abst
ract:lionardo~0.5&wt=json'
```

In both cases, the examples use misspelled words to be recognizable, but the same syntax can be used for intercept existing similar words.

What just happened?

Both the preceding examples work as expected. The first gives us documents containing the term `painting` and the second gives us documents containing `leonardo`. Notice that the syntax `plainthing^0.5` represents a query that matches with a certain confidence. So, we will also obtain occurrences of documents with the term `paintings`, which is good. But, we could receive weird results in a more general case. In order to set up the confidence value properly, there are not many options apart from doing tests.

> Using fuzzy search is a simple way of obtaining a suggested result for alternate forms of search query, just like when we trust some search engine's similar suggestions in the *did you mean* approach.

Time for action – writing a simple phrase query example

When using one of the internet search engines to search for a sequence of words, we can generally define the entire sequence as a unique term for search, wrapping it with the " character. With Solr, we are able to perform similar queries. We will call a sequence of words a phrase, and we will be able to handle it as a unique object:

```
>> curl -X GET 'http://localhost:8983/solr/paintings_readonly/
select?q=abstract:%22original%20oil%22~20&wt=json&indent=true'
```

Notice how in this example %22 is the encoding for the " character.

What just happened?

In this little example, we are using the `q=abstract:"original oil"~20` query with the proper HTTP encoding for characters. Notice that when using a phrase query, we could handle the entire phrase between double quotes as if it were a single term. So, we could search for exact match for it, boost it, apply wildcards, or use a fuzzy search, as we did in our example.

When used with phrases, the fuzzy search syntax denotes a particular kind of search that is generally defined as a *proximity search*. In our example, we will find both occurrences of the terms `original` and `oil` no more than 20 terms distant from each other. In our example, this could give us results for documents containing small paragraphs with either of the terms, or, for example, documents containing the phrase `originally painted as oil`.

Time for action – playing with range queries

Another good option for queries is the possibility to play over a certain range of data. This is particularly useful when dealing with numeric values (the `trie` types are designed to perform well in this case) and date/timestamp values too.

Just to give you an idea, we could test the following simple queries:

```
>> curl -X GET 'http://localhost:8983/solr/paintings_readonly/
select?q=width:[5 TO 8]&fl=title'
```

```
>> curl -X GET 'http://localhost:8983/solr/paintings_readonly/
select?q=timestamp:[* TO NOW]'
```

```
>> curl -X GET 'http://localhost:8983/solr/paintings_readonly/
select?q=timestamp:[NOW-20MINUTES TO NOW}'
```

What just happened?

The first case is really intuitive. In it, we search for documents with width values from five to eight.

For dates, on the other hand, things generally get a bit more complicated. Solr uses the default canonical representation for date types as given in the following link:

```
http://www.w3.org/TR/xmlschema-2/#dateTime-canonical-representation
```

We can use some modifiers to handle a relative period of time. In the third example, we search from 20 minutes ago to now. Notice that although the square bracket represents included values, the curly brackets represent values that are not to be included.

Time for action – sorting documents with the sort parameter

Another very common case is when we have to sort the results. This is very simple to obtain using a specific sort parameter. For example, to obtain the results ordered by `artist` in a descending order (so that we have the last ordered artist in the first position), and in particular to produce a document result list containing only the fields `uri` and `sameAs` (that represents the uri pointing to the same resource on another repository).

```
>> curl -X GET 'http://localhost:8983/solr/paintings/select?q=*:*&start=0
&rows=200&sort=artist desc&fl=sameAs,uri&wt=json&indent=true'
```

What just happened?

The `sort` parameter needs a very simple syntax, as you have seen in the previous example. It needs the name of the field on which we want to sort, and the type of sorting. Here, `asc` is used for ascending order and `desc` for descending order. It is important to remember that *we can append a new sort definition for every field* on which we want to sort (we could combine them as we need). Moreover sorting makes sense only on single valued field, not on multivalued ones.

> Using `sort=artist desc` is similar to `SORT BY artist DESC` in SQL.

Sorting should be used only when strictly necessary. Please be aware of the impact of sorting operations in terms of memory consumptions, refreshing of cache, and garbage collector invocations.

> One of the typical usage for function query (for more information in function query visit `http://wiki.apache.org/solr/FunctionQuery`) is sorting. We could sort a collection over a value calculated by a specific function query (similar to using pseudo-fields).

Playing with the request

A **RequestHandler** is a component used to expose a new service. It is designed to receive a specific type of query. This way, it's also possible to define two different services with the same component, changing only the parameters values or the list of parameters they are designed to parse. The list of the possible handlers is on the wiki at `http://wiki.apache.org/solr/SolrRequestHandler`. The update components are already enabled by default. So, we can post the data to be indexed using CSV, json, or XML, as we have already seen. Other components are designed to be used for advanced query capabilities that we will see in the *Looking at different search parsers – Lucene, Dismax and Edismax* and *Introducing the spellcheck components* section of *Chapter 5, Extending Search*, and in *Chapter 6, Using Faceted Search – from Searching to Finding*. The `DataImportHandler` will be used in *Chapter 8, Indexing External Data Sources*, for acquiring external data.

Remember that we can switch among different handlers using the `qt` parameter, and when we have not defined any handler's name, we are actually using the default one (`/select/` on `StandardRequestHandler`). In the next example, we will create a new endpoint using some specific configuration on `StandardRequesHandler`.

Time for action – adding a default parameter to a handler

All the parameters seen till now can also be used to configure a new request handler.

1. It's very simple to configure new search handlers, and add some default parameters to them. For example we could add a new configuration to our `paintings` core (to its `solrconfig.xml` file):

```
<requestHandler name="/search_by_width/" class="solr.
StandardRequestHandler">
  <lst name="defaults">
    <int name="rows">3</int>
    <str name="wt">json</str>
    <str name="indent">true</str>
    <bool name="omitHeader">true</bool>
  </lst>
```

```
    <lst name="appends">
      <str name="fq">abstract:painting AND sea</str>
      <str name="fq">title:* AND artist:*</str>
    </lst>
    <lst name="invariants">
       <str name="fl">title,artist</str>
       <str name="fq">width:{0 TO 4]</str>
    </lst>
  </requestHandler>
```

2. This time we will not need to re-import data, as we are only adding a new handler to a predefined `solrconfig.xml` file. We restart the core, and then perform the following query:

```
>> curl -X GET 'http://localhost:8983/solr/paintings/search_by_
width?q=*:*'
```

3. We will receive an output as shown in the following image:

```
>>curl -X GET 'http://localhost:8983/solr/paintings/search_by_width?q=*:*'
{
  "response":{"numFound":17,"start":0,"docs":[
      {
        "artist":["http://dbpedia.org/resource/Winslow_Homer"],
        "title":["Breezing Up"]},
      {
        "artist":["http://dbpedia.org/resource/Henri_Matisse"],
        "title":["Beasts of the Sea"]},
      {
        "artist":["http://dbpedia.org/resource/Gentile_da_Fabriano"],
        "title":["Adoration of the Child"]}]
  }}
>>
```

Here, we are obtaining only the first three documents from the results.

What just happened?

In our configuration, we will use three different list of parameter values (`<lst />`), containing values that will be defined by their data types (`str`, `bool`, `int`, and so on). We can recognize the following three different parts:

- ◆ **default**: We use this part to define default values for various parameters, in particular regarding the format for the results. These values can be easily overridden during query, as we normally do.

◆ **appends**: Here we put parameters that should be appended to every request. In our case, we want to consider only documents containing the term `painting` and `sea` in their abstract field. We also want to be sure that every document in the result has a value for the fields `artist` and `title`. Notice that these choices are restrictive and they should be read in the beginning. We can add as many parameter choices as we like to obtain narrower searches.

◆ **invariants**: In this part, we specify fields that we don't want to be changed. In our case, we want to search documents describing paintings with a specific size proportion and we will output only two predefined fields (artist and title), no matter what `fl` values are passed during querying.

We can look at `http://wiki.apache.org/solr/SearchHandler#Configuration` for a complete reference.

Both the `fl` and the `fq` parameters can be passed many times as we would need to add a new criteria at the time. For example, by using some client library for frontend. However, in the invariant part, only the `fq` parameter can be customized during query.

Playing with the response

A **Response Writer** is a component to write results from a query in a different way. Using the writer type parameter `wt`, we can obtain results in some different formats, including CSV, XML, json, and also php-like formatted array. But, depending on how it's made, Response Writer can be also used to create different presentations of data. It can be managed internally on the server by Solr using XSLT, velocity templates, or other technologies.

You can read more on the reference guide at:

`https://cwiki.apache.org/confluence/display/solr/Response+Writers`

> One of the most interesting alternative Response Writer is the **VelocityResponse Writer**. For more information on VelocityResponseWriter, visit `https://wiki.apache.org/solr/VelocityResponseWriter`). We will not use it here as it involves a little knowledge of the velocity syntax and writing some specific templates. But, it is a very good tool for prototyping. I suggest you look at it when you are a bit more confident about Solr configuration, proceeding one step at a time.

We will focus mainly on directly using the services for our purposes, so that you can define your own frontend on those. For example, it's simple to construct a basic example of frontend showing only a list of documents preview using the Solrstrap JavaScript library:

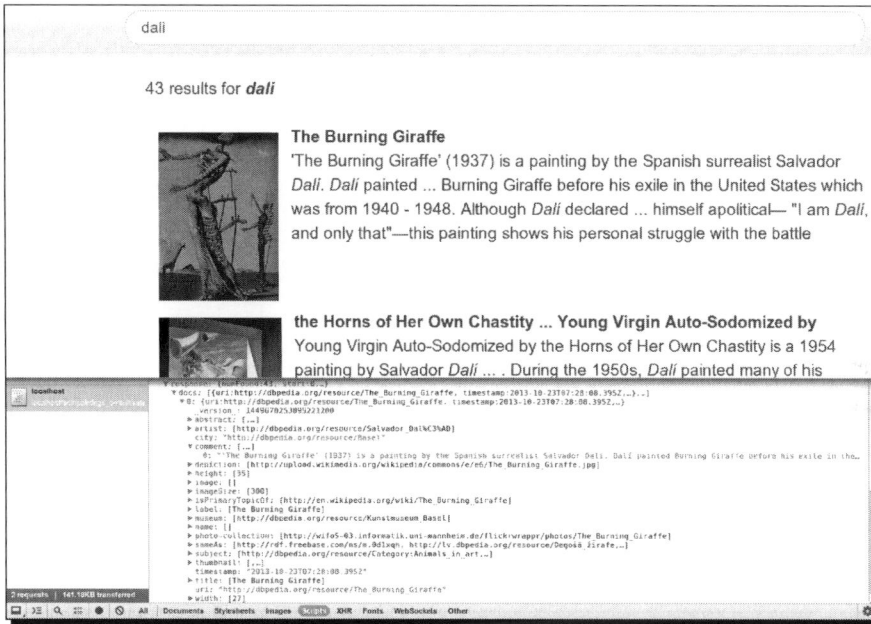

You can find this small draft constructed on a single HTML page by following the path `/SolrStarterBook/test/chp04/paintings/html`, which can be used as a skeleton for starting your own experiments with customizations. In the example shown here, you can easily see a structured version of the results obtained from the server by using the browser (Chrome, in this case) console.

Summarizing the parameters that affect result presentation

We have already seen and used the couple `start` and `rows` that gives us the possibility to play with the pagination of results. We also did a few tests with the fields list parameter `fl` and the parameter `fq` to restrict the collection of documents on which we perform searches.

The `pageDoc` and `pageScore` parameters expose two different level of scores, and are important if you need to select documents with a score value higher than a certain amount.

At last, we can simply hide the header part of a response with the `omitHeader` parameter. This could be useful when in production.

Analyzing response format

We can obtain a simple remainder of the main section of a common response by executing the following simple query:

```
>> curl -X GET 'http://localhost:8983/solr/paintings/select?q=*:*&rows=0&
facet=true&mlt=true&mlt.fl=&highlight=true&stats=true&debug=true&wt=json'
```

This simply returns a simple structure for a common response:

```
{
 - responseHeader: {
        status: 0,
        QTime: 1
    },
 - response: {
        numFound: 4621,
        start: 0,
        docs: [ ]
    },
 - facet_counts: {
        facet_queries: { },
        facet_fields: { },
        facet_dates: { },
        facet_ranges: { }
    },
    moreLikeThis: { },
 - stats: {
        stats_fields: { }
    },
 - debug: {
        moreLikeThis: { },
        rawquerystring: "*:*",
        querystring: "*:*",
        parsedquery: "MatchAllDocsQuery(*:*)",
        parsedquery_toString: "*:*",
        explain: { },
        QParser: "LuceneQParser",
        timing: { }
    }
}
```

Here, we can easily recognize the `response` section that will generally contain the list of the docs returned. In this case, the result is empty (like the other lists for faceted search highlights, and so on) because of the use of `rows=0` for simplicity.

Apart from the initial `responseHeader` section, the latter sections (`facet_counts`, `moreLikeThis`, `stats`, and `debug`) correspond to specific search handlers that we can also activate using the `qt` parameter. In this case, we expose the response via the json formatter `wt=json`, but we can also switch to other kind of representations, as you already know.

Time for action – enabling XSLT Response Writer with Luke

An example of an interesting alternative is the XSLT Response Writer. For instance, we could use the one designed to enable XSLT processing over the XML responses.

1. To do this, first of all we define a new core that we will name `paintings_xslt`. In its own `solrconfig.xml` file, we will add a simple new definition:

```
<queryResponseWriter name="xslt" class="solr.XSLTResponseWriter">
  <int name="xsltCacheLifetimeSeconds">0</int>
</queryResponseWriter>
```

2. Once we have enabled it, we can use an XSLT file. For this, we could use a copy of the `luke.xsl` file provided in the default Solr examples.

3. Now we can ask for the Luke analysis:

```
>> curl -X GET 'http://localhost:8983/solr/paintings_xslt/admin/
luke?q=*:*&wt=xslt&tr=luke.xsl'
```

4. Obtaining the output shown in the following image:

As you see, the output is more readable in this case. It can be used and improved to create a sort of report and help us in the analysis phase. However, the XSLT processor is good for testing, but it's not the best choice for a production environment. It's much more flexible and simple to scale on using JavaScript or other languages from the client-side to consume services.

What just happened?

Now that the Luke Request Handler is enabled, we can easily call it to obtain a simple formatted analysis of the fields in use in our index by using the following command:

```
>> curl -X GET 'http://localhost:8983/solr/paintings_xslt/admin/
luke?q=*:*&wt=xslt&tr=luke.xsl'
```

Notice that the parameter `wt=xslt` tells Solr to use this Response Writer, and the `tr=luke.xsl` parameter is used to retrieve the `XSLT` file from the `conf` directory of the core itself.

> Another very good source of information for field analysis can be obtained from the *FieldAnalysisRequestHandler*, but it is a bit more complex to read. Refer to it at: `http://lucene.apache.org/solr/4_5_0/solr-core/org/apache/solr/handler/FieldAnalysisRequestHandler.html`.

Listing all fields names with CSV output

Sometimes it's useful to obtain a list of the available field, and this is very simple to obtain if we use the CSV output format:

```
>> curl -X GET 'http://localhost:8983/solr/paintings/schema?wt=csv'
```

In this way, we obtain a simple plain text result. In this case, it will be a single row text containing a simple list of field names divided by commas.

Listing all field details for a core

On the other hand, we can always obtain details about specific fields—not only name but datatypes, specific schema attributes, and others:

```
>> curl -X GET 'http://localhost:8983/solr/paintings/schema/
fieldtypes?wt=json'
>> curl -X GET 'http://localhost:8983/solr/paintings/schema/fields'
>> curl -X GET 'http://localhost:8983/solr/paintings/schema/
dynamicfields'
>> curl -X GET 'http://localhost:8983/solr/paintings/schema/copyfields'
```

I suggest you play with these simple services on your example as they can be useful in the development phase, depending on your needs.

Exploring Solr for Open Data publishing

Combining some of the latter options exposed till now, it's very simple to expose our results using two formats that are very useful in the context of **Open Data** integration.

Reading the widely known definition of Open Data from Wikipedia:

> *"Open data is the idea that certain data should be freely available to everyone to use and republish as they wish, without restrictions from copyright, patents or other mechanisms of control".*

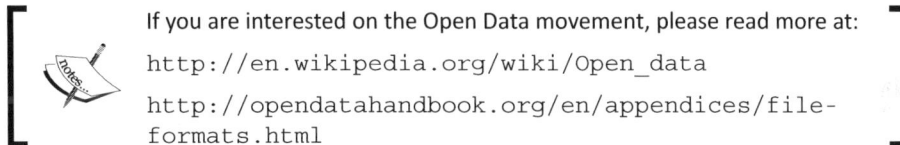

> If you are interested on the Open Data movement, please read more at:
>
> http://en.wikipedia.org/wiki/Open_data
>
> http://opendatahandbook.org/en/appendices/file-formats.html

Let's look at two simple recipes that can be used to expose Solr results directly in formats widely adopted in the Open Data context. While it is generally not a good idea to expose Solr results directly, these methods can be useful in some specific context as they are very easy to use.

Publishing results in CSV format

First of all, we could easily expose the data in *CSV format*:

```
>> curl -X GET 'http://localhost:8983/solr/paintings/
select?q=*:*&wt=csv&csv.mv.separator=|'
```

Notice that we have not only specified `wt=csv`, but also `csv.mv.separator=|` that stands to define the character | as a separator for values in multivalued fields.

Publishing results with an RSS feed

A second, interesting option, will be constructing an *RSS feed* over our data:

```
>> curl -X GET 'http://localhost:8983/solr/paintings/select?q=artist:Dal%
C3%AC&wt=xslt&tr=rss.xsl'
```

For example, here we have created a feed for searches of `Dalì` so that if new document were added to the index, they will be shown in the results. We could also use the `timestamp` field here if we want.

Notice that in this way we could define several RSS feeds, one for every kind of search we want to define. For the XSLT manipulation, we are using a slightly customized version of the original rss.xsl from the default Solr examples.

Good resources on Solr Query Syntax

Finally, I'd like to strongly suggest you to do some reading on a few good resources to obtain a different point of view of understanding Solr Query Syntax:

◆ http://www.solrtutorial.com/solr-query-syntax.html

◆ http://solr.pl/en/

◆ http://www.typo3-media.com/blog/solr-search-request-handlers.html

◆ http://java.dzone.com/articles/apache-solr-get-started-get

◆ http://www.solrtutorial.com/solr-query-syntax.html

◆ http://www.supermind.org/blog/378

Pop quiz

Q1. For what are the parameters start, rows used?

1. Pagination: request results from start to start+rows

2. Pagination: request results from start to rows

3. Selecting results which has an index greater than start value, but no more than rows times

Q2. Is it possible to perform searches over misspelled terms?

1. Yes, with fuzzy search

2. Yes, with wildcard (*) search

3. Yes, with phrase search

Q3. Can we use more than one search handler in Solr?

1. Yes

2. No

Q4. What is a Boolean query?

1. A query which uses only Boolean values

2. A query which returns only true/false results

3. A query which uses Boolean operators

Q5. Is it possible to perform searches over incomplete terms?

1. Yes, with fuzzy search

2. Yes, with wildcard (*) search

3. Yes, with phrase search

Q6. In what scenarios would it be useful to handle phrase searches?

1. When a user wants to search over a specific sequence of terms, including putting it in double quotes

2. When a user is searching for an exact phrase match

3. When we need to search for multiple words at the same time

Summary

In this chapter, we started using the same configuration we used for *Chapter 3, Indexing Example Data from DBpedia – Paintings*.

We introduced the basic parameters for a Solr query (`q`, `start`, `rows`, `fl`, `fq`, and others), then we saw how to create more complex query by combining them. We saw how it's possible to paginate results, how we can "pin" conditions to query over more small (and more specific) collections of documents using filter queries, and we also had a chance to explore different result formats.

In order to play a little with different Response Writers using XSLT, we analyzed the index structure with the Luke analyzer. We then exposed the data returned from Solr in the direction of Open Data export of the data, providing the output as CSV as well as an RSS feed for every search we want.

In the next chapter, we will extend the kind of search we can perform to be able to go further in the direction of a more real use-case.

5
Extending Search

In this chapter we will focus on understanding how a search experience can be more user-oriented: the focus will be on user experience for search, we can call it "user search experience". We are not prototyping any real front end; there will not be any HTML here, but we simply start considering on one hand how a common, non-advanced user will perform a query and on the other hand how to construct a result structure suitable for the front-end process.

We will briefly introduce some examples with a real approach, implementing patterns such as autosuggestion and giving, for example, an idea on how a geolocalized search would perform.

We also have a chance to get an idea on how to use Solr again for prototyping, by introducing a concept such as editorial boosting of results and augmenting data from external data sources during the update process.

Looking at different search parsers – Lucene, Dismax, and Edismax

It does not matter whether you use it as a standalone application or as an embedded framework, the main aim of an Apache Solr application is generally to index over a wide mix of structured and unstructured data, and provide powerful search capabilities to the users of an enterprise application.

In order for this to work, it's important to remember that all the data indexed in a Solr application needs to be denormalized as they are actually stored in the form of vectors of terms, in the same way Apache Lucene does. But if Lucene was designed to offer advanced and fast search to experienced users, and it is a component designed to be plugged into the development of an application, a Solr application should be able to take care of a common user's needs and real-world enterprise tasks.

Solr applications are also designed for searching on specific domains and more specialized data than the whole Web. From a mathematical point of view, this reduces the space represented by our vectors to a great extent, so that we cannot simply use them without further small corrections. From the domain point of view, a user doesn't need to take care of things such as synonyms or misspelled words, or the misuse of some basic operators. Sometimes we need to be less precise and yet to provide results that the users can find useful, thus matching their needs.

For all these reasons, I like to think that the main aim of a Solr application is providing support for some kind of search experience.

Starting from the previous core definition

We can use a copy of the core definitions seen earlier in *Chapter 3, Indexing Example Data from DBpedia – Paintings*: we can copy them to define our new core in `/SolrStarterBook/solr-app/chp05/paintings/core`. For starting with the example of the multicore definition for this chapter, you can use the following script again in `/SolrStarterBook/test/`:

```
>> ./start.sh chp05
```

In order to populate this index for the examples, you can proceed with the steps seen in *Chapter 3, Indexing Example Data from DBpedia – Paintings* or use the scripts you'll find in the corresponding `/SolrStarterBook/test/chp05/paintings/` folder.

Time for action – inspecting results using the stats and debug components

We have already seen some examples using the debug components while introducing the response format. Here we will start from that, and see it in action, introducing also the stats components:

1. Suppose we want to debug a query in which we are searching for paintings that contain the term `vatican` inside the `city` field, we can do it as follows:

    ```
    >> curl -X GET 'http://localhost:8983/solr/paintings/select?q=city
    :vatican&rows=1&debug=true&wt=json&indent=true&json.nl=map'
    ```

2. We can easily make some tests with the stats components as follows:

```
>> curl -X GET 'http://localhost:8983/solr/paintings/selec
t?q=city:vatican&rows=0&stats=true&stats.field=width&stats.
field=height&stats.facet=city&wt=json&indent=true&json.nl=map'
```

3. Executing this really simple query with both the components will help us in understanding how they are designed to expose two different yet complementary kinds of information: one about field's values and the other about components.

4. In the following screenshot you'll see them in action, **stats** on the left side, and **debug** on the right side:

```
"debug":{
  "rawquerystring":"city:vatican",
  "querystring":"city:vatican",
  "parsedquery":"city:vatican",
  "parsedquery_toString":"city:vatican",
  "explain":{
    "http://dbpedia.org/resource/Deliverance_of_Saint_Peter":"
    2.8737047 = (MATCH) weight(city:vatican in 61) [DefaultSimilarity], result of:
    2.8737047 = fieldWeight in 61, product of:
    1.0 = tf(freq=1.0), with freq of:
    1.0 = termFreq=1.0
    7.6632123 = idf(docFreq=15, maxDocs=12529)
    0.375 = fieldNorm(doc=61)
  "},
  "QParser":"LuceneQParser",
  "timing":{
    "time":61.0,
    "prepare":{
      "time":17.0,
      "query":{"time":17.0},
      "facet":{"time":0.0},
      "mlt":{"time":0.0},
      "highlight":{"time":0.0},
      "stats":{"time":0.0},
      "debug":{"time":0.0}
    },
    "process":{
      "time":44.0,
      "query":{"time":35.0},
      "facet":{"time":0.0},
      "mlt":{"time":0.0},

                                            "stats":{
                                              "stats_fields":{
                                                "width":{
                                                  "min":"1200", "max":"?",
                                                  "count":14, "missing":1,
                                                  "facets":{
                                                    "city":{
                                                      "vatican":{
                                                        "min":"1200", "max":"?",
                                                        "count":14, "missing":1,
                                                        "facets":{}
                                                      }
                                                    }
                                                  }
                                                },
                                                "height":{
                                                  "min":"1370", "max":"?",
                                                  "count":14, "missing":1,
                                                  "facets":{
                                                    "city":{
                                                      "vatican":{
                                                        "min":"1370", "max":"?",
                                                        "count":14, "missing":1,
                                                        "facets":{}
```

5. If you are curious about what kind of information you can obtain with the same query using the pseudo field `[explain]`, it's easy to test it using the following command:

```
>> curl -X GET 'http://localhost:8983/solr/paintings/selec
t?q=city:vatican&rows=1&stats=true&stats.field=width&stats.
field=height&stats.facet=city&fl=[explain+style=nl]&indent=true&wt
=json'
```

6. In the following screenshot, you'll see it in action:

```
"responseHeader":{"status":0,"QTime":1},
"response":{
  "numFound":15,"start":0,"docs":[
    {
      "[explain]":{
        "match":true,
        "value":2.8726256,
        "description":"weight(city:vatican in 3421) [DefaultSimilarity], result of:",
        "details":[
          {
            "match":true,"value":2.8726256,"description":"fieldWeight in 3421, product of:",
            "details":[
              {
                "match":true,"value":1.0,"description":"tf(freq=1.0), with freq of:",
                "details":[{"match":true,"value":1.0,"description":"termFreq=1.0"}]
              },
              {"match":true,"value":7.660335,"description":"idf(docFreq=15, maxDocs=12493)"},
              {"match":true,"value":0.375,"description":"fieldNorm(doc=3421)"}
            ]
```

7. This screenshot clearly shows how the [explain] pseudo field is not directly related to debug or stats, but it can still be used to debug the actual parsing. We will look at query parsing in detail using both of them, and the analogous explain section exposed by the debug component, in the next sections, using more complex and interesting queries.

What just happened?

On the left side of the first screenshot, we can recognize different stages in the query parsing and execution, from the text typed by the user (rawquerystring) to the explain section where we can look at the internally expanded syntax. We will use the syntax later with more complex examples; remember that the explain section will include a line for every row (in this case, rows=1, so one line). In addition to this information, we can obtain an explicit reference to the parser used for the query (QParser, in this case is the default Lucene one) and to the time spent for the execution of the various components.

The stats component in the second example (on the right side of the first screenshot) provides a sequence of values about a specific field; for example, stats.field=width is used to show statistics about the values for the specific field width (minimum, maximum, how many are there, how many are missing, and so on), and stats.facet=city can be used to enable faceting of statistical values over this field. It's easy at the moment to think about stats.facet as a way to add statistics of the terms on a per-field basis. Every facet in this example will represent statistics starting from a particular field, used as our central point of interest.

For example, searching for paintings and asking for statistics about them with a `facet` attribute on `city` can be done as follows:

```
>> curl -X GET 'http://localhost:8983/solr/paintings/select?q=abstract:po
rtrait&rows=0&stats=true&stats.field=width&stats.field=height&stats.facet
=city&wt=json&indent=true&json.nl=map'
```

The preceding command will give us many lines in the facet section of every stats section, one for each term in the `city` field (the terms are actually indexed depending on the particular chosen tokenizers). Note also how these results are independent of the number of rows as they refer to general statistics for fields in a specific schema, and we can use them to gain a wide view of the data, starting from a specific point.

The usage of the pseudo field `fl=[explain+style=nl]` actually gives us some more structured visualization of the debug metadata about the terms in the result, as you can see in the second screenshot. We will use these kinds of results in particular for more complex queries, but you can also combine the two different results if you want to compare them by simply adding both the parameters into your requests.

Looking at Lucene and Solr query parsers

The Lucene query parser has been extended in Solr to take care of some recurring use cases. For example, it is possible to provide more flexibility for ranged queries, leaving them open ended, by using a * character to indicate that there is no lower or upper limit, or explicitly specify queries that must not include a specific term. We can look at the differences between the Lucene parser and the Solr default parser, based on Lucene: `http://wiki.apache.org/solr/SolrQuerySyntax`.

Moreover, there are pseudo fields that are used as fields but are actually computed by some functions. This way we can, for example, embed subqueries (with the `_query_:text-of-subquery` syntax) and function queries (with the `_val_:text-of-functionquery` syntax). You can easily note that `_field_` denotes a pseudo field or an internal field, as we have already seen for `_version_`.

For a real-world application, however, we need to manage queries that cannot contain special operators, as they can be too much complex for common users, and we'd like to have some more robust parsing over errors and typos in the queries. While it is always possible to define some kind of pre/post processing of a query at application level, there are two more query parsers that we can use because they are designed specifically for common users: Dismax and Edismax.

Time for action – debugging a query with the Lucene parser

We will now debug a basic query using the standard Lucene parser, in order to use it later as a reference for thinking about what will happen while using other parsers.

Using the default Lucene parser, suppose we are searching for a painting without remembering its title: we remember that it has something to do with Dali or Vermeer, there was a giraffe in it, and one or more female figures. A simple way to search for it is to go to the search box on our site and type in something similar to giraffe dali "female figure" vermeer. Note how we are using the double quotes to pass two terms as a single complex term: this is what is generally called a phrase query.

1. We can simulate this search as usual by using the web interface, or cURL using the following command:

```
>> curl -X GET 'http://localhost:8983/solr/paintings/select?q=gira
ffe+dali+%22female+figure%22+vermeer&start=0&rows=10&fl=title+arti
st+city&wt=json&indent=true&debugQuery=true'
```

2. Note that the %22 encoding stands for double quotes, and we have not defined a specific field to search in. For simplicity, we have to choose some values at the start, rows, fl and wt parameters, in order to obtain a more readable result, and we add the debugQuery=true parameter to activate the debug search component. The latter permits us to see how the query is internally parsed:

```
- response: {
    numFound: 91,
    start: 0,
  + docs: […]
  },
- debug: {
    rawquerystring: "giraffe dali "female figure" vermeer",
    querystring: "giraffe dali "female figure" vermeer",
    parsedquery: "fullText:giraffe fullText:dali PhraseQuery(fullText:"female figure")
    fullText:vermeer",
    parsedquery_toString: "fullText:giraffe fullText:dali fullText:"female figure" fullText:vermeer",
  - explain: {
        http://dbpedia.org/resource/The_Burning_Giraffe: " 28.326546 = (MATCH) product of: 37.768726 =
        (MATCH) sum of: 14.682315 = (MATCH) weight(fullText:giraffe in 7953) [DefaultSimilarity],
        result of: 14.682315 = score(doc=7953,freq=8.0 = termFreq=8.0 ), product of: 0.53296727 =
```

Here we can recognize a standard query in the parsedQuery field.

What just happened?

I strongly suggest to play with the different query handlers and define your own examples for them: you don't have to be concerned about using the "wrong" parameters here, as there can only be configurations that can be improved.

It's possible to write a request with cURL with the following syntax:

```
>> curl -G 'http://localhost:8983/solr/paintings/select?start=0&rows=1
0&fl=title+artist+city&wt=json&indent=true&json.nl=map&debugQuery=true'
--data-urlencode 'q=giraffe dali "female figure" vermeer'
```

This is better to look at the query parameters in a more readable way.

In our example we have found `91` matching documents, and the first is the one that most probably fits our searches (in the preceding screenshot I only projected it for improving readability). Reading with some patience all the results, we can find some other documents where the `veermer` term is found in the `artist` field, but its score is probably less than the first of the results. This is because while imposing other conditions the parser tries to find some documents that fits all of these, and omits them one by one only if a match is not found this way. In this case, the presence of a painting by `Dalì` with the `Veermer` name in its title is probably the best choice.

> I suggest you do this kind of evaluation as an exercise, using the same parameters over the web interface, then verifying the values, also adding and removing documents. A very interesting point to notice is that the Lucene score is not in a percentage, as it is designed for an open collection, where items can have a different relative score, depending on documents being removed or added. We will look again at the Lucene score later.

If you prefer, we can look at the query parameter individually. One of the example is as follows:

```
q=giraffe dali "female figure" vermeer
start=0, rows=10
fl=title artist city
wt=json, indent=true
debugQuery=true
```

You must have noticed the debug section, where you can read the `parsedQuery` and `parsedQuery_toString` output that gives us an idea of how the query is actually parsed by the internal components. It's important to see what is happening: we are obtaining a series of field searches (in the default `fullText` field) for both the terms and the phrase search, combined as a single Boolean query using the implicit default inclusive "or" condition. This is interesting, because this suggests us the possibility of thinking about decomposing a single query into several independent parts that will be recombined to offer the final one.

The Dismax query parser is focused specifically on this behavior, and moves a step further on it.

Time for action – debugging a query with the Dismax parser

Disjunction Max Query (Dismax) searches for every pair of the field/term separately, and then combines the results in order to calculate the maximum score value of the results. By default, it performs searches on every field.

1. Let's start again by using cURL for a Dismax query as follows:

```
>> curl -X GET 'http://localhost:8983/solr/paintings/select?q=gira
ffe+dali+%22female+figure%22+vermeer&start=0&fl=title+artist+city
&wt=json&indent=true&debugQuery=true&defType=dismax&qf=artist+abs
tract^2&mm=3&pf=abstract^3'
```

2. When we find good parameter values in our experiments, we can, for example, configure a new request handler with these values predefined in solrconfig.xml.

3. Looking at the following screenshot, extracted from the complete results, we can see different DisjunctionMaxQuery objects, one independent from the other:

```
((
    +((
        DisjunctionMaxQuery((abstract:giraffe | artist:giraffe^2.0))
        DisjunctionMaxQuery((abstract:dali | artist:dali^2.0))
        DisjunctionMaxQuery((abstract:"female figure" | artist:"female figure"^2.0))
        DisjunctionMaxQuery((abstract:vermeer | artist:vermeer^2.0))
    )~3)
    DisjunctionMaxQuery((abstract:"giraffe dali female figure vermeer"^3.0))
)/no_coord
```

4. In this example, the choice of parameters' values is used to produce some different and independent searches, using the DisjunctionMaxQuery component, and then assemble the result vector into a final combination.

What just happened?

In this kind of search, obtaining a list of good matches is somewhat more important than a higher precision of the result; avoiding powerful (and sometimes ugly) operators, and searching by a simple keyword sequence will correspond to a more natural query for a common user.

We have used some more new parameters here specific to Dismax as follows:

◆ defType:dismax: This is used to activate the Dismax query parser. It is equivalent to checking on the Dismax entry in the web interface, to activate and open it.

◆ qf:artist^2 abstract: This is a list of query fields. Here we are restricting the searches to some specific fields, than give to the field artist some more importance than abstract in the results.

- ◆ mm:3: Here, we search (if possible) for a document with a minimum match of three terms.

- ◆ `pf:abstract^3 defines a phrase field`: We want to boost the phrase search more that has some match in the abstract field.

> Note that by activating the Dismax parsing without specifying values for its own parameters, you will have the same results as with the standard Lucene parser.

The more readable and final parsed version of the same query is exposed by the `parsedquery_toString` field, as shown in the following screenshot:

```
+(
    (
        (abstract:giraffe | artist:giraffe^2.0)
        (abstract:dali | artist:dali^2.0)
        (abstract:"female figure" | artist:"female figure"^2.0)
        (abstract:vermeer | artist:vermeer^2.0)
    )~3)
(abstract:"giraffe dali female figure vermeer"^3.0)
```

The choice of query fields produces an explicit Boolean query for every term. This small series of independent queries are then assembled as a unique proximity search query, using a minimum match of 3 (which corresponds to mm=3).

Finally, the phrase and term boost are taken into account separately and only the second one is considered optional (there is no + sign), so that if no match is found the output will be less precise on that condition, but still there will be some result. Generally speaking, we can think about using this query parser as we always want some result, even less precise, but still pertinent.

Using an Edismax default handler

Extended Dismax Parser (Edismax) has been designed as an evolution of the Dismax parser, so it's probably the best choice as a default query handler in our project for common queries. It is almost identical to Dismax, but introduced with some more fine tuning parameters; for example, the possibility to choose how to act differently with bigram and trigram phrase searches (for example, `pf2`, and `pf3` for sequences of two and three terms respectively), and the chance to define a user field (the `uf` parameter) where it's still possible to make use of the Lucene syntax.

The most important of all is that it is even more robust on errors, incomplete conditions, missing operands, and so on. It has been also designed to perform automatic escaping and to use lowercase values when possible, as well as to be flexible enough to let us use Boolean parameters with different syntax: AND, and, &&, OR, or, ||. The "fail-fast" behavior of this query parser is thus a good compromise between the Lucene power and the behavior expected by a common user in real scenarios.

You can find an explanation of parameters at http://wiki.apache.org/solr/ ExtendedDisMax.

> If you are interested in a good explanation of the origin of this parser, please consider reading this introduction at http://searchhub. org/2010/05/23/whats-a-dismax/.

Configuring an Edismax query handler as the default one in our schema is as simple as adding the following code in our solrconfig.xml (you will find it along with a specific /SolrStarterBook/solr-app/chp05/paintings_edismax core in the examples):

```
<requestHandler name="standard" class="solr.SearchHandler"
default="true" >
  <lst name="defaults">
    <str name="defType">edismax</str>
    <str name="echoParams">explicit</str>
    <str name="qf">artist^2 abstract</str>
    <str name="pf">abstract^3</str>
    <int name="mm">3</int>
    <str name="fq">abstract:painting*</str>
    <str name="fq">title:*</str>
    <str name="fq">artist:*</str>
    <str name="uf">paint~4</str>
    <str name="fl">title artist</str>
    <str name="wt">json</str>
  </lst>
</requestHandler>
```

Note that if some of the parameters' values were fixed in the queries, a filter query can be used for performance reasons; for example if we added fq=abstract:painting* in our case, if we added fq=comment:painting, we will omit those results that do not have the term painting in the comment, so please use this parameter carefully. Using title:* and artist:* is just a way to obtain only the documents that actually contain the values for those fields. Note that we can pass as many fq single values as we want, and they will be cached internally for the performance. We will see filter queries again later in *Chapter 6, Using Faceted Search – from Searching to Finding*.

Lastly, since in this example we don't want to use a different handler for our Edismax search from the default one, we need to remove the original default handler as follows:

```
<requestHandler name="standard" class="solr.StandardRequestHandler"
default="true" />
```

The choice of having the handlers working together or changing the default one will generally depend on your application.

> An interesting article by *Nolan Lawson* (`http://nolanlawson.`
> `com/2012/06/02/comparing-boost-methods-in-solr/`)
> can give us some suggestions on how to combine boosting with different
> types of parsers such as Edismax and the Lucene one.

However, if we don't substitute the default handler with the Edismax handler, we can of course use both Lucene and Edismax at the same time, as we will see in the next sections.

Time for action – executing a nested Edismax query

Using the `defType=edismax` parameter, it's possible to combine the usage of Edismax and Lucene together at the same time. Moreover, we can execute more restrictive queries nested one into another by performing the following steps:

1. In the following example, we ask for documents containing the term `painting` in the abstract field, and then we define a nested query using the Edismax query parser (`{!dismax ...}`) as follows:

    ```
    >> curl -X GET 'http://localhost:8983/solr/paintings/
    select?q=abstract:painting%20AND%20_query_:%22{!dismax%20
    qf=artist^2%20qf=abstract%20pf=abstract^3%20mm=3%20
    v=$qq}%22&fl=title%20artist&wt=json&qq=giraffe%20dali%20
    %22female%20figure%22%20vermeer'
    ```

2. Note how this example looks very ugly at first, due to nested elements and HTTP encoding, but now we will see that it's not so complicated as it may seem.

3. Even if we use cURL for transcribing examples, I suggest you to try to reproduce the same example by inserting the parameter values on the web interface or on your browser's console, as it's always useful to have multiple and different access to read the data.

What just happened?

If you look carefully at the parameter sequence of this simple nested query, you will find that the most interesting part is the following code:

```
q=abstract:painting
AND
_query_:"{!dismax qf=artist^2 qf=abstract pf=abstract^3 mm=3 v=$qq}"
qq=giraffe dali "female figure" vermeer
```

We are actually performing two different kinds of queries and then combining them with an AND condition, so that they have to be verified at the same time. Please consider that the qq parameter name cannot be changed at the moment, and it's used to define what you can see as a sort of local variable, useful for writing the nested query text in a clearer form.

A short list of search components

We already briefly introduced the idea behind the Solr components workflow, and we see that it's possible to use multiple query handlers at the same time by specifying a defType parameter. The defType parameter helps us to choose between some different query handlers, including our customized ones, if there are. We will focus on the next paragraphs of the standard and Dismax query handlers.

The defType and qt parameters that we have already seen are similar but different: the qt parameter can be used to define and customize a search handler in the solrconfig.xml file while defType is a parameter that's used to inform a search handler what type of query parser to use.

For example, for using Edismax, it is possible to adopt some different equivalent syntax as follows:

```
q={!dismax qf=query-filter-condition} some-query-terms
q={!type=dismax qf=query-filter-condition} some-query-terms
q=some-query-terms&defType=dismax&qf=query-filter-condition
```

We have already seen how to select different response writers using a simple wt parameter.

Both request handlers and response writers are particular types of SolrPlugin that are available at http://wiki.apache.org/solr/SolrPlugins.

> One of the possible ways to extend Solr components is to write a new Java class that should subscribe one of the SolrPlugin interfaces defined in the `org.apache.solr.util.plugin` package.
>
> Furthermore, if a plugin implements `ResourceLoaderAware` or `SolrCoreAware`, it can easily share some configurations handled by the main core.

For our purposes, it's important to have some more experience with the search-specific components: `http://wiki.apache.org/solr/SearchComponent`; in order to have a much wider point of view, we can think about Solr out-of-the-box capabilities in search and related actions. For your convenience I have summarized some of the most important ones in the following table, with references to the chapters where we have the chance to play a bit with them:

Reference	Parameter	Component	Chapters
Search Handlers: `http://wiki.apache.org/solr/SearchHandler`			
Query using some of the query parsers	`query`	Query component	3,4,5
Add the highlight results section	`highlight`	Highlight component	5
Add the more like this results section	`mlt`	MoreLikeThis component	6
Provide faceted results	`facet`	Facet component	6
Add some statistics to the results	`stats`	Stats component	5
Add a debug section for inspecting queries	`debug`	Debug component	5
Others			
Provide a spellchecker, useful as autosuggester		SpellCheck component	5
Promote some term or phrase		QueryElevation component	5
Provide Bloom index capabilitiy		BloomIndex component	5
Expose the IDF and TF Lucene vector weights		TermVector component and Termscomponent	6
Provide clustering capabilities for fields and documents		Clustering component	6

We will see faceted searches and other related topics in *Chapter 6, Using Faceted Search – from Searching to Finding*, such as grouping results or defining a "more like this" handler. Moreover, we will have the chance to get an introductory idea about some advanced and still evolving topics such as clustering terms and documents, and Lucene terms vector weights suitable to functions and similarity queries.

Adding the blooming filter and real-time Get

Lastly, a blooming filter can be seen as a look-up for the existence of a specific value in a read-only collection: Solr uses this especially for verifying the presence of a value in a distributed cloud instance. Adding a blooming filter handler in our configuration is easy, as shown in the following code:

```
<searchComponent name="bloom" class="org.apache.solr.handler.
component.BloomIndexComponent">
   <str name="field">uri</str>
</searchComponent>
<requestHandler name="/bloom" class="org.apache.solr.handler.
component.SearchHandler">
   <arr name="components">
     <str>bloom</str>
   </arr>
</requestHandler>
```

And all we should do is check for the existence of a specific resource using the following command:

```
>> curl -X GET 'http://localhost:8080/solr/bloom?q=uri:http\://dbpedia.
org/resource/Drawing_Hands'
```

At the moment of writing this book, there were issues in the current implementation of bloom filters, so I suggest you not use them; but it's interesting to follow this idea because, with this functionality, you can check not only for the existence of a specific resource but you can obtain false positives (which "maybe" existing) that can be used as a test for finding your own resources.

However, we don't need a bloom filter if we want to look up a specific resource in a faster way, without the cost of doing a search in the index (and then reopening a new searcher). In this case, we can simply use the RealTimeGetHandler as follows:

```
<requestHandler name="/get" class="solr.RealTimeGetHandler">
    <lst name="defaults">
      <str name="omitHeader">true</str>
      <str name="wt">json</str>
      <str name="indent">true</str>
    </lst>
  </requestHandler>
<updateHandler class="solr.DirectUpdateHandler2">
  <updateLog class="solr.FSUpdateLog">
    <str name="dir">${solr.ulog.dir:}</str>
  </updateLog>
</updateHandler>
```

And we can verify whether a document has been added to the index by using the following command:

```
>> curl -X GET 'http://localhost:8080/solr/get?q=uri:http\://dbpedia.org/
resource/Drawing_Hands'
```

Note that using this command, we will know if a specific document has been added to the index before a commit operation is performed, since they have already been added with some soft commit. This can be very useful in many situations, especially while using sharding with SolrCloud, which we will see in *Chapter 8, Indexing External Data Sources*.

Time for action – executing a simple pseudo-join query

More recently, due to requests from the community, pseudo-join queries have been added to filter documents at runtime by applying conditions to another document value. A pseudo-join query can be executed as follows:

1. It's very easy to execute a pseudo-join query, as you will find it very similar to the nested queries seen earlier:

```
>> curl -X GET 'http://localhost:8983/solr/paintings/select?fl=ti
tle,artist&q=abstract:paintings%20AND%20\{!join%20from=artist%20
to=title\}artist:vermeer'
```

This query simply returns again the document for Dalì's painting *The Ghost of Vermeer of Delft Which Can Be Used As a Table*.

2. Note that the characters { and } need to be escaped with \ or substituted by the correct HTTP encoding. If we rewrite the cURL command as follows, the query will be much more readable, and we can still contain the output format in the usual way, separating it from the parameters containing the query itself:

```
 >> curl -X GET 'http://localhost:8983/solr/paintings/
select?fl=title,artist&wt=json' --data-urlencode
'q=abstract:paintings AND {!join from=artist to=title}
artist:vermeer'
```

What just happened?

Here we are querying in the documents containing the term painting in the abstract field, and then joining them over the documents that contain the vermer term in the artist field, and has some match in the title with the artist field. This is a very particular case, and gives us the possibility of using it for some considerations.

If you have some experience with SQL, you will be familiar with the following code:

```
/solr/paintings/select?
fl=title,artist
q=abstract:paintings AND {!join from=artist to=title}artist:vermeer
```

The following is a slight analogy to an inner SQL query:

```
SELECT title,artist
FROM paintings
WHERE (abstract:paintings AND (title IN (SELECT artist FROM paintings
where artist:vermeer))
```

This does not suggest that we should start using Solr with a pseudo-SQL approach, but there can be cases where we need to filter out some documents from the result, if they don't match a certain criteria in another document field. I must inform you that these are usually some very particular use cases.

Highlighting results to improve the search experience

One of the most recurring and recognizable front-end patterns while performing searches is the ability to provide results to the users with the matching terms obvious, in order to make them more recognizable. Using such an ability together with the flexibility of an Edismax parser would probably be the best choice for several simple applications.

Time for action – generating highlighted snippets over a term

As an example, let's define a new query for highlighting a term we are currently searching for using the following steps:

1. The following is the query used for searching the document containing an artist term similar to "salvatore":

```
>> curl -X GET 'http://localhost:8983/solr/paintings/select
?q=artist:salvatore~0.5&fl=uri,title,artist&rows=2&hl=true&
hl.fl=abstract&hl.simple.pre=%3Cstrong%3E&hl.simple.post=%3C/
strong%3E&hl.snippets=4&wt=json'
```

What we are expecting to see in the results are snippets of texts, extracted from the actual texts in the documents, so a user can recognize a matched term, as shown in the following screenshot:

```
{
 - responseHeader: {
     status: 0,
     QTime: 19
   },
 - response: {
     numFound: 25,
     start: 0,
   - docs: [
     - {
         uri: "http://dbpedia.org/resource/The_Basket_of_Bread",
       - artist: [
           "http://dbpedia.org/resource/Salvador_Dalí"
         ],
       - title: [
           "The Basket of Bread"
         ]
       },
     - {
         uri: "http://dbpedia.org/resource/The_Burning_Giraffe",
       - artist: [
           "http://dbpedia.org/resource/Salvador_Dalí"
         ],
       - title: [
           "The Burning Giraffe"
         ]
       }
     ]
   },
 - highlighting: {
   - http://dbpedia.org/resource/The_Basket_of_Bread: {
     - abstract: [
         "The Basket of Bread is a painting by Spanish surrealist <strong>Salvador</strong> Dalí. The painting
         depicts four",
         "-bitten. The basket sits on a white cloth. The painting resides at the <strong>Salvador</strong> Dalí
         Museum, St"
       ]
     },
   - http://dbpedia.org/resource/The_Burning_Giraffe: {
     - abstract: [
         "The Burning Giraffe (1937) is a painting by the Spanish surrealist <strong>Salvador</strong> Dalí.
         Dalí painted"
       ]
     }
   }
 }
}
```

Clearly the values projected by the highlighting component are not designed to be used directly by users, but by a front-end component of the application, in order to "decorate" the results with an appropriate formatting for highlighting. Generally speaking, the snippets proposed on the highlighted results can be returned by themselves or more often they will be used, for example, to find the portion of text to be emphasized, and replace it when we need it for formatting.

What just happened?

In the example, you can recognize that the highlights in the returned snippets are surrounded by XML tags, even if the format is JSON. The format for highlighting is independent from the result format.

We have reduced the rows returned to only 2, in order to make the results more readable. As you can see there is a highlighted item for every document, so it's important to remember to return the unique key field, too (in our case, it's the URI; in a common scenario, it will be an ID field) in order to be able to assemble the highlights and the actual results, without the need for referring to position.

- ◆ `hl=true`: This is used for activating the highlighting component.

- ◆ `hl.fl=abstract`: This lets us return only text snippets from the abstract field.

- ◆ `hl.simple.pre=<strong>`, `hl.simple.post=</strong>`: This defines the tags to surround the matching term (we can, of course, replace the characters < and > with `%3C` and `%3E`).

- ◆ `hl.snippets=4`: This will produce four snippets at the most for every document. This is important since there can be more than one snippet from a long text field, such as our abstract field; in the example, the first item in the highlighted results actually contains two snippets.

Moreover a snippet is useful because it not only contains the term to be highlighted, but also a text fragment useful for identifying its context. We can also decide how much text this snippet should contain in the results via a specific parameter.

You can find a complete list of all the usable parameters at:
`http://wiki.apache.org/solr/HighlightingParameters`

Some idea about geolocalization with Solr

Geolocalization has made a great improvement in the last few years in every kind of user experience. The process of placing and visualizing data on a map has been generally a very useful, and it is also best suited for mobile applications. Providing geolocalization means at least finding out what coordinates should be used to link our data at some point in the geographic space; when we are using a smartphone these coordinates can be taken from its sensors, but if we are developing a search application, this data should be chosen more carefully.

In our `paintings` example, it's simple to imagine performing searches over the geographical location where a painting is actually located, as this can be an additional way to see the data. Unfortunately, the data we have used so far does not contain the information about coordinates. The best we can find is only the name (the English name, to be precise) of the city where a painting is actually stored, probably the city of the museum or private collection where it is located. Assuming that there are lot of services that provide coordinates for a specific city name on the Internet, a common task is to retrieve this kind of information from one of those services, and simply add them to our index. Some of the most well-known services, probably at the moment, providing geocoding information are as follows:

- The Google Maps API
- The OpenStreetMap API
- Geonames downloadable dataset
- The Linked Geo Data API and downloadable dataset

I only cited here some of the most used, but there are many others. A good one is, for example, the Nominatim API, provided by Open Street Map: `http://wiki.openstreetmap.org/wiki/Nominatim`

If you look at the information they collect for `Paris` from `http://nominatim.openstreetmap.org/search?city=Paris&dedupe=1&format=json`, you will see that there are many matches, but the first is indeed the `Paris` we are thinking about, and we have then the chance to retrieve its latitude and longitude, to be able to use them later for constructing a map of how our data should be geographically disposed.

Time for action – creating a repository of cities

Our work is then very simple. We have a city name in our index, but we don't have its coordinates. We can check in the Nominatim Open Street Map API to obtain its coordinates if present, and some extra metadata. The procedure for this is as follows:

1. I decided that you need not worry about retrieving that data, so I put a very simple Scala script called `import_cities_osm.sh` in the `/SolrStarterBook/test/chp05/cities` directory. The script will search for the list of cities in your running `paintings` core and then ask Nominatim if there are matches to it, importing them if present into a new core, which we will simply call `cities`. Obviously this will produce some extra noise, but it's good as we are still experimenting.

2. Before you run the script we not only have to define the new `cities` core, we need to define a new `solrconfig.xml` file (this is nothing new. We define a new core with usual capabilities) and the schema will be really minimal, as shown in the following code:

```
<schema name="cities" version="1.1">
  <types>
    <fieldtype name="string" class="solr.StrField" />
    <fieldType name="long" class="solr.TrieLongField" />
    <fieldType name="location" class="solr.LatLonType"
subFieldSuffix="_lat_lon" />
    <fieldType name="text" class="solr.TextField"
positionIncrementGap="100">
      <analyzer>
        <charFilter class="solr.MappingCharFilterFactory"
mapping="mapping-ISOLatin1Accent.txt" />
        <tokenizer class="solr.StandardTokenizerFactory" />
        <filter class="solr.LowerCaseFilterFactory" />
      </analyzer>
    </fieldType>
  </types>

  <fields>
    <field name="id" type="long" required="true" />
    <field name="city" type="text" required="true" indexed="true"
stored="true" />
    <dynamicField name="*" type="string" multiValued="false"
indexed="true" stored="true" />
    <dynamicField name="*_coordinates" type="location"
indexed="true" stored="true" />
  </fields>
  <uniqueKey>id</uniqueKey>
</schema>
```

3. When we have defined our new core, we can restart the Solr instance and run the following script:

```
>> ./import_cities_osm.sh
```

4. And in a while, we will have our small repository of city information. To verify that we can simply perform a filtered range query over values for latitude and longitude fields:

```
>> curl -X GET 'http://localhost:8983/solr/cities/
select?&q=*:*&wt=csv&fq=lat:\[46.00+TO+50.00\]+AND+lon:\
[2.00+TO+3.00\]'
```

5. Using this we can find out that we now have information about `Paris` and other places.

What just happened?

The only new part in this small experiment was the introduction of a new type of field, specifically for handling spatial search, as given at: `http://wiki.apache.org/solr/SpatialSearch`

Note that we are using a filtered query (we will see it again in the next chapters), in which we are actually defining two range queries in the latitude (`lat`) and longitude (`lon`) field separately. We saved the coordinate values both as a couple of separated fields and as a unique field, which is internally handled and divided into two numerical parts, optimized for this kind of search. This is what we have defined with the new schema field and field types, if you look carefully at the example in which I have maintained both the solutions; you can test it as you want.

Playing more with spatial search

Then, remembering the introduction of this new type of field, we can perform more or less the same search by using a bounded box search, in order to capture all the cities in a specific area:

```
>> curl -X GET 'http://localhost:8983/solr/cities/
select?&q=*:*&fq=coordinates:\[46.00,2.00+TO+50.00,3.00\]&wt=csv'
```

But we can also perform queries based on an assigned distance radius (for example, 190 km), given a certain central point:

```
>> curl -X GET 'http://localhost:8983/solr/cities/
select?q=*:*&fl=city,display_name&q=*:*&fq={!bbox}&sfield=coordinates&pt=
48.8565056,2.3521334&d=190&spatial=true&wt=json&indent=true'
```

In the latter case, in my dataset I obtained again Paris with other two cities in France (Le Liège, Rueil-Malmaison) that are within the radius. This kind of search is quite useful when used in the back end of some HTML widget that permits defining searches, for example, with a slider.

Looking at the new Solr 4 spatial features – from points to polygons

In the previous example, we saw how Solr is able to manage coordinates with basic distance and spatial functions. These functions were introduced to offer a more structured approach. Instead of using two distinct floating point values for latitude and longitude, we can handle them together in a single type, designed to internally store the values separately for queries in range and other operations using a syntax designed for geolocalization.

Since Lucene 4 introduced a new spatial module, Solr itself adds new spatial features based on it. These components are changing fast, and I suggest you follow the updates on the page `http://wiki.apache.org/solr/SolrAdaptersForLuceneSpatial4`.

Starting from Solr 3 spatial points handled with LatLonType, it's now possible to index the following shapes:

- **Points (latitude, longitude)**: This has the same syntax as `LatLonType`.
- **Rectangles**: This is used with syntax `minX`, `minY`, `maxX`, and `maxY` (the same used for bounding box queries).
- **Circles**: This is used with syntax `Circle(latX, lonX, d=distance)`. Note that this kind of object extends `LatLonType` with the distance functions already supported in Solr 3 as query parameters.
- **Polygons, LineString, and other shapes**: These are written using the **Well Known Text (WKT)** syntax `POLYGON ((LatLon1, LatLon2, Latlon3, …))`.

The basic idea is to construct complex objects (and shapes) over the simplest, as expected.

> Well Known Text is a text markup format originally defined by **Open Geospatial Consortium (OGC)**, and since then adopted by many databases and systems with spatial support, for example, PostGis, GeoServer, Oracle, and others. WKT formats can represent various kinds of spatial concepts, from points to complex polyhedral surfaces. The Wikipedia page `http://en.wikipedia.org/wiki/Well-Known_Text` also contains some examples and references to the standards.

In order to properly handle ploygons in the queries, new spatial predicates have been introduced: `Contains`, `Intersects`, `IsWithin`, and `IsDisjointTo`.

The new components extend the Lucene 4 spatial component with features from spatial4J and **JTS (Java Topology Suite)** libraries. There are still some minor problems with dependencies at the moment, and if you want to test by yourself these features, you have to do a little hacking of the Solr application. You have to add the libraries into the standard WAR file in `SOLR_DIST/example/webapps/solr.war`, or in the expanded application, `SOLR_DIST/example/solr-webapp/webapp/WEB-INF/lib`, remembering that if you change the WAR file, the expanded folder will also be changed by Jetty. Another option is to use Maven, and in this case you can take a look at the sample application at GitHub: `https://github.com/ryantxu/spatial-solr-sandbox`, which can be used to test these features.

The most notable addition in these new features is the the introduction of the PrefixTree type. This is basically a structured type that represents the world as a grid, and internally decomposes each grid recursively into more fine grained cells. This fractal-like approach is interesting since it can be also used to store other kinds of content (not only strictly related to spatial data), still using the topology functions on them.

Time for action – expanding the original data with coordinates during the update process

Defining an external and specific dedicated index is not unusual in a real context, when sometimes you would like to index and search for specific kind of entities. Thus, you will be able to recognize them and annotate them in your own data in a way similar to what we already did for highlighting, but in a more controlled way and with more semantics. A good experiment at this time, involving just a bit of scripting, could be expanding the information we have about our city at the time of posting them to be indexed.

1. Suppose we have already collected information about cities, and we want to use it to expand the information about every new document when it contains a known city. I have defined a new `paintings_geo` core that extends the usual painting with updating capabilities, as in the following snippet of `solrconfig.xml`:

```xml
<updateHandler class="solr.DirectUpdateHandler2">
  <updateLog>
    <str name="dir">${solr.ulog.dir:}</str>
  </updateLog>
  <autoCommit>
    <maxTime>100</maxTime>
    <openSearcher>false</openSearcher>
  </autoCommit>
</updateHandler>
<requestHandler name="/update" class="solr.UpdateRequestHandler">
  <lst name="defaults">
    <str name="update.chain">script</str>
  </lst>
</requestHandler>
<updateRequestProcessorChain name="script">
  <processor class="solr.StatelessScriptUpdateProcessorFactory">
    <str name="script">cities_from_osm.js</str>
  </processor>
  <processor class="solr.LogUpdateProcessorFactory" />
  <processor class="solr.RunUpdateProcessorFactory" />
</updateRequestProcessorChain>
```

2. For the `schema.xml` file we left all unchanged, but added the field seen before `location`:

```xml
<fieldType name="location" class="solr.LatLonType"
subFieldSuffix="_lat_lon" postingsFormat="SimpleText" />
<dynamicField name="*_coordinates" type="location" indexed="true"
stored="true" />
```

3. Now let's start the core with the usual scripts and post some data on that, using a simple update example on CSV, using the following command:

```
>> curl -X GET 'http://localhost:8983/solr/paintings_geo/
update?stream.body=TEST_01,Mona+Lisa,Leonardo+Da+Vinci
,Paris&stream.contentType=application/csv;charset=utf-
8&fieldnames=uri,title,artist,city'
```

4. Here we are posting as an example a small record about the `Mona Lisa` located at `Louvre, Paris`.

What just happened?

If you start the usual importing process on this new core with the provided script and look at the running log in the open console, you can easily find that we are adding some extra information to the document. During the update process, we attached an update processor to the update chain, so that every document will be processed by the script `cities_from_osm.js`. Here we can use every scripting language supported by JVM: Jruby, Groovy, JavaScript, Scala, Clojure, and others. We decided to use JavaScript for two reasons: it has a well-known syntax and it's already used in many HTML front ends. It's good to have somebody in the team who can use it and give us some help if needed.

We can easily explain what happened there with some simplified pseudo code (please refer to the following example for the complete script):

```
function processAdd(cmd) {

  var doc = cmd.solrDoc;
  doc.setField("museum_entity", museum-value);
  doc.setField("[QUERY]", "/"+other.getName()+"?q="+query.toString());
  doc.setField("[DOCS HITS]", docset.size());

  var other = getCore(cmd, 'cities');
  var searcher = other.newSearcher("/select");
  var term = new org.apache.lucene.index.Term("city", city);
  var query = new org.apache.lucene.search.TermQuery(term);
  var docset = searcher.getDocSet(query);

  var doc_it = docset.iterator();
  while (doc_it.hasNext()) {
  var id = doc_it.nextDoc();
    var doc_found = searcher.doc(id);
    var lat = doc_found.getField("lat").stringValue();
    var lon = doc_found.getField("lon").stringValue();
```

```
    doc.setField("coordinates", normalize(ns, lat)+","+normalize(ns,
  lon));
  }

  searcher.close();
}
```

Note that even if we are using JavaScript as a language, the general API (name and parameters of the methods) corresponds to the original Java one to make things easier. Once we retrieve a `SolrInputDocument` doc from the `UpdateRequestProcessor` object command, we will be able to add to it new fields at runtime (remember that we have defined dynamic fields; this simplifies things as we are not bound to specific field's name and type here). In particular, we retrieve data from the already populated `cities` core with data from Open Street Map and perform on it a search for obtaining the coordinates of a matching city name. This approach is not optimal, as we are actually opening a new searcher every time, and can be optimized by saving a reference to a searcher. The simplest way to do that could be, for example, using some global variable, but we don't need to do this now.

Finally we can construct the coordinate field with the right syntax; this time the coordinates are physically stored within the `painting` resource.

We also decided to put two extra fields ([QUERY] and [DOCS_HITS]) in the results to represent the original query and the number of documents. These represent only other examples of field creation at runtime, but they are useful again to see how to handle a Java object within Javascript. Note that here we are adopting the naming convention of pseudo-fields used with transformers just to let them be recognizable from the original ones; but the fields are, in this case, actually saved in the index, they are not created "on the fly".

Performing editorial correction on boosting

There are some cases in which it can be useful to give more visibility to certain documents in particular: for example, because they are indicated as more relevant, or because we want to do some reranking of results, thus boosting the more popular documents by using the search logs, or, again, to append at the end document which refer to terms and words that seems not to be very pertinent in general to our searches, even if they are precise in terms of full-text search. This kind of "revised results" should be done in a team with some expert on the domain data, who can possibly help us in deciding how much a process will fit the problem.

We can easily introduce an editorial correction by adding the following simple configuration into Solr:

```
<searchComponent name="elevator" class="org.apache.solr.handler.
component.QueryElevationComponent">
  <str name="queryFieldType">string</str>
```

```
    <str name="config-file">elevate.xml</str>
</searchComponent>

<requestHandler name="/elevate" class="solr.SearchHandler">
  <arr name="last-components">
    <str>elevator</str>
  </arr>
</requestHandler>
```

As you can see, we are basically defining a new, independent `searchComponent`, and we will "plug" it into a specific `requestHandler` chain, just to avoid using the default one. The search component makes use of an external simple XML file in which we will define what document should be added or removed from the results, similar to the following code, which you can easily expand:

```
<elevate>
  <query text="dali">
    <doc id="http://en.wikipedia.org/wiki/Metamorphosis_of_Narcissus"
/>
  </query>
  <query text="leonardo">
    <doc id="http://en.wikipedia.org/wiki/Lisa_del_Giocondo"
exclude="true" />
  </query>
</elevate>
```

In this simple example, we want a specific painting (`narcissus` by `dali`) to be "promoted" to the top of the result, while for the second example, we want to give lesser visibility to a specific painting (another portrait of the same subject of *Mona Lisa*, but for some reason we would not have it in the first result). We have searched using the term `leonardo`.

Introducing the spellcheck component

When we refer to the spellchecker, we think about a component that is able to recognize small typos and errors over a term inserted by a casual user. In short, the component works by applying some distance between the terms in search and the terms indexed. When the distance will give results lesser than a certain value, a suggestion will be returned. Nothing is conceptually complicated then, and the component works generally almost well out of the box. Still it's important to do some fine tuning in order to have it work as expected; we always have to remember that if we use only the terms in our index, our precision can degrade very fast due to the domain-specific nature of our application, and to the quantity of the terms we have indexed.

Spellchecking can be seen somehow similar to obtaining suggestions for similar topics. This is one of the most commonly used ways to implement with Solr a functionality similar to the well-know "did you mean" by Google.

The most important spellcheckers that can be used are as follows:

♦ `IndexBasedSpellChecker`: This will check for the terms in the index.

♦ `WordBreakSolrSpellChecker`: This does the same function but it's able to handle sequences of words. This can be seen as a sort of "phrase" spellchecker if you want.

♦ `DirectSolrSpellChecker`: This introduces some adjustments over the `IndexBasedSpellChecker` one, by taking care of spaces, punctuations, and other things. This spellchecker doesn't need to re-index the terms.

♦ `FileBasedSpellChecker`: This can be used to provide suggestions starting from a file of controlled words.

You can find details about the SpellCheck component in the following official wiki page:

`http://wiki.apache.org/solr/SpellCheckComponent`

There is also a specific page with hints on how to use it for "did you mean" autosuggestions at `http://wiki.apache.org/solr/Suggester`.

Time for action – playing with spellchecks

A very simple way to play with spellchecking is to define a new request handler to manage this kind of result apart from the common ones. On a real application, you should consider concatenating them directly after the main results, as usual using the appropriate component chain.

1. We can start by defining a new `paintings_spellchecker` core, derived from the previous core, and add to its `solrconfig.xml` file the configuration for a multiple spellchecker using the following code:

```
<searchComponent name="spellcheck" class="solr.
SpellCheckComponent">
  <str name="queryAnalyzerFieldType">text_auto</str>
  <lst name="spellchecker">
    <str name="name">direct</str>
    <str name="field">artist_entity</str>
    <str name="classname">solr.DirectSolrSpellChecker</str>
    <str name="distanceMeasure">internal</str>
    <float name="accuracy">0.8</float>
    <int name="maxEdits">2</int>
```

```
      <int name="minPrefix">1</int>
      <int name="maxInspections">5</int>
      <int name="minQueryLength">3</int>
      <float name="maxQueryFrequency">0.01</float>
      <str name="spellcheckIndexDir">./spellchecker</str>
   </lst>
   <lst name="spellchecker">
      <str name="name">wordbreak</str>
      <str name="field">artist_entity</str>
      <str name="classname">solr.WordBreakSolrSpellChecker</str>
      <str name="combineWords">true</str>
      <str name="breakWords">true</str>
      <int name="maxChanges">3</int>
      <str name="spellcheckIndexDir">./spellchecker</str>
   </lst>
</searchComponent>
```

2. As you can see, we are operating in a field called `text-auto`, which we will define in a while. Moreover we are using two different spellcheckers at the same time, as each one of them simply adds its suggestions to the results section, without causing problems for the other. For every component, we are using different parameters' values. The search component for spellchecking can be easily used by a specific request handler as usual:

```
<requestHandler name="/suggest" class="org.apache.solr.handler.
component.SearchHandler">
   <lst name="defaults">
     <str name="df">artist_entity</str>
     <str name="spellcheck">on</str>
     <str name="spellcheck.dictionary">direct</str>
     <str name="spellcheck.dictionary">wordbreak</str>
     <str name="spellcheck.extendedResults">true</str>
     <str name="spellcheck.count">10</str>
     <str name="spellcheck.alternativeTermCount">5</str>
     <str name="spellcheck.maxResultsForSuggest">5</str>
     <str name="spellcheck.collate">true</str>
     <str name="spellcheck.collateExtendedResults">true</str>
     <str name="spellcheck.maxCollationTries">10</str>
     <str name="spellcheck.maxCollations">5</str>
     </lst>
   <arr name="components">
     <str>spellcheck</str>
   </arr>
</requestHandler>
```

3. Note that here we are defining a `/suggest` request handler that will make use only of the components in the spellcheck chain, and we have put in it several predefined arbitrary values for its parameters.

4. Let's now define the new type we are going to use for spellchecking in our `schema.xml` file:

```
<fieldType class="solr.TextField" name="text_auto"
positionIncrementGap="100">
  <analyzer>
    <tokenizer class="solr.WhitespaceTokenizerFactory" />
    <filter class="solr.WordDelimiterFilterFactory"
generateWordParts="1" generateNumberParts="1" catenateWords="1"
catenateNumbers="1" catenateAll="0" splitOnCaseChange="1" />
    <filter class="solr.LowerCaseFilterFactory" />
  </analyzer>
</fieldType>
<dynamicField name="*_entity" type="text_auto" multiValued="false"
indexed="true" stored="true" />
```

5. Furthermore, for the field that will get this type, we can use `omitTermFreqAndPositions="true"` to save a little space and time during indexing.

6. When everything is configured, we can start Solr in the usual way (don't forget to add the core in the list of the `/SolrStarterBook/solr-app/chp05/solr.xml` file), and build the spellcheck specific index using the following command:

```
>> curl -X GET 'http://localhost:8983/solr/paintings_spellchecker/
suggest?spellcheck.build=true&wt=json'
```

7. Then we can play with some example queries; feel free to try several queries on your own. I suggest using a query with a lot of typos. (this has no real meaning), For example purposes you can use `pollok some-text salvator some-text lionardo some-text georgio`, as given in the following command:

```
>> curl -X GET 'http://localhost:8983/solr/paintings_spellchecker/
suggest?q=artist_entity:pollok%20salvator%20lionardo%20georgio&row
s=1&spellcheck=true&wt=json&indent=true'
```

What just happened?

While playing with our funny example query, we will receive an output similar to the one shown in the following screenshot:

```
"spellcheck":{
  "suggestions":{
    "pollok":{
      "numFound":1,"origFreq":0,
      "startOffset":14,"endOffset":20,
      "suggestion":[{"word":"pollock","freq":2}]
    },
    "salvator":{
      "numFound":1,"origFreq":0,
      "startOffset":21,"endOffset":29,
      "suggestion":[{"word":"salvador","freq":32}]
    },
    "lionardo":{
      "numFound":1,"origFreq":0,
      "startOffset":30,"endOffset":38,
      "suggestion":[{"word":"leonardo","freq":7}]
    },
    "georgio":{
      "numFound":1,"origFreq":0,
      "startOffset":39,"endOffset":46,
      "suggestion":[{"word":"giorgio","freq":8}]
    },
    "correctlySpelled":false,
    "collation":{
      "collationQuery":"artist_entity:pollock salvador leonardo giorgio",
      "hits":0,
      "misspellingsAndCorrections":{
        "pollok":"pollock",
        "salvator":"salvador",
        "lionardo":"leonardo",
        "georgio":"giorgio"
```

In these results, you can easily recognize one suggestion for each of the misspelled terms `pollok`, `salvator`, and `lionardo`, and two for `georgio`. Every suggestion also contains the positional information, which is useful to point the suggestion into the actual results when we will play the suggester in conjunction with a normal query.

Note that the XML format is slightly different from the JSON one, as it will contain some more information; for example, you will see it in action in the following screenshot, where I have isolated the part for the last suggestion:

```
▼<lst name="georgio">
    <int name="numFound">1</int>
    <int name="startOffset">39</int>
    <int name="endOffset">46</int>
    <int name="origFreq">0</int>
  ▼<arr name="suggestion">
    ▼<lst>
        <str name="word">giorgio</str>
        <int name="freq">5</int>
      </lst>
    </arr>
  </lst>
  <bool name="correctlySpelled">false</bool>
▼<lst name="collation">
    <str name="collationQuery">artist_entity:pollock salvador leonardo giorgio</str>
    <int name="hits">0</int>
  ▼<lst name="misspellingsAndCorrections">
      <str name="pollok">pollock</str>
      <str name="salvator">salvador</str>
      <str name="lionardo">leonardo</str>
      <str name="georgio">giorgio</str>
    </lst>
  </lst>
</lst>
```

As you have seen, we have adopted several arbitrary parameters; I don't want you to think too much about everything now; I prefer suggesting you to play with examples by changing their values and repeat using your query. This way you can start your analysis, and you can find a complete list of the parameters that can be used here: `http://wiki.apache.org/solr/SpellCheckComponent#Request_Parameters`

The following are the most interesting ones:

- `queryAnalyzerFieldType`: This is the type on which the spellchecker query will be analyzed.
- `field`: This is the field used to build spellchecker results.
- `name`: This is the name for the chosen spellchecker component. There can be more than one in the same chain.
- `classname`: This is the class that implements the spellchecker component interface.
- `maxEdits`: This represents the maximum number of changes enumerating a term. At the moment, this value can be 1 or 2. You can think of this value as the quantity of small typos that can be considered for a suggestion.
- `distanceMeasure`: This is the algorithm that will be used to calculate term distance; the default one is the well-known algorithm by Levensthein.
- `accuracy`: This is the precise value to be achieved for a suggestion to be added as a proper one in the results.
- `spellcheckIndexDir`: This is used to define where to save the index specific for spellchecking.

The best way to find good configurations for a spellchecker is ideally to ask real users to give comments on the results, and how they differ from what they expect. In order to do this, we can log users' requests and analyze them to find the uncovered case.

Using a file to spellcheck against a list of controlled words

Another very interesting spellchecker can be adopted to perform suggestions starting from a file-based list of controlled words:

```
<lst name="spellchecker">
  <str name="name">file</str>
  <str name="field">artist_entity</str>
  <str name="classname">solr.FileBasedSpellChecker</str>
  <str name="sourceLocation">spellings.txt</str>
  <str name="characterEncoding">UTF-8</str>
...
</lst>
```

In this example, the `spellings.txt` file is a simple plain-text file, where every line will contain a word that can be used for spellchecking. This kind of suggestion can be again very crucial when adopted on prototyping, as it is quite simple to add terms in it during an incremental development. For example, you can incorporate log analysis and other user feedback, review them, and then try to add some terms derived from the supervised terms into your spellchecker.

Collecting some hints for spellchecking analysis

While playing with spellchecking, it's always important to do a good analysis on a specific spellchecker component before putting it in the default chain.

After that, when we will be confident about the accuracy of the results, we can bind the spellchecker component in the standard query handler by using the usual chain parameters in the request handler as follows:

```
<arr name="last-components">
    <str>spellcheck</str>
    ...
</arr>
```

Moreover, we can explicitly choose which class actually takes the term in the query from the user and maps it to the suggested ones. For example, the standard component will be as follows:

```
<queryConverter name="queryConverter" class="solr.
SpellingQueryConverter" />
```

This is generally the most obvious choice and you may not need to explicitly write a configuration for it, but you should consider this syntax in case you will have to write your own `queryConverter` class.

If needed, it is possible to rebuild the index for spellchecking when committed as follows:

```
<searchComponent name="spellcheck" class="solr.SpellCheckComponent">
  <str name="buildOnCommit">true</str>
</searchComponent>
```

This is, however, not a good choice for many applications, since it can become a performance issue, so try to consider this kind of choice carefully.

While talking about the performance of these kinds of components, one has to also reduce the footprint they have in memory, for example, by omitting normalization and by not having them stored.

Furthermore, a good option is decoupling the spellchecked field to the fields used for other purposes. This can be easily done as usual by `<copyField>`, and this can also be useful to adopt different strategies in the destination field, thus making it more appropriate for the spellchecking process. When we do analysis for the configuration of this component, it's always a good idea to consider removing stemming and similar decomposition of terms from the fields to be used, as they can have a negative influence on the metrics adopted and then on the accuracy. The best will be adopting a word-based n-gram decomposition during the analysis of the field in order to have a good phrase suggestion.

Pop quiz

Q1. What is the `debug` component designed for?

1.   It is designed to inspect the parsing of a query while it is executed

2.   It is designed to inspect the results in details, focusing on the values in the documents returned

3.   It is designed to inspect the results in details, focusing on the values in the documents returned

Q2. What is the context in which we want to adopt spellchecking?

1.   When we need to be able to perform queries flexible enough to match the same term in different languages

2.   When we need to be able to perform queries flexible enough to match misspelled words

3.   When we want to be able to match incomplete words

Q3. What are the main differences between the Lucene query parser and the Dismax one?

1.   The Lucene parser provides powerful operators for advanced users; it can return more precise results at the cost of queries which are more difficult to write

2.   The Dismax and Edismax parsers are designed for common users; they can return less precise results, expanding simple user queries

3.   They are the same, and Dismax and Edismax only introduced some more specific parameters over the Lucene parser

Q4. What are pseudo-fields?

1. Pseudo-fields are internal fields that can be used directly in the queries
2. Pseudo-fields are a way to call functions, using them with the same syntax used for fields
3. Pseudo-fields are a way to call specific components (for example, the `explain` component), using the same syntax used for fields

Q5. How can you describe an editorial boosting to a client, during a meeting?

1. With editorial boosting, we can promote some specific document at the beginning of our results
2. With editorial boosting, users can directly give feedback on the results, changing the ranking of it
3. With editorial boosting, the documents in the results are designed by us, and they cannot be changed by queries

Summary

In this chapter we have finally started considering real-world user needs and, most important of all how to start shaping what I like to call a *user search experience*.

We learned how to write our own update scripts for augmenting results with data from external sites or from others cores also (we saw how to do this in the context of the spatial search, but this technique can be used in several ways). Many of these techniques can be a strategic improvement in our development process, if we will become experts in using the editorial corrections in a correct way for boosting results and suggesting them from a controlled vocabulary.

Finally we have seen in more detail what the usable search components are, how to configure queries for common non-advanced users using Dismax, how to analyze statistical data and debug metadata over a common standard query, and how to provide highlighting that can be used to construct "more like this" presentations.

In the next chapter we will introduce faceting, which can be used in conjunction with all this functionality to extend searches to a wider usage level.

6
Using Faceted Search – from Searching to Finding

In this chapter, we will have the chance to play with facets, text similarity and recommendations. We will again proceed back and forth from toy prototypes to the analysis of specific examples in order to give some direction and ideas for extended studies and improvements. I will also suggest some reading on math and information design theory for those who want to go further.

In order to explore the relation between these different approaches, we will see two different suggesters. We will start by using faceted search, which we have seen in action, without too much explanation, in the earlier examples. This is one of the most simple and yet complex features of Solr.

We will gradually shift our focus to findability and its implications for common users, introducing concepts such as similarity and recommendations.

Exploring documents suggestion and matching with faceted search

Auto-completing terms will be a great improvement in user experience. We have already used an auto-suggester approach in *Chapter 5, Extending Search*. But an autocompletion approach could also be useful as a strategy to suggest **navigation paths**, because this could be adopted not only in the context of a traditional search but also for *serendipity*-based approaches. It gives the user the chance to discover some very different stuff while searching. These two directions can be implemented with several strategies, focusing on terms or some kind of data aggregation, from **automatic clustering** to **faceting**, that we will see in a while.

We can think about facets in analogy to categories, which can be used to collect many different documents sharing the same value. As we will see, however, facets do not need to be predefined of precomputed as categories generally are, but they can be requested on the fly, because they will be computed on term values that exist in the index. We can then think of facets as a way of narrowing down searches, while at the same time collecting suggestions useful to a broader exploration of the data.

A facet can also be seen as a sort of data clusterization on a specific term.

We will introduce *Carrot2* in *Chapter 7*, *Working with Multiple Entities*, *Multicores, and Distributed Search*, which is a tool for document clustering and can be used with Solr. The clustering tools use documents' similarities or ranking metrics to compute data aggregation. This can involve complex processes, because every similar value can be computed using complex mathematical models, while the process of facet computation is simple. It's best to see a little introductory example to start.

Time for action – prototyping an auto-suggester with facets

Let's imagine a free search box on a simple HTML prototype (we will play with it later). When we are writing our term, we write Hen and pause a little for the interface to start suggesting something to us. The screen we see will be similar to what we see on the left side of the following screenshot:

On the left, we can see a simple prototype that gives an idea of how the results will be suggested to users when they write their terms for a search. To get the output shown in the previous screenshot, we perform the following steps:

1. When the user writes the term Hen, some suggestion is prompted, showing how many document results are available and also reporting the fields on which some matches are actually found.

2. On the right, I put an example that includes only the raw suggestion results for the `artist_entity` field, just to give an idea of what is behind the scenes.

3. We do not have a prototype yet, but we can easily simulate the output shown on the right by the request:

```
>> curl -X GET 'http://localhost:8983/solr/paintings/selec
t?q=*:*&rows=0&facet=true&facet.field=artist_entity&facet.
prefix=hen&wt=json'
```

4. As usual, remember to start the appropriate core first; for example here, I suppose, we have defined a new core in `/SolrStarterBook/solr-app/chp06/paintings`, restarting from the configuration used in *Chapter 5*, *Extending Search*.

Here we retrieve a short list of suggestions for the field `artist_entity`. As you can see, the response format gives us a suggested term, followed by the number of documents that currently *match* that request.

What just happened?

In this small example, we are not interested in obtaining results (`rows=0`). Instead, we want to obtain a small list of items for a certain field (in the example, the field is `artist_entity`) and get information about how many documents contain that term in particular. In order to do this, we have to activate the **faceting capabilities** of Solr using `facet=true` (it's possible to use `facet=on` as for most Boolean parameters) and restrict the list of items to the ones that starts with a particular text, using `facet.prefix=hen`. Note that we have to write the term in lowercase due to our previously adopted approach for analyzing the `artist_entity` field, but we can change this if we want.

Time for action – creating wordclouds on facets to view and analyze data

1. Using the faceting capabilities of Solr, it is really simple to produce a **wordcloud** or **tagcloud**. These are very good visualization tools, because they can be used not only for their aesthetics but also to synthesize visually a weighted list of terms from the domain in which we are moving into. I have prepared some really simple examples of this using only HTML and JavaScript code, using the simple and powerful **jqcloud** (`http://www.lucaongaro.eu/demos/jqcloud/`) library:

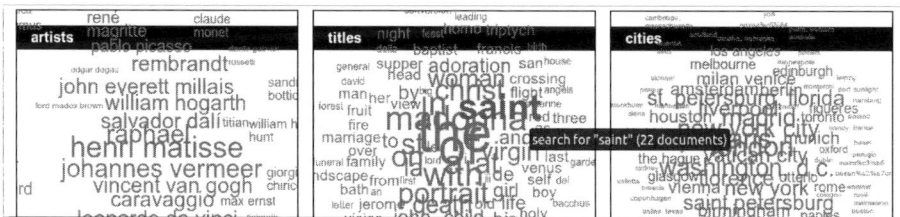

2. All we have to do to play with them, and eventually customize the examples is to start Solr in the usual way (for example, calling `start chp06` from the `/SolrStarterBook/test/` directory), and then open the page located at `/test/chp06/html/wordclouds`.

3. In this example, we can see that terms are presented in a sparse visualization, and the word size visually represents its relevance in the context. For example, the terms presented in the middle box are collected from the title field using the faceting capabilities of Solr:

```
>> curl -X GET 'http://localhost:8983/solr/paintings/select?q=*:*&
rows=0&facet=true&facet.field=title&wt=json'
```

In this simple request, we have omitted the documents from the result of (`rows=0`), because we simply want to obtain facets' results.

What just happened?

When selecting the term **saint**, we will be prompted for the possibility to perform a query for the term, while we already know that there will be 22 documents matching that term. If we click on the link, a basic query will be produced:

```
>> curl -X GET 'http://localhost:8983/solr/paintings/
select?q=title:saint&wt=json'
```

Where, as expected, we find 22 documents with their fields and details. This is a really simple approach, but can give a lot of interesting ideas on the context, during the prototyping phase, and can also be improved in several different ways.

> If you have some experience with SQL, you can probably recognize some similarity between the faceting mechanism and the usage of the GROUP BY clause in SQL. For example, using `facet.field=artist` can be seen more or less similar to the SQL expression, SELECT P.artist, COUNT(P.artist) FROM paintings AS P GROUP BY P.artist. With Solr, however, we can obtain results from many facets at once. (The same results will require different queries in SQL.) Moreover, the facets can be easily combined with other criteria, and they offer very good performance, because they collect values from the saved index.

Thinking about faceted search and findability

From the previous two examples, we have seen that it is simple to obtain a list of recurring terms for a specific field using facets, including information about the number of documents involved. The tagcloud example, in particular, is similar to what we usually see in action with folksonomies, but all the collection of terms projected here is from a single field at once. If we want to perform a search once a term has been selected, we will make a new query on that term. This is interesting because in some ways it can gives us *specific directions* of the search, improving find ability.

> **Findability** is a definition often used in **Information architecture (IA)** and **User experience (UX)** contexts, which relies not only on the process of doing a "good" search but mostly on the possibility for a common user to be able ideally to reach every *relevant* resource of information on a site by navigational patterns.
>
> There is a good collection of articles that could be used as a source and inspiration for the topic at `http://findability.org/`.

Starting from that idea, I'd like to think about facets in Solr as ways to obtain a wider view of the same data, which we are able to manage using complex search criteria. This may sound confusing, because once a facet criteria will be added to our query, it will actually narrow the search. But it is important to focus on the idea that a *facet* is not a mechanism to perform searches by itself (if you look at the response, you will find that the facet results are on a specific section), but it is more intended to provide a shallow, *fluid classification system* in contrast to the traditional taxonomies-based approaches, which are predefined, fixed and hierarchical.

> A **facet** comprises "clearly defined, mutually exclusive, and collectively exhaustive aspects, properties, or characteristics of a class or specific subject".
>
> `http://en.wikipedia.org/wiki/Faceted_classification`

In this perspective, a facet is a simple aggregation of metadata referred to a group of resources that can be seen as related to each other from the perspective of their reference and usage of the same terms, moving our interest *from searching to matching,* as we will see later.

Faceting for narrowing searches and exploring data

A good idea is to again use prototyping to construct, in this case, a simple navigation over facets that can help us focus on one of the most simple ways to use them in many contexts. I have prepared a simple example using the very good `ajax-solr` library, which we will see in action again in further chapters. Feel free to use it as a base for creating prototypes on your data too:

You will find this example by navigating to `/SolrStarterBook/test/chp06/paintings/html/index.html`. You can play with it directly with your web browser, without any web server, after you have started your Solr painting core in the usual way.

The simple interface, on the left-hand side of the page, gives us the chance to *collect* one or more terms from different facets in order to produce a collection of resources, on the right hand side of the page as a visual preview that changes, reflecting the choice we have made. This is very similar to the concept of *filtering* the list of resources, as we are accustomed to do on e-commerce sites, but it can be used backwards to explore different search paths from the original simply by removing a selected criteria from the list.

In other words, this approach can expand the traditional "bag of words" - based search for full text into a more wide search capability that mixes the fulltext advanced search functionality with a kind of detour-based exploring of the same relevant data. A user can, at some point, find that Louvre contains many paintings, and decide to explore the list by simply clicking the interface. As a general case, this leads to performing queries of which we as users had not originally thought. These queries are of interest to us as we will be informed in advance on how many relevant documents we will find using the selected criteria, and every time we add or remove a selection, a new series of criteria (and their related results) is triggered.

In our example, the query uses the parameters tabulated as follows:

`q:*:*`	We are not searching for specific terms
`facet:true`	The faceting support has to be enabled
`facet.field:museum_entity`	The HTML interface asks for the facets' results on the `artist_entity`, `museum_entity`, and `city_entity` fields.
`facet.field:artist_entity`	
`facet.field:city_entity`	
`fq:city_entity:paris`	We are already using a **filter query** based on the selection made. This is an improvement of the same idea behind the tagcloud example.
`fq:museum_entity:"musée du louvre"`	

If you want to directly play with the query using facets, you can use the following command:

```
>>  curl -X GET 'http://localhost:8983/solr/paintings/
select?facet=true&q=*:*&facet.field=museum_entity&facet.field=artist_
entity&facet.field=city_entity&facet.limit=20&facet.mincount=1&f.city_
entity.facet.limit=10&json.nl=map&fq=city_entity:paris&fq=museum_entity:"
mus%25c3%25a9e+du+louvre"&wt=json'
```

Here, note the use of lower case, HTTP entity substitution (for example, for accented chars and double quotes), and + for spaces.

Note that we can decide how many results we will obtain for every facet (`facet.limit`) or even customize the number of results for a specific field (`f.field_name.facet.limit`, in our case `f.city_entity.facet.limit`).

If you analyze the parameters used, and test the query directly in your browser, you will see that is not too complicated. Unfortunately, sometimes it is not easy to read using cURL, and I suggest creating small prototypes on HTML, for example, using the ajax-solr library, as in the previous example. (You will find references to ajax-solr in the *Appendix, Solr Clients and Integrations*.) We will see filter query later in this chapter. A filter query is very often used as a method to perform a search using the criteria selected from a previous faceted search. This widely adopted navigational pattern is useful as it provides a simple interaction for an easy-to-understand user interface (the user can enable/disable filters), and it is even a better performer.

There is a good overview on the wiki page, `http://wiki.apache.org/solr/ SolrFacetingOverview`, which can be used as an introduction, and as you can imagine, there are a lot of resources on this topic, not only on the Solr site, but also on the Web.

If you want to read something to gain a deeper theoretical knowledge of faceted navigation, I strongly suggest reading the article, written in 2009, by William Denton at `http://www. miskatonic.org/library/facet-web-howto.html`. This article gives clear definitions and practical patterns to understand deeply where and how to adopt a faceted navigation. You will find it very useful for a better understanding of the concepts behind the Solr faceting capabilities and where to use them in your projects.

The following are some other sites where you can find articles that could offer some good perspective:

- `http://alistapart.com/article/design-patterns-faceted-navigation`
- `http://www.uxmatters.com/mt/archives/2009/09/best-practices-for-designing-faceted-search-filters.php`
- `http://www.uie.com/articles/faceted_search/`

For the moment, we will practice using simple examples on our data.

Time for action – defining facets over enumerated fields

Faceted search is generally used with enumerations: The faceted results can be used, as we saw, for suggesting a sort of "horizontal" classification. Moreover, we can play with different fields and enable/disable terms from them as in the HTML prototype seen before. This is very useful to produce a guided navigation for the user using filters.

1. To use facets this way, we should use `solr.KeywordTokenizerFactory` in the `schema.xml` file as given in the following code:

```
<fieldType name="text_facets" class="solr.TextField">
  <analyzer>
```

```
      <charFilter class="solr.MappingCharFilterFactory"
          mapping="mapping-ISOLatin1Accent.txt" />
      <tokenizer class="solr.KeywordTokenizerFactory" />
      <filter class="solr.LowerCaseFilterFactory" />
    </analyzer>
  </fieldType>


  . . .


  <dynamicField name="*_entity" type="text_facets"
  multiValued="false" indexed="true" stored="true" />
```

2. Once we have modified our `schema.xml` file for the core at `/SolrStarterBook/solr-app/chp06/paintings`, we simply populate it with the example data and then start it from the `/SolrStarterBook/test/chp06` path (remember that you can use the corresponding `.bat` if you are on a Windows machine):

```
>> start.sh
```

```
>> post.sh (from another terminal window)
```

3. When the core has been started and populated with our data, we will have to populated the fields to be used for entity enumeration with the facets. For example, if we want to obtain a list of all the artists, we will use the following command:

```
>> curl -X GET 'http://localhost:8983/solr/paintings/select?q=*:*&
rows=0&facet=true&facet.field=artist_entity&facet.limit=-1&facet.
mincount=2&facet.sort=count&wt=json&json.nl=map'
```

What just happened?

In the example, we have activated facets, and then requested faceting results for the field **artist_entity**. Here, the role of keyword tokenization is crucial. We have to be sure that the original term (or terms) is preserved; so, in most cases, we need to adopt a copyfield in order to play with different text analysis on the source and destination fields.

In our scenario, we decided not to use copyfields, but to play with a simple external script during the update phase as we saw in the previous examples. We need to put in our `solrconfig.xml` file to populate the fields defined for enumeration, as shown in the following code:

```
<requestHandler name="/update" class="solr.UpdateRequestHandler">
  <lst name="defaults">
    <str name="update.chain">script</str>
  </lst>
</requestHandler>
  . . .
```

```
<updateRequestProcessorChain name="script">
  <processor class="solr.StatelessScriptUpdateProcessorFactory">
    <str name="script">normalize_entities.js</str>
  </processor>
  <processor class="solr.LogUpdateProcessorFactory" />
  <processor class="solr.RunUpdateProcessorFactory" />
</updateRequestProcessorChain>
```

An important aspect to consider if you plan to consume the results from JavaScript into an HTML interface is the format of the response. Here, we used the parameters wt=json and json.nl=map to request the Json format with a named list in the format of a map, as shown in the following screenshot:

```
- facet_fields: {                - facet_fields: {                - facet_fields: {
  - artist_entity: [               - artist_entity: [               - artist_entity: {
    - [                              "leonardo da vinci",              leonardo da vinci: 11
        "leonardo da vinci",         11                             }
        11                         ]
      ]
    ]
```

In the screenshot, you can see the respective output structure for an array of an array (json.nl=arrarr), simple array alternating name and value (json.nl=flat), and finally the map (json.nl=map).

We decided to obtain a list of the artists who are related to at least two documents (facet. mincount=2) and the complete list too (facet.limit=-1). You can easily obtain the list of terms ordered from the most recurring ones to the lesser recurring ones using facet. sort=count or have them in a lexicographic order using facet.sort=index. Sometimes, it is useful for the frontend to have the complete list even if a term has no matching documents. In this case, we can simply add the facet.missing=true parameter.

Performing data normalization for the keyword field during the update phase

We can easily verify whether the update script is working well by asking for a list of recurring subjects:

```
>> curl -X GET 'http://localhost:8983/solr/paintings/select?q=*:*&
rows=0&facet=true&facet.field=subject_entity&facet.limit=-1&facet.
mincount=2&facet.sort=count&json.nl=map&wt=json'
```

In this case, we are producing a facet over a more readable version of the data, which is produced during the update phase on the `subject_entity` field, stripping the namespace part off the original `subject` field data. If you want, you can play the same query by changing the faceted field to `facet.field=subject`, and you will return the original complete value.

Reading more about Solr faceting parameters

The faceting functionality can be combined with the default search capability, but this involves using several different parameters at once. The list of parameters can be found on the official wiki page:

```
http://wiki.apache.org/solr/SimpleFacetParameters
```

I strongly suggest you to play with different parameter combinations to understand how they perform on our data. Sometimes turning off the actual results (`rows=0`) to think only about the facets can be very useful. While we showcase only a few parameters in our examples, you can find the whole list on the reference page:

```
https://cwiki.apache.org/confluence/display/solr/Faceting
```

These parameters shown in the reference page can be very useful for evaluating the best choice for performance. For example, it's possible to adopt different strategies for faceting over a field. The type of strategy/algorithm used can be chosen by the `facet.method` parameter on a per field basis, and the parameter permits us to choose among the enum, field cache, or even field cache per segment strategies (which is the same as field cache, but more fine grained on different segments).

Time for action – finding interesting topics using faceting on tokenized fields with a filter query

While we are working on our sites, it is generally useful to use faceted search over taxonomies, tag collections, or other kinds of enumerated terms; there are cases in which it could be useful to look at the most recurring and interesting words in a certain field. This kind of search can be played on all the documents in the index or, more interestingly, on a specific search, restricting the size of the documents' collection we are playing on. The steps for finding interesting topics using faceting on tokenized fields with filter query are as follows:

1. In this particular scenario, we need to move in the opposite direction as before. We need to use tokenization in a similar way as for the "common" text field; so, we will use a tokenized field here instead of a keyword field to show this particular exception to the normal adoptions of faceting.

2. Since we have already defined our field for the `*_entity` fields, we only need to check the configuration for a common tokenized field, which will be used to create a list of recurring terms.

3. For our needs, a good configuration can be as shown in the following code:

```
<fieldType name="text_general" class="solr.TextField">
  <analyzer>
    <charFilter class="solr.MappingCharFilterFactory"
        mapping="mapping-ISOLatin1Accent.txt" />
    <tokenizer class="solr.WhitespaceTokenizerFactory" />
    <filter class="solr.WordDelimiterFilterFactory"
        generateWordParts="1" generateNumberParts="1"
        catenateWords="0" catenateNumbers="0" catenateAll
        ="1" splitOnCaseChange="1" preserveOriginal="0" />
    <filter class="solr.StopFilterFactory" words
        ="stopwords.txt" ignoreCase="true" />
    <filter class="solr.LowerCaseFilterFactory" />
    <filter class="solr.SynonymFilterFactory" synonyms
        ="synonyms.txt" ignoreCase="true" expand="false" />
  </analyzer>
</fieldType>
```

4. We then need to restart the core in order to use the new configuration (for example, we will use it for fields such as `subject` and `abstract`), and I suggest you also clean and populate the index again. This can be easily achieved with the usual commands or by using the provided `clean` and `post` scripts (for example, `clean.sh` if you are on *NIX or `clean.bat` if you use Windows).

5. Since the abstract field contains some detailed information on a specific painting, this is the ideal candidate for this kind of experimentation. If we want to obtain a list of the most used terms in this field, we can use the following query:

```
>> curl -X GET 'http://localhost:8983/solr/paintings/select?q=*
:*&rows=0&facet=true&facet.field=abstract&facet.limit=-1&facet.
mincount=50&json.nl=map&wt=json'
```

6. But, we can also play with two more parameters: the *standard query* and the *filter query*. For example, if we want to obtain the same results, not on the full collection of documents but only on documents that have a mention of the term **oil** in their abstract description, we can change the query a little, as shown in the following code:

```
>> curl -X GET 'http://localhost:8983/solr/paintings/select?q=*
:*&rows=0&facet=true&facet.field=abstract&facet.limit=10&facet.
mincount=50&json.nl=map&wt=json&fq=abstract:oil'
```

7. The standard and filter queries can generally produce simple differences in the results, and even if these differences are important for the score evaluation, they will not affect our experiments. In the left side of the following screenshot, you will see the results from the first query, and on the right side, the results from the second:

```
{                                         {
  - responseHeader: {                       - responseHeader: {
      status: 0,                                status: 0,
      QTime: 20                                 QTime: 63
  },                                        },
  - response: {                             - response: {
      numFound: 5069,                           numFound: 433,
      start: 0,                                 start: 0,
      docs: [ ]                                 docs: [ ]
  },                                        },
  - facet_counts: {                         - facet_counts: {
      facet_queries: { },                       facet_queries: { },
      - facet_fields: {                         - facet_fields: {
          - abstract: {                             - abstract: {
              painting: 777,                            painting: 406,
              his: 433,                                 oil: 271,
              artist: 334,                              his: 212,
              one: 329,                                 artist: 177,
              which: 315,                               one: 173,
              painted: 306,                             work: 159,
              art: 301,                                 painted: 156,
              work: 289                                 which: 154
          }                                         }
      },                                        },
      facet_dates: { },                         facet_dates: { },
      facet_ranges: { }                         facet_ranges: { }
  }                                         }
}                                         }
```

We will see filter queries later in this chapter. As a general rule, it is preferable to use them in combination with facets when you need to "pin" a certain term in order to restrict the space used on a subdomain; for example, the collection of documents containing the term `oil`.

What just happened?

When comparing the results from the previous two examples, it is worth noting that the hits change for every term. These differences produce a different order of the results; thus, terms proposed in the first example simply disappear in the second.

In the first example (on the left), we are asking for eight facet results (using `facet.limit=8`, but we can ask for all with `facet.limit=-1`), but we feel that we are only interested in terms that have a certain recurrent use in the documents (`facet.mincount=50`).

In the second example (on the right side of the image), we *pin* the term **oil**, which should be present in the `abstract` field, and use the same query again. This could be quite useful, because in this way we are restricting the actual documents' collection on which we play the query. We can ask for facets over the fields that are different from the one used for this kind of restriction; for example, we could facet on the title (`facet.field=title`), while we apply a restriction on the abstract field (`fq=abstract:oil`):

```
>> curl -X GET 'http://localhost:8983/solr/paintings/select?q=*:*&rows
=0&facet=true&facet.field=title&facet.limit=10&facet.mincount=50&json.
nl=map&wt=json&fq=abstract:oil'
```

You probably don't have an idea yet on how this could be important for implementing an effective user interface. Consider the fact that we don't want to loose the flexibility of narrowing searches and navigation with facets, while we still want to add some restrictions with filter queries and eventually search in the usual way with the standard query. You may want to read the following page on wiki:

```
http://wiki.apache.org/solr/SimpleFacetParameters#Multi-Select_
Faceting_and_LocalParams
```

I also suggest you to play with the examples again, changing the fields we are currently using. For example, you might be interested in the result when using the `title_entity` field instead of the `title` field.

Using filter queries for caching filters

A `FilterQuery` can be used, as shown, to dynamically include or exclude a document from the documents' collection. This can also improve the speed for retrieving documents as the filters could be internally cached for later use. In fact, only the internal Lucene document identifiers are actually stored to perform the lookup in order to have a small memory footprint.

Moreover, filter queries have a strong impact when calculating scores, because by introducing filters, we change the size of the collection over which we play the queries.

To see this in detail, we can use a simple Boolean query asking for documents that contain the term `vermeer` in the title field and the term `dali` in the artist field:

```
>> curl -X GET 'http://localhost:8983/solr/paintings/
select?q=(title:vermeer%20AND%20artist:dali)&fl=title,score&start=0&rows=
2&indent=true&wt=json&json.nl=map&debug=true'
```

The result combining these two conditions will contain only one document; then we can play a little with the other combinations of parameters. The idea is to see what happens to the score when changing the way of combining common and filter queries to obtain results.

The following table shows score variations on different tests:

Parameters	Score Variations
q=(title:vermeer AND artist:dali)	score: 4.3593554
q=title:vermeer fq=artist:dali	score: 3.369493
q=artist:dali fq=title:vermeer	score: 2.7659535
q=*:* fq=title:vermeer fq=artist:dali	score = 1
q=*:* fq=(title:vermeer AND artist:dali)	score = 1

Starting from the example query, it's possible to use the parameter combinations proposed in the table to obtain different scores. An important fact to note here is that scores are not absolute, but relative to an entire collection of results.

> The concept of an absolute score does not make sense in this context because score values are not directly comparable through different searches. Scores could be comparable if they were normalized at some point, but this should be avoided as the document can be updated, removed, or added to the index, thereby changing the scores.

On reading the table starting from the end, you will clearly notice that in the last two examples, we are excluding all the documents that do not match these constraints using only filter queries. In this case, the score does not need to be higher than any other hypothetical document's score as we know there is only one single document, so we will obtain a default value of 1.

As long as we are introducing parameter combinations that are less restrictive, combining filter queries with standard query, we find the score which boosts our document towards the start of the result in particular (which will be always the same). This is needed to have the first result for a hypothetically wider collection of documents.

Indeed, in the first example, even if we are obtaining the same single document as a result, we are actually searching over all the documents (the entire index), and our document will have a greater score value.

Just to be more clear, if you are not satisfied with having a simple numeric result and want to go a step further in understanding what's behind that, you can simply look at the debug details by adding `debug=true`, which I have omitted here for simplicity and readability.

For example, the first combination (no filter queries) will be internally expanded as:

```
4.359356 = (MATCH) sum of: 2.6043947 = (MATCH) weight(title:vermeer in
456) [DefaultSimilarity], result of: 2.6043947 = score(doc=456,freq=1.0
= termFreq=1.0 ), product of: 0.77293366 = queryWeight, product of:
8.985314 = idf(docFreq=1, maxDocs=5875) 0.086021885 = queryNorm
3.369493 = fieldWeight in 456, product of: 1.0 = tf(freq=1.0), with
freq of: 1.0 = termFreq=1.0 8.985314 = idf(docFreq=1, maxDocs=5875)
0.375 = fieldNorm(doc=456) 1.754961 = (MATCH) weight(artist:dali in
456) [DefaultSimilarity], result of: 1.754961 = score(doc=456,freq=1.0
= termFreq=1.0 ), product of: 0.6344868 = queryWeight, product of:
7.3758764 = idf(docFreq=9, maxDocs=5875) 0.086021885 = queryNorm
2.7659535 = fieldWeight in 456, product of: 1.0 = tf(freq=1.0), with freq
of: 1.0 = termFreq=1.0 7.3758764 = idf(docFreq=9, maxDocs=5875) 0.375 =
fieldNorm(doc=456)
```

While the last (only a single Boolean filter query, with the common query matching all the documents) will be expanded as:

```
1.0 = (MATCH) MatchAllDocsQuery, product of: 1.0 = queryNorm
```

I hope that seeing these results will convince you to pay attention when you want to use filter queries. Lastly, don't forget that it is really important to consider scores when thinking about document similarity. We will introduce that later in this chapter.

Time for action – finding interesting subjects using a facet query

Let's now look at the other possible applications of faceting. For example, we can use a facet query to find the most-recurring terms. If this recurring term is on the subject field, this could be used for example to obtain suggestions on interesting topics.

1. Now, we want to obtain a simple facet result for the subjects; thus, enter the following query:

    ```
    >> curl -X GET 'http://localhost:8983/solr/paintings/select?q=*:*&
    rows=0&facet=true&facet.field=subject_entity&facet.limit=-1&facet.
    mincount=2&facet.sort=count&json.nl=map&wt=json'
    ```

    We will find that the most common subject in our data is related to the religious theme of `Annunciation`. This result is not particularly surprising, because this is one of the most widely represented themes in classic European art.

2. If we started from the opposite direction, and ask ourselves if the annunciating action is present in the collection, we could easily write the following facet query:

```
>> curl -X GET 'http://localhost:8983/solr/paintings/select?q=*:*
&rows=0&facet=on&facet.query=subject_entity:annunciating~5&facet.
mincount=1&wt=json'
```

3. We will obtain the same results: five matches in facet query counts on 5069 documents. Note that we can ask for the same information while we are querying on other facets, for example:

```
>> curl -X GET 'http://localhost:8983/solr/paintings/select?q=
*:*&rows=0&facet=on&facet.field=city_entity&facet.field=artist_
entity&facet.query=subject_entity:annunciating~5&facet.limit=10&f.
artist_entity.facet.limit=2&wt=json&json.nl=map&fq=abstract:angel'
```

4. We can restrict the number documents to those that contain a reference to an angel figure (`fq=abstract:angel`). We will ask facets for cities and artists related to it (`facet.field=city_entity` and `facet.field=artist_entity`) and to the number of documents that could possibly be related to our search on the subject too (`facet.query=subject_entity:annunciating~5`).

In this case, we will obtain two facet query counts.

What just happened?

We started from the list of terms in the facet for the `subject_entity` field. We found that the term annunciation has been used most on our dataset. Note that the `subject` field plays a similar role here as tags in a controlled vocabulary. This could be used as an idea to play with your fixed, controlled tag vocabulary if you have one. Once we have found an interesting term, we play in reverse just to understand how the facet query works. What we see here is if we use a similar term in the same field (`subject_entity:annunciating~5`), we will obtain the same expected results. Starting from that acquisition, the next step will be to use the facet query without restricting it to a single field, using the following query:

```
>> http://localhost:8983/solr/paintings/select?q=*:*&rows=0&facet=on&fac
et.query=annunciating~5&facet.mincount=1&wt=json
```

In this case, we will obtain 50 matches over all the fields.

If we introduce more than one field for faceting, and perform a facet query, as in the last example, it is simple to notice that every result is independent of the other. Even if we write a query in the `facet.query` field, it will be not used outside its context to filter the other results. Instead, the filter and common queries will produce changes to the facet and facet query results too as they will restrict the collection on which the facets will operate their counts.

Using a filter query is best when we have to fix some criteria to restrict the collection size. We can then use facets as a way to provide suggestion for navigation paths. A typical user interface will add a filter to our query when we select a specific facet suggestion, thus narrowing the search. In contrast, when a filter is removed, the collection on which we search will be broader, and the faceting results will change accordingly.

As a last note, it's possible to specify parameters on a per field basis when needed, for example, using `f.artist_entity.facet.limit=2` we are deciding to have no more than two facet results for the `artist_entity` field. Note that `facet.mincount` does not imply any semantics; it's only an acceptable minimum ground value for a text match, but it can still be used as if it implies some specific simple *relevance*.

Time for action – using range queries and facet range queries

Starting from the faceting principles seen, we may be curious about the possibility to obtain terms in the facets by range. This is possible and very simple to test on numerical values, such as height and width in our case:

```
>> curl -X 'http://localhost:8983/solr/paintings/
select?q=*:*&fq=height:[100%20TO%20200]&fl=title&rows=1&facet=true&facet.
range=height&facet.range=width&facet.range.start=0&facet.range.
end=400&facet.range.gap=40&json.nl=map&wt=json'
```

What just happened?

By now, the facet mechanism has become clearer, and it should seem much simpler than in the beginning. The fact is, when using facets, we look at data "in advance", or if you prefer, we could think we are collecting data classified in some way, in order to choose a direction to move into this simple classified word. To be honest, I don't like the usage of the term classification in the context of faceting. I'd rather prefer using terms such as aspects or similar but at the moment, I'm more interested in focusing on the idea behind it.

Here, it's important to avoid missing a simple principle here; facet ranges are best used when you play with them from a web interface, and specifically, a slider widget is very often the best interaction to give to the user for changing the range parameters.

The parameters, by themselves, are quite simple; with `facet.range=width` we decided to use the field width for range faceting, and we will need a start, end, and step value, which we will define using `facet.range.start`, `facet.range.end`, and `facet.range.gap` respectively. It's not a big deal. Once more we will use this functionality in conjunction with filter query (in this case, the query is a range query too) in order to construct a navigation inside the data by performing subsequent queries. The filter query part could also be seen as a kind of memory of where we are now on the data, in some way, as it temporarily fixes our context. The filter query could change from time to time, depending on what we will discover using facets, facet ranges, and facet queries.

Time for action – using a hierarchical facet (pivot)

If we are using facets, we probably need to move horizontally on the data without imposing a specific, single hierarchy, even for a single field. This is useful and very flexible as the facets could also be combined with each other, but this should not be seen as a limit when we want to manage taxonomy or a structured, controlled dictionary. The usage of hierarchical faceting is rather simple, and it is based on the well-known pivot column navigation pattern, yet to be available in some database applications.

The idea is that we will provide a list of of field names, and the results will be constructed over them. We can use the following query:

```
>> curl -X 'http://localhost:8983/solr/paintings/
select?q=artist:dali&facet.pivot=artist_entity,city_entity,museum_
entity&facet=true&facet.field=city_entity&facet.limit=10&rows=0&wt=json&i
ndent=true&facet.pivot.mincount=1'
```

Another example for the query is shown as follows, and it will probably be more restrictive:

```
>> curl -X GET 'http://localhost:8983/solr/paintings/select?q=artist:dali
&rows=0&facet=on&facet.field=city_entity&facet.pivot=city_entity,museum_
entity,artist_entity&facet.limit=1&facet.mincount=3&wt=json'
```

What just happened?

In the first example, we are asking you to use a hierarchy of artists, cities, and museums as *pivots*. So, we will expect a result where for every artist we search over cities, and then over museums. We should expect, in most cases, to find some different nested results, with low result count. If we use a different criteria for pivoting, such as city_entity, museum_entity, and artist_entity, we will not be surprised to obtain less pivot results, with a good relative match count, as shown in the following screenshot:

```
- facet_counts: {
    facet_queries: { },
    - facet_fields: {
        - city_entity: [
            "st. petersburg, florida",
            4
          ]
      },
    facet_dates: { },
    facet_ranges: { },
    - facet_pivot: {
        - city_entity,museum_entity,artist_entity: [
            - {
                field: "city_entity",
                value: "st. petersburg, florida",
                count: 4,
                - pivot: [
                    - {
                        field: "museum_entity",
                        value: "salvador dali museum",
                        count: 4,
                        - pivot: [
                            - {
                                field: "artist_entity",
                                value: "salvador dali",
                                count: 4
                              }
```

In this case, we are indeed looking for paintings by a specific artist at a specific museum, which is probably a more natural approach and it will be faster to read the results too. Note that when we are interested in adopting this particular approach, we are also able to offer a sort of breadcrumb to the users in order to make it easy for them to remember the current selection. We should avoid confusion with an actual navigation on the data. We are still using facets and their capabilities to give us suggestions on directions for moving *later* into the data.

Introducing group and field collapsing

Once you have played with some examples, at some point, you will probably be curious about the possibility to view results, grouped by a certain field value, in a similar way to what is possible with SQL.

From Solr's point of view, this functionality is intended to be used in two scenarios:

- **Field collapsing**: It is used when we want to collapse a group of results into a certain amount of entries, aggregating them by a common field value. This is a typical case for search engines or internal engines on large datasets, and it is generally useful to provide only the top results for some value choices to give an idea on what the users should expect with some link to the complete series of results. This is somewhat similar (from a different point of view) to what we have done with the `wordclouds` prototype; so, this approach will be useful when you have lots of shared values, and it's not complex to use some HTML or JavaScript to produce the query for the complete results.

- **Result grouping**: In this case, we are grouping documents with a common field value and show only at the top of the results. This is widely used in the e-commerce context for providing the most viewed or bought products. On a news or OPAC site, it would show the most recent or more interesting resource.

You are certainly not missing some analogies with facets, but the main difference here is that we are playing with actual data, not with counts of matching documents. Another very interesting aspect that you won't miss is relative to what kind of relevancy function is used to produce the top elements for a group or even the group itself. (We could even construct a group for documents that return the same value when applying a certain function.) Going deeper with these functions can force us to use vectors and similar types but, at the moment, you are probably more interested in having an idea of which parameters can be used while grouping results. Refer to the following link for more info:

```
http://wiki.apache.org/solr/FieldCollapsingsolr
```

There is another related resource at the LucidWorks documentation site:

```
http://docs.lucidworks.com/display/solr/Result+Grouping
```

Time for action – grouping results

Let's work a bit with grouping, just to jump start your own experimentation. First of all, we will search for the documents that simply contain the word `painting`, and group the results by city, then obtain the first result and finally move to the next.

```
>> curl -X GET 'http://localhost:8983/solr/paintings/select?q=abst
ract:painting&start=2&rows=1&fl=artist_entity,title&group=on&group.
facet=false&group.field=city_entity&group.limit=1&group.offset=0&group.ng
roups=false&wt=json&indent=true'
```

The output of this query is as shown in the following screenshot:

```
>> curl -X GET 'http://localhost:8983/solr/paintings/select?q=abstract:painting&start=2&rows=1&fl=artist_entity,title&group=on&group.f
acet=false&group.field=city_entity&group.limit=1&group.offset=0&group.ngroups=false&wt=json&indent=true'
{
  "responseHeader":{
    "status":0,
    "QTime":10},
  "grouped":{
    "city_entity":{
      "matches":777,
      "groups":[{
        "groupValue":"new york city",
        "doclist":{"numFound":17,"start":0,"docs":[
          {
            "artist_entity":"Henri Matisse",
            "title":["The Young Sailor II"]}]
        }}]}}}
>> curl -X GET 'http://localhost:8983/solr/paintings/select?q=abstract:painting&start=2&rows=1&fl=artist_entity,title&group=on&group.f
acet=false&group.field=city_entity&group.limit=1&group.offset=1&group.ngroups=false&wt=json&indent=true'
{
  "responseHeader":{
    "status":0,
    "QTime":9},
  "grouped":{
    "city_entity":{
      "matches":777,
      "groups":[{
        "groupValue":"new york city",
        "doclist":{"numFound":17,"start":1,"docs":[
          {
            "title":["The Nostalgia of the Infinite"],
            "artist_entity":"Giorgio de Chirico"}]
        }}]}}}
>>
```

The result will contain a section, as shown in the following screenshot:

```
"grouped":{
  "city_entity":{
    "matches":777,
    "groups":[
      {
        "groupValue":"new york city",
        "doclist":{
          "numFound":17,"start":0,
          "docs":[
            {
              "artist_entity":"Henri Matisse",
              "title":["The Young Sailor II"]
            }
          ]
```

On executing the query again, asking for the second group this time (remember that the second group will have `group.offset=1`), we will get the following result:

```
"grouped":{
  "city_entity":{
    "matches":777,
      "groups":[
        {
          "groupValue":"new york city",
          "doclist":{
            "numFound":17,
            "start":1,
            "docs":[
              {
                "title":["The Nostalgia of the Infinite"],
                "artist_entity":"Giorgio de Chirico"
              }
            ]
```

It's clear that this is not the best visualization for our data, but I feel we have to play again with these kind of JSON raw results before putting them into appropriate HTML in order to have a good understanding of what's happening. The next step for sorting the group results would probably be to use these results from a carousel HTML widget or similar UX patterns.

What just happened?

We started with the first query, where we activated the grouping capability (`group=on`) and projected only three fields in the results (`fl=artist_entity,title`). At this point, we need to choose a field whose values will be used to group the results (`group.field=city_entity`).

The first part is needed for the process to start working, then we need to think about results in a similar way to what we usually do when paginating. We are only selecting a certain amount of results (`start=2`, `rows=1`) but not dividing the groups in pages. The group pagination is then required with separate parameters; for example, the parameters `group.offset=1` and `group.limit=1` will start from the second result (we always start from 0!) and offer only one result at a time. You may think about `group.offset` and `group.limit` as a sort of the `start` and `rows` parameters to be used internally in the groups.

For example, we moved to the next result for the same group by simply incrementing the `group.offset` value (imagine accomplishing this by clicking on an HTML widget):

```
>> curl -X GET 'http://localhost:8983/solr/paintings/select?q=abst
ract:painting&start=2&rows=1&fl=artist_entity,title&group=on&group.
facet=false&group.field=city_entity&group.limit=1&group.offset=1&group.ng
roups=false&wt=json&indent=true'
```

Finally, I have added two parameters that we have not used earlier: `group.facet` to create faceting over groups and `group.ngroups` to manage nested groups.

Playing with terms

When we started with the first example, and then explored some of the possibilities in the configurations for text analysis of a field type, we saw that it is important to handle terms correctly in Lucene and Solr. We saw this again when using facets as we could obtain very different results by simply handling terms on the same data with different approaches. And we have often seen that terms are very important for the construction of the final score of the results. We don't want to go too far in handling terms directly. Instead, we prefer to use higher-level approach, but this approach can still give some idea in case you want to study more on this later.

Time for action – playing with a term suggester

A very simple way to start playing directly with terms is to configure a small auto-suggester (the third now), this time directly based on term enumeration and somewhat similar to the facet-based suggester seen at the beginning of this chapter.

1. For simplicity, we will define a new core named `paintings_terms`. We need not post new data here, so we will point it to the index at `/SolrStarterBook/solr-app/chp06/paintings/data`. We will copy the same `schema.xml` configuration, but we need to modify our `solrconfig.xml` file a little in order to enable a search handler specific for handling terms, as shown in the following code:

   ```
   <searchComponent name="terms" class="solr.TermsComponent" />
   <requestHandler name="/terms" class="solr.SearchHandler"
   startup="lazy">
     <lst name="defaults">
       <bool name="terms">true</bool>
       <bool name="distrib">false</bool>
     </lst>
     <arr name="components">
       <str>terms</str>
     </arr>
   </requestHandler>
   ```

2. With this simple configuration, we are enabling the terms component and linking it to a new search component. Once we have restarted the core, we will be able to make queries.

3. For example, we want to make a request similar to the auto-suggester with the facets seen at the beginning of this chapter. It is useful when playing with a suggest-as-you-type approach. Suppose we have typed the term `hen`; the command will be as follows:

   ```
   >> curl -X GET 'http://localhost:8983/solr/paintings_terms/
   terms?terms.fl=artist_entity&terms.prefix=hen'
   ```

4. Another way to obtain a similar result is using a *regular-expression*-based approach, as shown in the following command:

```
>> curl -X GET 'http://localhost:8983/solr/paintings_terms/
terms?terms.fl=artist_entity&terms.regex=pa.*&terms.regex.
flag=case_insensitive&wt=json&json.nl=map&omitHeader=true'
```

In both the cases, we are asking for results using the `artist_entity` field for simplicity.

What just happened?

The `TermsComponent` is a search component, which iterates over the full terms dictionary and returns the frequencies of every term in the documents' collection for the entire index without being influenced by the current or filter query.

In short, this functionally is very similar to what we already saw using faceting for autosuggestion as this component is actually faceting over the entire terms' collection for the current index, but there are a couple of differences. This is very fast (it uses low-level Lucene functions) and provides term-level suggestions that are independent from the current search and restrictions. However, there is a drawback: Documents that have been marked for deletion but have not been deleted yet are also returned.

The first example needs no further explanation as it is based on the use of a prefix in the same way as with facets.

In the second example, we are looking for results that start with pa using **regex (regular expression)**. We have also decided to ignore case with regex, and can omit the header to simplify the way to consume results from the HTML frontend.

If you want to study more about regular expression, start with a simple tutorial, which can be found at

```
http://net.tutsplus.com/tutorials/javascript-ajax/you-
dont-know-anything-about-regular-expressions/.
```

Then move on to something more specific to Java (remember, Solr is written in Java), such as the following link:

```
http://www.vogella.com/articles/
JavaRegularExpressions/article.html
```

For the second example, we will obtain the following result:

```
{
  - terms: {
      - artist_entity: {
            pablo picasso: 10,
            paolo veronese: 2,
            parmigianino: 2,
            paul c%c3%a9zanne: 2,
            paul gauguin: 1,
            paul peel: 1,
            paul philippoteaux: 1
        }
    }
}
```

Note that the presence of an escaping HTTP entity is not an error here. It is needed to correctly handle special characters. In most cases, you have to manage these characters by decoding them during the construction of the HTML counterpart.

> When using terms, there are a lot of options that can be used. For example, `terms.mincount` and `terms.sort` act the same as the analogous options seen before for facets. On the other hand, `terms.raw` designates a specific behavior on terms, and will give us the chance to see the actual format of the data (that could mean very low readability, in particular, for dates and numbers). For more understanding, we can refer to the official wiki page:
>
> `http://wiki.apache.org/solr/TermsComponent`

Using regular expressions, we can also achieve matching in the middle of the keyword. By searching the `artist_entity` field, which is keyword-based, we want to obtain results that contain the substring `mar`:

```
>> curl -X GET 'http://localhost:8983/solr/paintings_terms/
terms?terms.fl=artist_entity&terms.regex=.*mar.*&terms.regex.flag=case_
insensitive&wt=json&json.nl=map&omitHeader=true'
```

The following code will not necessarily be at the beginning:

```
{
  - terms: {
      - artist_entity: {
            john martin (painter): 3,
            mary cassatt: 2,
            coppo di marcovaldo: 1
        }
    }
}
```

Here, we have used `terms.regex=.*mar.*`, which roughly remembers the usage of the `LIKE` syntax in SQL. (Let's imagine writing something similar to `LIKE '%mar%'`.) Note that the regex expressions in Solr are based on Java with some minor changes. If you want to check them in detail, I suggest you look directly at the JavaDocs pages, for example, `http://lucene.apache.org/core/4_4_0/queryparser/org/apache/lucene/queryparser/classic/package-summary.html#Regexp_Searches`. This, however, is not needed for handling facets.

Thinking about term vectors and similarity

When adopting Solr, you probably want to introduce an advanced full-text search and a faceted navigation support on your site or application. In many cases, you don't want to go any further on deeper theoretical study and only want to learn how to manage an efficient tool. On the other hand, Solr is built on top of Lucene, that uses a term's or document's multidimensional sparse matrix for its internal representation. It is important to remember that we are actually handling *vectors of terms* as these are the internal data structures that give us the fast and flexible lookup capabilities we are starting to manage. Please do not get scared of some reading involving a bit of math theory, which will be proposed for taking you to the next step in your journey on Solr, when you have played enough with the basic functions.

When playing with the examples and developing your own, I hope you are more and more cognizant of the fact that our attention should shift from the need for a *search engine* to the actual management of a *match engine*. The text queries give us results based on internal metrics, so that the calculation of a match score is crucial. This approach is based on the widely adopted "bag of words" hypothesis, which suggests to approximate the relevance of the document to a query by calculating the frequencies of words for the documents in the collection. In other words, if we see queries as pseudo-documents, and if they have similar vectors for a specific term, we will assume that they tend to have similar meaning.

This is a strong hypothesis, and yet is functioning in most cases, introducing us to the concept of *similarity* of vectors. Use a mathematical function to find out what vectors (and then what terms, since every term has its own vector) are mostly related to each other. This kind of term-vector-based matching is used in Lucene for highlighting, implementation of partial updates, and suggesting other terms in a "more like this" fashion, as we will see in while at the end of this chapter.

Moving to semantics with vector space models

Moreover, the concepts behind similarity involve some studies about *vector space models* (http://en.wikipedia.org/wiki/Vector_space_model) and move us to think about *semantics*. This is far beyond the scope of this book, and involves advanced concepts, but if you are interested in reading something about this, I suggest you read *From Frequency to Meaning: Vector Space Models of Semantics*, by *Turney and Pantel* (http://www.jair.org/media/2934/live-2934-4846-jair.pdf), where the authors talk about the different kinds of *semantic similarities*.

The point here being when we approach similarity between entire documents or a group of fields, it may be possible to define other kinds of document similarities when exploring the context in which the terms live. This can be done using latent (implicit) relations or explicit dictionaries, frames, and models. In this direction, there are a growing number of libraries that can be integrated with Solr for machine learning or clusterization (for example, Carrot2, Mahout, Weka, and so on) and for the integration of natural language processing features on the Solr workflow (for example, UIMA or OpenNLP).

The Solr workflow permits us to write custom wrapper components at every stage for integrating external libraries, even when they need to use precomputed models, for example, using the Stanford NER component, which we will see in action in *Chapter 9, Introducing Customizations*.

Moreover, in *Chapter 8, Indexing External Data Sources*, we will look at the Data Import Handler library, which will be probably refactorized in the near future using a document processing pipeline framework. This will be another good start for the introduction of external component's integration.

Looking at the next step – customizing similarity

An important progress with Solr 4 is the possibility to choose among different similarity implementations. For every implementation, a factory is provided and all the concrete classes will inherit the default `similarity` Java class:

```
http://lucene.apache.org/core/4_3_1/core/index.html?org/apache/
lucene/search/similarities/Similarity.html
```

The default implementation, based on the vector space model, is the `TFIDFSimilarity` one:

```
http://lucene.apache.org/core/4_3_1/core/org/apache/lucene/search/
similarities/TFIDFSimilarity.html
```

From this point, it's possible to implement custom similarities with a class (and its own factory) in the same way as with all the provided classes, which are still experimental, for most, at the time of writing: BM25Similarity, MultiSimilarity, PerFieldSimilarityWrapper, SimilarityBase, and TFIDFSimilarity.

Just to give you an idea, we could choose a different similarity implementation; for example, our hypothetical custom one by putting:

```
<similarity class="some.package.MySimilarityFactory">
  <str name="parameter1_name">a-string-value</str>
  <float name="parameter2_name">a-numeric-value</float>
...
</similarity>
```

An interesting fact is that from Solr 4.0, there are also similarity factories that support specifying specific implementations on individual field types.

We could, for example, have adopted cosine similarity, which is very widely used. It is a measure of the angle between two term vectors, the smaller the angle, the more similar the two terms. This is simple to calculate, and will work very well in most cases, but could eventually fail on some simple peculiar cases, which can be found at http://www.p-value.info/2013/02/when-tfidf-and-cosine-similarity-fail.html. We can have the need for some even more specific and customized measure. If you are a Java programmer and need some theory to define your own customized score, a good place to start is the classic book on *Information Retrieval* (http://nlp.stanford.edu/IR-book/pdf/irbookprint.pdf). However, it's important to note that similarity calculations generally involve offline computations as a document will have a value computed over the whole collection.

Time for action – having a look at the term vectors

If we want to look directly at term vectors, there is the possibility to enable a simple search component, which will return them in the results. In this case, we first need to be sure to put some specific parameters for a field in schema.xml; this is shown in the following steps:

1. Then we need to enable a specific component and a handler for the term vectors:

```
<searchComponent name="termVector"
   class="solr.TermVectorComponent" />
<requestHandler name="/tvc" class=
   "solr.SearchHandler" startup="lazy">
   <lst name="defaults">
     <bool name="tv">true</bool>
   </lst>
   <arr name="last-components">
```

```
    <str>termVector</str>
  </arr>
</requestHandler>
```

2. Once we have enabled this new handler, we are able to search something (for example, the term `vermeer` in the abstract field) and look at the results that will contain the vector parts:

```
>> curl -X GET 'http://localhost:8983/solr/paintings_terms/select?q=abstract:vermeer&start=0&rows=2&fl=abstract,fullText&qt=/tvc&tv.all=true&tv.fl=fullText&wt=json&json.nl=map&omitHeader=true'
```

   Here again, for simplicity, we use the JSON format for output and omit the header.

What just happened?

We can look at the results directly. By extrapolating some interesting bits, we can see `uniqueKey`, which is reported to give us the chance to relate the vector results to related documents. It's important to remember that term vector results act as metadata in our response. If we use a `rows=0` parameter, we will not obtain any results for the vectors either as they are, in fact, behind the proposed actual result and used in the calculation of the matching score. The result is shown in the following screenshot:

```
{
 - response: {
     numFound: 21,
     start: 0,
   - docs: [
     - {
       - abstract: [
           "The Ghost of Vermeer of Delft Which Can Be Used As a Table (1934) is a painting by Spanish surrealist Salvador Dali. The title refers to the Dutch painter Johannes Vermeer and the image of Vermeer viewed from his back is a reference to Vermeer's paintings The Art of Painting and The Little Street. In this image Vermeer is represented as a dark spindly figure in a kneeling position. The figure's outstretched leg serves as a table top surface, on which sits a bottle and a small glass. This leg tapers to a baluster-like stub, however there is a shoe nearby."
         ]
       },
     - {
       - abstract: [
           "The Little Street (Het Straatje) is a painting by the Dutch painter Johannes Vermeer, executed c. 1657-1658. It is housed in the Rijksmuseum of Amsterdam, and signed left below the window with the writing "I V MEER". The exact location of the scene Vermeer painted is not known. However, recent study by the Delft professor F.H. Kreuger found the Voldersgracht as the location of Vermeer's The Little Street. Nowadays, the Vermeer Centre Delft is located here."
         ]
       }
     ]
 },
 - termVectors: {
     uniqueKeyFieldName: "uri",
   - http://dbpedia.org/resource/The_Ghost_of_Vermeer_of_Delft_Which_Can_Be_Used_As_a_Table: {
       uniqueKey: "http://dbpedia.org/resource/The_Ghost_of_Vermeer_of_Delft_Which_Can_Be_Used_As_a_Table",
     - fullText: {
       - 3: {
           tf: 4,
           df: 357,
           tf-idf: 0.011204481792717087
         },
       - 4: {
           tf: 3,
           df: 933,
           tf-idf: 0.003215434083601286
         },
       - 11: {
           tf: 1,
           df: 5069,
           tf-idf: 0.00019727756954034326
         },
```

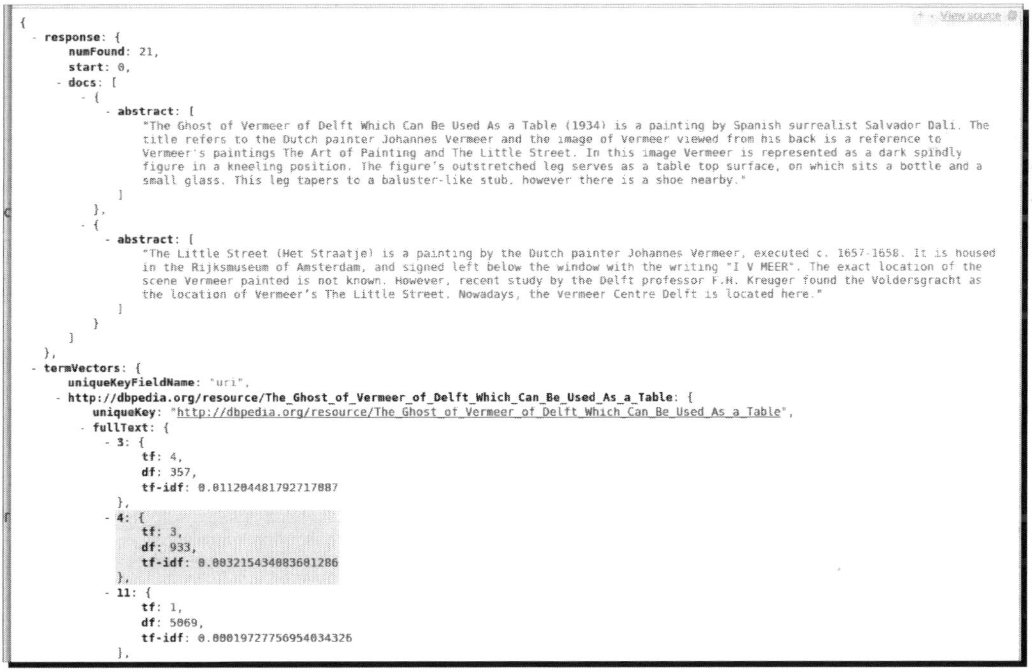

The `tf-idf` parameter is simply an approximation value for calculating the score of a document, which is a ratio between term frequency (how many times a term recurs in the index) and document frequency (how many documents contain the term). This is calculated by multiplying `tf*idf`, where `tf` is the term frequency, and `idf` is the inverse document frequency. Because Solr returns the term frequency and document frequency (`df`) values instead, we can simply use the ratio `tf/df` to calculate.

Just to give you an idea, if we search for the values related to the term `vermeer` itself in the results, we will find that there is a score for the "lacemaker" resource, as shown in the following screenshot:

```
- vein: {
      tf: 1,
      df: 3,
      tf-idf: 0.3333333333333333
  },
- vermeer: {
      tf: 24,
      df: 71,
      tf-idf: 0.3380281690140845
  },
- vermeera: {
      tf: 1,
      df: 4,
      tf-idf: 0.25
  },
- very: {
```

Note that when taken outside its context, the score value by itself gives us no information. We have to compare this value with others values to give it some meaning.

Reading about functions

Solr provides several built-in functions that can also be extended with functions of your own. The built-in functions could play some important roles, such as ranking, because they can be used as *local parameters* to boost the score of a document.

You will find an almost complete (and growing, I suppose) list of functions here:

```
http://wiki.apache.org/solr/FunctionQuery#Available_Functions
```

Here, you will mostly find scalar functions as the functions that return vectors are experimental. Most of the vector functions will return simple numeric scalar results calculated over term vectors, such as `docFreq`, which return the number of documents that contain the term in the field (this is a constant as it assumes the same value for all documents in the index). Other notable examples will be the maximum or minimum evaluation, some mathematical functions, or the euclidean distance between two vectors, which can be seen again as some kind of surrogate against a similarity measurement.

A very simple way to play with functions is using them as local parameters, for example:

```
...&defType=func&q=docfreq(text,$myterm)&myterm=dali
```

Introducing the More Like This component and recommendations

What we have seen so far is the ability to look at an entire index and search for statistics about terms in order to be able to create aggregation of similar terms when needed for a natural and flexible data navigation. We saw that combining an advanced search with filters and facets can produce a good navigation on data. Furthermore, we can move from searching to matching by focusing on some kind of similarity calculation over the internal Lucene term vectors, which can really help us in finding interesting documents.

Starting from the same concept, Solr provides a *More Like This* component, which is designed to offer the user a selection of interesting, relevant documents similar to the ones returned as a result of the search. In short, Solr can also be used to obtain *recommendations*. As suggested in the article, *Building a real-time, Solr powered recommendation engine*, by *Trey Granger*:

```
http://www.slideshare.net/treygrainger/building-a-real-time-
solrpowered-recommendation-engine
```

The recommendations are not the actual results of a query in itself as they will also occur in the results at some point, but they are recommended in particular by a specific similarity calculation.

We can imagine many strategies here, starting from a simple boosting of interesting attributes (as we saw earlier for editorial boosting to change the ranking of results) to approaches based on *hierarchies*, *controlled vocabulary*, and *taxonomies*. In the latter cases, the interest moves from an enumeration-based approach (similar to what we saw with facets before) to a weight-based boosting, where every level of a tree could have a specific and different boosting value. Moving further, there can be other kinds of textual similarities. Some will be based on a snippet of text that acts as the context, and some will be based on vector-based computations, as seen before. It's even possible to introduce unsupervised machine learning algorithms to cluster documents and dynamically discover concepts. This is achievable using Weka, Mahout, or Carrot, for example.

Time for action – obtaining similar documents by More Like This

In the case of `MoreLikeThis`, we can imagine performing an internal query for every term that seems to be relevant by computing the similarity based on its vectors. The document extracted from the collection by the lookup will be included in the `MoreLikeThis` results list.

We can easily play with a small, simple example. Search for the term `boy` in the title field, and ask the results to be sorted by descending score (`sort=score+desc`) from the most relevant to the least as shown in the following query:

```
>> curl -GET 'http://localhost:8983/solr/paintings/select?q=title:bo
y&start=0&rows=1&mlt=on&mlt.fl=artist_entity,title&mlt.mindf=1&mlt.
mintf=1&mlt.minwl=3&fl=uri,title,score&sort=score+desc&omitHeader=true&wt
=json'
```

Note that we will not need to add new handlers to `solrconfig.xml` as More Like This will work on term vectors, and can be used by default. It is preferable to use stored term vectors for fields that will be used for calculating similarity. If term vectors are not stored, `MoreLikeThis` will generate terms from the stored fields.

What just happened?

Once we have enabled the More Like This component (`mlt=on`), we are able to obtain results for our example query, as shown in the following screenshot:

In our example, we asked for recommendations with a minimum document frequency of 1 (`mlt.mindf=1`), a minimum term frequency again equal to 1 (`mlt.mintf=1`), and ignored words that are shorter than a length of three characters as we feel that are not so significant (`mlt.wl=3`).

We can refer to the wiki page to look for a list of parameters and use cases:

`http://wiki.apache.org/solr/MoreLikeThis`

If you look at the image, you will find that there are many proposed recommendations, and the first one seems to be very pertinent, but still there is a odd error on the third position. This is probably due to the textual distance between the term `boy` and the term `bee`, and we could have configured it better in our example by enabling term vectors on the fields for which we calculated the similarities (`mlt.fl=artist_entity,title`).

Adopting a More Like This handler

Even if we are not required to define a new handler for the `MoreLikeThis` component, this is still possible by adding a simple configuration to the `solrconfig.xml` file:

```
<requestHandler name="/mlt" class="solr.MoreLikeThisHandler">

</requestHandler>
```

This could be helpful in some case and is easy to configure. For more details, please visit:

`http://wiki.apache.org/solr/MoreLikeThisHandler`

Pop quiz

Q1. Which components can be used for an auto-suggester?

1. Facets component, data import handler component, and terms component

2. More Like This component, facets component, and filters component

3. Facets component, terms vector component, and More Like This component

There seem to exist different versions of the 'adoration of the magi' theme:

```
>> curl -X GET 'http://localhost:8983/solr/paintings/select?q=subject_ent
ity:adoration+of+the+magi&fl=title,artist,comment&wt=json'
```

Q2. How can we discover this only using facet suggestions?

1. We can use facet.field=subject_entity

2. We can use facet.field="adoration of the magi"

3. We can use facet.prefix="adoration"

Q3. How can we obtain a list of all the possible cities and museums in the index?

  1. Using facet.field=city,musem

  2. Using facet.field=city AND facet.field=museum

  3. Using facet.field=city&facet.field=museum

Q4. For what is the More Like This component designed?

  1. To provide recommendations of similar documents

  2. To provide recommendations of documents with similar terms

  3. To provide recommendations of documents with similar terms for a specific field

Q5. What is the meaning of `tf-idf`?

  1. It represents the ratio between the terms frequency and inverse document frequency

  2. It represents the ratio between the terms frequency and document frequency

  3. It represents the product between the inverse document frequency and terms frequency

Summary

In this chapter, we explored the idea of how it could be possible to improve the search experience in a wider perspective, from searching for some specific terms to finding *relevant* documents.

We started by introducing the Solr faceting capabilities to create a dynamic search experience for the user. By mixing the common usage of advanced parameters, operators, and function combinations with facets, we started to consider ways for moving into the data collection. This changes how we understand searches; every query could be seen as a pseudo-document, and we used Solr as a *match engine* rather than a *search engine*.

Filter queries have a crucial behavior, improving performance on the technical side and restricting the domain in which we execute our searches on the more abstract side. They have also led us to introduce the concept of *similarity*. We saw similarity in action by using the built-in `MoreLikeThis` component to obtain recommendations, adding value to common search results.

7
Working with Multiple Entities, Multicores, and Distributed Search

In this chapter we will again see how to define our entities. We will start from multiple cores (one for entity), then we will eventually index different types of resources in the same denormalized core. This will be useful for suggesting some more similarity analysis for the data, introducing new directions in the schemaless approach we have adopted so far for our prototypes.

In this context it's important to introduce concepts such as replication and shards, in order to understand the basic features of SolrCloud.

Working with multiple entities

When using Solr (or several other information retrieval tools), one of the most recurring open questions is, "What are the best practices to adopt for the analysis of the entities we are working with?"

In the previous chapters of this book we had a chance to start playing with Solr, adopting a multicore approach from the beginning, simply thinking about a core as an index for every single entity. This way we could define more and more cores to explore some different index configurations for the same entity (for example, painting). But, when we played with the `cities` core to augment our data on the `paintings` core, we were already using two cores at the same time, each of them defining an index for a different entity. The point is, we are always able to index our data on different cores and manage them as independent services.

There are times, however, when it could be more useful to manage data in a single index, avoiding too much relational thinking between different cores. In the next sections, we will explore how to handle multiple entities on different indexes, or with a single index.

Time for action – searching for cities using multiple core joins

One of the more recently added features is the so-called **pseudo-join**. This functionality permits us to explore queries that contain constraints on values between different fields. The term join is partially misleading, but makes sense if we consider the possibility of using this feature on fields from two different indexes.

Let's look at a simple example, using the paintings_geo and cities examples from *Chapter 5*, *Extending Search*.

1. Let's start with the examples from *Chapter 5*, *Extending Search* by executing

   ```
   >> cd /your-path-to/SolrStarterBook/test/
   >> ./start.sh chp05 (*NIX)
   >> start.bat chp05 (win)
   ```

   Please always remember to populate the cores with your data, for example, using the provided scripts in the path /SolrStarterBook/test/chp05 for each core.

2. Once the cores are running, we can search for cities where we will find some Caravaggio art:

   ```
   >> curl -X GET 'http://localhost:8983/solr/paintings_geo/select?q=
   artist:caravaggio+AND+{!join+from=city+to=city+fromIndex=cities}ci
   ty:*&fl=city,score&wt=json&json.nl=map&indent=on&debugQuery=on
   ```

3. A similar and more efficient query could be rewritten by using the following filters:

   ```
   >> curl -X GET 'http://localhost:8983/solr/paintings_geo/select?fq
   =artist:caravaggio&q={!join+from=city+to=city+fromIndex=cities}cit
   y:*&fl=city,score&wt=json&json.nl=map&indent=on&debugQuery=on'
   ```

   > Each of the examples will give us four results, including Berlin, Messina, Paris, and Naples.

4. Now we will try an almost opposite example:

   ```
   >> curl -X GET 'http://localhost:8983/solr/cities/
   select?q={!join+from=city_entity+to=city+fromIndex=paintings_geo}
   abstract:caravaggio+AND+city:*&fl=city,display_name,score&df=fullT
   ext&wt=json&indent=true&debugQuery=on'
   ```

5. In this case, we are searching the cities and we could expect to obtain the same results using a relation-like thinking. Wrong! We didn't obtain just four results as expected, but 48 results, because we are actually obtaining several false positives! In the following screenshot the first and second results are displayed to the left, and the first part of the results from the last example are displayed to the right:

```
- docs: [
  - {
      city: "http://dbpedia.org/resource/Messina",
      score: 3.989947
    },
  - {
      city: "http://dbpedia.org/resource/Berlin",
      score: 3.989947
    },
  - {
      city: "http://dbpedia.org/resource/Paris",
      score: 3.989947
    },
  - {
      city: "http://dbpedia.org/resource/Naples",
      score: 3.989947
    }
  ]
- docs: [
  - {
      city: "http://dbpedia.org/resource/Messina",
      score: 1
    },
  - {
      city: "http://dbpedia.org/resource/Berlin",
      score: 1
    },
  - {
      city: "http://dbpedia.org/resource/Paris",
      score: 1
    },
  - {
      city: "http://dbpedia.org/resource/Naples",
      score: 1
    }
```

```
- docs: [
  - {
      city: "Naples",
      display_name: "Napoli, NA, CAM, Italia",
      score: 1
    },
  - {
      city: "Naples",
      display_name: "Naples, Collier County, Florida, United States of America",
      score: 1
    },
  - {
      city: "Naples",
      display_name: "Naples, Cumberland, Maine, United States of America",
      score: 1
    },
  - {
      city: "Naples",
      display_name: "Naples, Greenup, Kentucky, United States of America",
      score: 1
    },
  - {
      city: "Naples",
      display_name: "Naples, Henderson, North Carolina, United States of America",
      score: 1
    },
  - {
      city: "Naples",
      display_name: "Naples, Scott County, Illinois, United States of America",
      score: 1
    },
  - {
      city: "Naples",
      display_name: "Naples, Uintah County, Utah, United States of America",
      score: 1
```

6. It's easy to note that the last result also includes false positives, which matches the name of a city (for example, Naples), but actually does not really refer to one of the paintings we are interested in. We searched for a reference on the Italian painter Caravaggio, but we also found cities in the United States!

What just happened?

In these examples we are using two cores with very different schema and configurations, each defining a `city` field, which can be used in our join queries. In the first query we are searching for documents on the `cities` core that contain values for the city fields (`city:*`); then we will match the results with documents in the `paintings_geo` core that have the same value. At the same time we want to apply the criteria `abstract:caravaggio` to our painting's results. We can obtain a similar result by using a filter query, as in the second example. In the second example using the `debugQuery=on&fl*,score` parameters it is simple to see how the score will differ. In particular, in the second example we will obtain the same results, but all the documents here have a score value `1`, while in the first example they have a greater value. The reason for this difference is that in the second case the filter query restricts the collection on which we are searching for `caravaggio` references. Also remember that score values are not normalized, so in the first case the results should have a score value greater than other documents in the collection.

Executing the last query, which is somewhat in the opposite direction (first search on `paintings_geo`, then match on `cities`), we saw that the results do not fit our expectations.

In order to understand what is happening, an option is to ask for the complete list of the city names for paintings matching our chosen criteria:

```
>> curl -X GET 'http://localhost:8983/solr/paintings_geo/select?q=abstrac
t:caravaggio+AND+city:*&rows=100&wt=json&debugQuery=on&fl=city'
```

We found 8 matching documents, referring to cities: `Messina`, `Valletta`, `Siracuse`, `Paris`, `Naples`, `Marseille`, `Berlin`, and `Toronto`. Note that, without excluding documents with the `city` field empty by using the `city:*` condition, we would instead obtain 38 results. If we simulate the matching process by executing individual queries on the cities core, we find 48 matching results, obtained by the following piece of code:

```
matching documents (48) = Messina (2) + Valletta (3) + Siracuse (0) +
Paris (10) + Naples (10) + Marseille (3) + Berlin (10) + Toronto (10)
```

This is very interesting, as we are producing results that may not match the `abstract:caravaggio` criteria clearly. Our misuse of the join has *increased our recall*, and the system is guessing some cities with the same name, loosing the initial criteria and also some *precision*. If you have some experience with a relational database, you may point out that this could be seen similar to what happened with *cartesian product*, but remember that we are not using actual relations here, but only *fields matching between documents*.

Preparing example data for multiple entities

It's useful to provide a couple of examples to think about how to shape our entities, including pros and cons, starting from multicore to denormalization into a single core, but first of all we need to download some more example data.

We will use a slightly rewritten version of the same script used to download data examples from DBpedia in *Chapter 3, Indexing Example Data from DBpedia – Paintings*. As long as the data collected grows there are chances that they could contain errors and problems of formatting. We can skip the problematic records when needed. I always suggest starting by isolating and skipping the tricky records from your prototypes, to remain focused, and later adjusting the process incrementally. In our case the RDF/XML serialization downloaded sometimes contains unwanted characters/tags, and we have to strip them off or ignore them in order to have our process running for most of the data collected. Then let's focus on acquiring as many data we can for our test examples, and don't worry if we miss something.

Downloading files for multiple entities

The first thing we need for populating our examples is a good data collection, which contains data to be used for different entities. If you are not interested in details about the downloaded data and creating the corresponding XML files for Solr, please skip directly to the *Playing with joins on multicores (a core for every entity)* section.

Following a similar approach to the one we used when we started with the first example on `paintings` data, we could easily start by downloading data for paintings using the following commands:

```
>> cd [path-to-SolrStarterBook]/test/chp07/arts
>> downloadPaintingsData.sh
```

If you have already done this or if you are not interested in this part, you could easily skip it and start using the already downloaded XML files you will find at `/SolrStarterBook/resources/dbpedia_paintings/downloaded`.

Once we have downloaded the files for paintings, we can easily download other data using the reference contained in the XML files we have downloaded so far. Every resource from DBpedia contains links to other resources that can be used to create a good playground of data.

In order to download data for artists, museums, and subjects, we will use another simple Scala shell script:

```
>> downloadMoreEntities.sh
```

The script (at `/SolrStarterBook/test/chp07/arts`) does nothing more than search for (in a painting resource) references of a certain type, and then download the corresponding representations. You don't need to use this script if you don't want to, as you will find some pre-downloaded files at `/SolrStarterBook/resources/`, divided into different `dbpedia_paintings`, `dbpedia_artists`, `dbpedia_musems`, and `dbpedia_subjects` folders.

Generating Solr documents

Once we have collected the XML/RDF representation for our data, it's time to produce the corresponding Solr XML representation, needed for populating the index. In my case I have collected about 5130 files in a few minutes, but be warned that these numbers could change if you execute the process by yourselves, as they depend on queries over a remote repository.

Here we can follow the same approach used before. We will use the simple `dbpediaToPost.sh` Scala script that transforms the XML sources into the Solr format using a specific `dbpediaToPost.xslt` transformation style sheet. All we have to do is call the script:

```
>> createSolrDocs.sh
```

This script will produce the corresponding `entity_name/solr_docs` field for every `entity_name/downloaded` directory.

The script is rather simple, containing a line for every resource type. For example, for creating Solr documents for artists:

```
>>./dbpediaToPost.sh ../../../resources/dbpedia_artists/downloaded/
../../../resources/dbpedia_artists/solr_docs/dbpediaToPost.xslt
'artists'
```

I don't want you to spend too much time on the programming details at the moment, but still I want you to notice that we are passing a parameter to the XSLT transformation sheet, that will be internally used by it to produce an `entity_type` field. For example, in the case of an artist the Solr document will contain:

```
<field name="entity_type">artists</field>
```

This will be very useful later, and please keep this field in mind while you start playing with the examples.

Playing with joins on multicores (a core for every entity)

The most simple approach can be creating a separate index for every entity. First of all we need to create a core for every entity (I call them `arts_paintings`, `arts_artists`, `arts_museums`, and `arts_subjects`), using a default configuration. In this case we will use one for every core, more or less a copy of the configuration previously used in *Chapter 6, Using Faceted Search – from Searching to Finding,* so I will omit the details here, and I invite you to look at the provided source in details.

After we have Solr running (using the `start.sh` file at `/SolrStarterBook/test/chp07/arts/`), we will post the Solr documents to the cores with the script `postCores.sh`. Once the cores are populated, the first thing we want to test is a very simple multicore join query, similar to the example discussed in *Chapter 5, Extending Search*:

```
>> curl -X GET 'http://localhost:8983/solr/arts_paintings/
select?q={!join%20from=city+to=city+fromIndex=arts_museums}dali&wt=json'
```

You don't need to expect very good performances when the index sizes increase, so I suggest you use it only when it's not possible to use another approach.

Using sharding for distributed search

Now that we have populated our data with four different cores, we can then use them to introduce the concept of **distributed search**.

A distributed search is a search that can be sent to a Solr instance, but will be actually executed while distributing queries over some different instances (and cores). This is generally intended to be used on a single schema definition that can be seen as a sort of very huge index, split for convenience on different parts (**shards**), on different Solr instances and cores.

Time for action – playing with sharding (distributed search)

Before talking about the implications of using shards, let's test this approach with two very simple example queries as follows:

1. First of all, let's try to simulate a distributed search over a single Solr instance, using the same Solr core twice (if you would like to give a name to the idea, we can name this an `identity shard`); in this case, we are executing the query on the `arts_paintings` core, and expanding the query with a distributed search over two simulated shards, which actually refers to the same core:

```
>> curl -X GET 'http://localhost:8983/solr/arts_paintings/
select?shards=localhost:8983/solr/arts_paintings,localhost:8983/
solr/arts_paintings&q=*:*&wt=json&debugQuery=on&fl=[shard],*'
```

2. Once this is proven to be working, we will move a step forward from the previous multicore join examples. We will simulate a *distributed* search over our cores as they were our shards. This time we are introducing other cores as shards, and we are using the pseudo-field `[shard]` to explicitly mark a document with its shard membership, as we can see in the screenshot following the command:

```
>> curl -X GET 'http://localhost:8983/solr/arts_
paintings/select?shards=localhost:8983/solr/arts_
paintings,localhost:8983/solr/arts_museums,localhost:8983/
solr/arts_subjects,localhost:8983/solr/arts_artists&q=fullT
ext:1630&start=0&rows=20000&debug=on&wt=json&fl=uri,entity_
type,[shard]&debugQuery=on'
```

```
- response: {
    numFound: 7,
    start: 0,
    maxScore: 11.708451,
  - docs: [
    - {
        uri: "http://dbpedia.org/resource/Category:1630_paintings",
        entity_type: "ENTITY_subjects",
        [shard]: "localhost:8983/solr/arts_subjects"
      },
    - {
        uri: "http://dbpedia.org/resource/Siege_of_Recife_(1630)",
        entity_type: "ENTITY_subjects",
        [shard]: "localhost:8983/solr/arts_subjects"
      },
    - {
        uri: "http://dbpedia.org/resource/Santa_Maria_della_Salute",
        entity_type: "ENTITY_museums",
        [shard]: "localhost:8983/solr/arts_museums"
      },
    - {
        uri: "http://dbpedia.org/resource/Ariane_in_Naxos",
        entity_type: "ENTITY_paintings",
        [shard]: "localhost:8983/solr/arts_paintings"
      },
```

3. In the previous screenshot you can see some of the results of the query, with details on the shard where a document is actually found (remember that in our case we have four distinct indexes, so it's easy to verify whether a document is present on a specific core or not).

> Note that here we are still executing a single query over a single machine, with a single running Solr instance, even if we are using multiple different cores as shards. This is not what shards are designed for; however, they should be used to distribute a single query over a single, huge index that can be *hosted* using several machines. You should have noticed that once we have adopted a compatible or identical schema definition, this can turnout to be only a conceptual distinction.

What just happened?

In the previous two examples, we are using parameters, such as `shards=host1/core1,host2/core2` to provide the list of shards where the query will be sent. The `[shard]` pseudo-field is used to mark a document with the explicit information about the shard that actually contains it. Here we need to specify a running Solr instance and a specific core name. There is no limit on using exactly the same schema definition or a slightly different one, as long as the schemas are compatible with each other. Two schemas can be compatible if they declare the *same fields* of the *same data types*, or if they only use the *same kind* of *dynamic fields* and the *same unique key*, just to cite two examples. There can be other specific cases, but the point is quite intuitive. Imagine using two shards that contain a year field, but one configured with a numeric type, and the other as a string type. When trying to retrieve values Solr should get an error. A less problematic case is when you will use fields that exist only on one of the two shards, as they will simply produce no match for some of the Solr instances. Moreover, be warned that if you really use different compatible schema definitions, you could even incur problems with different language analysis configuration, so I feel there is no point in using this approach.

Generally speaking, in our example, the query is being served by two Solr shards, which are essentially the same. This is a good start to considering using multiple shards, which have the same schema. When a document is present only on one shard, it can be replicated if needed (using a specific handler to enable one shard to communicate with the others), but it is generally not duplicated in the results.

This should give you the idea that shards are really designed to be used for splitting a large, huge index into more compact and distinct ones, and then being able to query them as if they were a single (logical) one. The maintenance of data on separate shards is up to us, and this has been proven by construction in this case, as we are in fact using exactly the same schema for the four cores, but *we have posted the data on that individually*, by type.

If you also want some deeper view of how this is working, we have adopted the parameters `fl=[shard]` to project the information of which shard actually contains a record, and of course `debugQuery=on`. This way we will see how the query is actually split and suprise! the query is not split at all by itself, but will produce 4 different matching results that will be collected.

Time for action – finding a document from any shard

Now that we have a principle, let's try to simulate a sharded query in a bit more realistic way, as given in the following steps

1. We can, for example, start two Solr instances and use cores from them as our shards. In order to simplify that, I have prepared a simple script (`/SolrStarterBook/test/chp07/arts/start_shards.sh`), which you can use after the usual `start chp07` script to have a new running Solr instance.

2. The new instance will need a different port, so I chose the `9999` port, which is simple to remember. I also decided to use the multicore definitions again from *Chapter 5, Extending Search*, and please remember to add data again before continuing.

3. Once we have our instances running (port `8983` for the current examples, port `9999` for the examples in *Chapter 5, Extending Search*), we need to add a new test document on a single shard to be able to prove that we will find it even by querying on a different one.

4. Let's add our test document (`/SolrStarterBook/test/chp97/arts/test_postSingleShard.sh`):

```
>> curl 'http://localhost:8983/solr/arts_paintings/
update?commit=true&wt=json' -H 'Content-type:application/json' -d
'
[{
    "uri" : "TEST_SHARDS_01",
    "title" : "This is a DUMMY title",
    "artist" : "Some Artist Name",
    "museum" : "Some Museum"
}]'
```

5. All we have to do then is to search for this particular document, starting our search on the `paintings` core from *Chapter 5, Extending Search*:

```
>> curl -X GET 'http://localhost:9999/solr/paintings/select?q=tit
le:dummy&wt=json&indent=true&fl=*,[shard]&shards=localhost:8983/
solr/arts_paintings,localhost:9999/solr/paintings'
```

> Note that we need to remove the `http://` part from the `host/core` definition in the shards list.

What just happened?

Looking at the results obtained by our test query, we will find the documents we are searching for, as expected:

```
- response: {
      numFound: 1,
      start: 0,
      maxScore: 5.6195335,
    - docs: [
      - {
             uri: "TEST_SHARDS_01",
           + fullText: […],
           - title: [
                 "This is a DUMMY title"
             ],
           + artist: […],
           + museum: […],
           + last_update: […],
             artist_entity: "Some Artist Name",
             museum_entity: "Some Museum",
             title_entity: "This is a DUMMY title",
             subject_entity: "This is a DUMMY title",
             _version_: 1443447862340878300,
             [shard]: "localhost:8983/solr/arts_paintings"
        }
      ]
   }
}
```

In this screenshot we can clearly recognize the shard source by the use of the `[shard]` field. An interesting point is that the `localhost:9999/paintings` core we are using is defined by a schema that is almost identical to the ones used in this chapter. If we test the same query (or any other query) on `localhost:9999/cities` core, we will get an error similar to the following output:

```
java.lang.NullPointerException at org.apache.solr.handler.component.
QueryComponent.mergeIds(QueryComponent.java:879)...
```

The errors remind us that the results obtained by different shards are actually merged, and the most important field for Solr to be able to merge those results is the one used as the unique key. In the cities example indeed we had no `uri` field, and even if our schema is very flexible using dynamic fields, the results cannot be merged this way. Note that if we repeat our query adding the `localhost:9999/cities` core in the shards list this time, it makes no difference, as there simply is no match.

This could give us some insight into how to use shards in a creative way, by defining a single nonrestrictive core to be used as a central query point, distributing requests all over different core definitions, used as shards. Even if we plan to force the use of shards this way, please note that we still have to manage the data in them *manually*, and *we cannot automatically split an existing index* in a simple way. These topics are well covered by adopting the features of SolrCloud, as we will see later in this chapter.

In these examples, we are using very simple queries to focus ourselves on the main aspects of using shards and to avoid too complex list of parameters that is too complex; but once we are querying on some Solr instance, we can use the common query parameters and components for faceting, highlighting, and stats and terms handling. However, there are some intuitive limitations: for example, you should have defined a field to be used as a unique key across all the shards and joins; scoring and similarity-oriented features will not work at the moment (for example, idf, MoreLikeThis, and so on). You will find more precise details on sharding on the official wiki page:

```
http://wiki.apache.org/solr/DistributedSearch
```

Collecting some ideas on schemaless versus normalization

Before we move to have a look at the main SolrCloud feature, I feel some more consideration of denormalization and the advantages of this approach will be useful when using Solr and similar tools. As we already pointed out, with distributed search we can obtain results even from a different shard. We could have, if needed, represented the data of different entities posted to different cores with compatible schema, and still the system should work. From this perspective, there seems to be no point in indexing data on different cores using an entity-relationship normalization approach. I tried to synthesize this simple idea in the following schema:

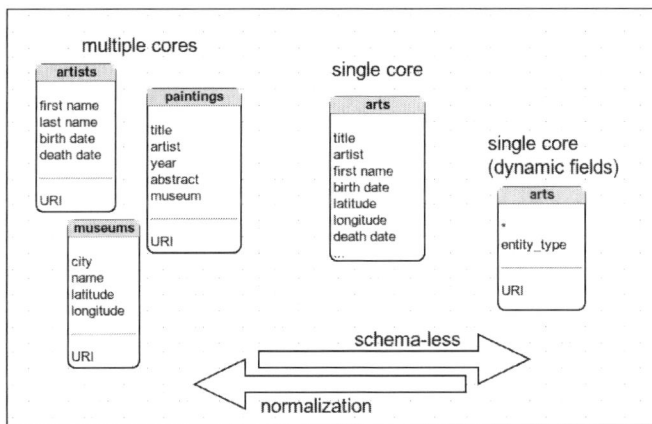

In the left part of this schema, we can find some suggested relationships between the different entities that could be used for joins if we were using a relational database. Note that Solr doesn't have a join functionality in the relational perspective as we have seen before, and it permits us to link together records representing different entity individuals by matching them on some criteria at runtime.

Looking at this schema I simply want you to remember again that *Solr isn't a relational database*, and even if we have some previous experience with those and it could be helpful to look at some analogies, we need to start thinking differently.

Although we are introducing some features from SolrCloud we are moving to adopt Solr not only as a search engine (and *match engine*, let's say), but as an effective NoSQL solution, and we should not be tempted to think too much in a relational way. I hope you will remember this simple fact. You can think about our schema in case of multiple entities as if we are creating a very long, huge vector with optional fields for every field of every entity. We will put only the values we have from time to time without harming the inverted index (there will be no "holes"). Thus we will ideally have no memory loss and duplications of fields to avoid by normalizing using a more rigid pre-defined schema.

Creating a single denormalized index

In this chapter I am intentionally not describing the configuration we are adopting, since it's basically the same as in the previous chapters, and it's not so important for us to test.

Adding a field to track entity type

You probably have not missed the adoption of an `entity_field` in the single core represented when reading our schema from left to right. This is the typical scenario in every model that adopts normalization. At the same point you will need a field or a property to keep track of the entity the data is referred to. We had given a specific value to this field with the XSLT used to produce our Solr documents. I suggest you to always adopt such a field when using different data representing different entities in your single core definition. You will be able to track that data from the beginning, or optimize your querying filtering them by type with `fq` parameters (remember that this can be appended on every request, if configured in `solrconfig.xml`), even if at some point you change some schema configuration.

Moreover, you can easily use faceting on this field to have a fast overview of the different data inserted, and even try to represent some hierarchy, but this is up to you.

In order to post the data on the single core definition, we will use the script (`/SolrStarterBook/test/chp07/postAll.sh`):

```
>> java -Dcommit=yes -Durl=http://localhost:8983/solr/arts/update -jar
post.jar ../../../resources/dbpedia_paintings/solr_docs/*.xml
```

I strongly suggest adopting this approach in the first stage of a project, in order to proceed with rapid prototyping and to be able to produce something testable in a couple of hours of work. But when you have this single melting-pot index running, you could start seeing it from different perspectives that will be specific to your project, from better shaping your domain, to starting to consider what kind of architecture should be used to expose the services.

Analyzing, designing, and refactoring our domain

Even if we are often using a schemaless approach for our prototypes, we still need to analyze our **domain** deeply, which is important to fully understand what kind of searches we need and how we can configure a correct text analysis for every field.

I suggest you to refer to: `http://www.infoq.com/resource/minibooks/domain-driven-design-quickly/en/pdf/DomainDrivenDesignQuicklyOnline.pdf`. This book can give you some insights into how to manage the domain analysis as a central part of our design.

Using document clustering as a domain analysis tool

If we have a unique big index containing data from different entities we could perform advanced analysis on it, which can give us a very interesting perspective of our data based on advanced metrics of similarity.

Once we have a single arts core running (you can find the details of the configuration in `/SolrStarterBook/solr-app/chp07/arts`), we can then define an `arts_clustering` twin core, which can be used with the same data and configuration, but exposing them to *document clustering analysis*. Solr 4 includes integration with the very good tool *Carrot2*, which you can download following the instructions on the site `http://download.carrot2.org/head/manual/index.html`.

Once you unzip the Carrot2 Web App, add the configurations for our examples; for your convenience I have placed in the path `/SolrStartedBook/carrot`.

> **Carrot2** is an Open Source Search Results Clustering Engine, which can automatically organize collections of documents into thematic categories.
>
> You can find all the references and the manual of the project on the official site:
>
> `http://project.carrot2.org/`
>
> It can fetch data from various sources, including wikipedia, results from search engines, and Solr itself. It can also be used with other data collections, adopting its XML format; so I suggest you to take a look at its API.

Note that we are interested in exposing data from Solr to Carrot2, but it's also possible to use Solr for indexing on the Carrot2 data itself, so the process can be customized in different ways, depending on your needs.

Once you have Carrot2 running, it's simple to define what we need to expose for Solr to talk to carrot:

```
<searchComponent name="clustering" enable="true" class="solr.
clustering.ClusteringComponent">
  <lst name="engine">
    <str name="name">default</str>
    <str name="carrot.algorithm">org.carrot2.clustering.
      lingo.LingoClusteringAlgorithm</str>
    <str name="LingoClusteringAlgorithm.
      desiredClusterCountBase">4</str>
    <str name="MultilingualClustering.
      defaultLanguage">ENGLISH</str>
  </lst>
  <lst name="engine">
    <str name="name">stc</str>
    <str name="carrot.algorithm">org.carrot2.
      clustering.stc.STCClusteringAlgorithm</str>
  </lst>
</searchComponent>

<requestHandler name="/clustering" class="solr.SearchHandler">
  <lst name="defaults">
    <bool name="clustering">on</bool>
    <bool name="clustering.results">true</bool>
    <str name="clustering.engine">default</str>
    <!-- Solr-to-Carrot2 field mapping. -->
    <str name="carrot.url">uri</str>
    <str name="carrot.title">uri</str>
    <str name="carrot.snippet">fullText</str>
  </lst>
```

```
    <arr name="last-components">
      <str>clustering</str>
    </arr>
  </requestHandler>
```

As you can see this is as simple as defining a new request and search handler couple of components, and put some (initial!) configuration for choosing algorithms and fields to be used from Carrot2.

The next step will be configuring Carrot2 to acquire data from Solr. We need to edit the `source-solr-attributes.xml` file at `/SolrStarterBook/carrot/webapp/WEB-INF/suites/`:

```
  <attribute-sets default="overridden-attributes">
    <attribute-set id="overridden-attributes">
      <value-set>
        <label>overridden-attributes</label>
        <attribute key="SolrDocumentSource.serviceUrlBase">
          <value value="http://localhost
            :8983/solr/arts_clustering/clustering"/>
        </attribute>
        <attribute key="SolrDocumentSource.solrSummaryFieldName">
          <value value="fullText"/>
        </attribute>
        <attribute key="SolrDocumentSource.solrTitleFieldName">
          <value value="uri"/>
        </attribute>
        <attribute key="SolrDocumentSource.solrUrlFieldName">
          <value value="uri"/>
        </attribute>
      </value-set>
    </attribute-set>
  </attribute-sets>
```

Finally we need to add our new Solr source in the `suite-webapp.xml` file at `/SolrStarterBook/carrot/webapp/WEB-INF/suites/` (we can add as many instances as we want):

```
  <source component-class="org.carrot2.source.solr.SolrDocumentSource"
  id="solr" attribute-sets-resource="source-solr-attributes.xml">
    <label>arts (Solr)</label>
    <title>Solr Search Engine</title>
    <icon-path>icons/solr.png</icon-path>
    <mnemonic>s</mnemonic>
    <description>our Solr instance.</description>
  </source>
```

When we have both `arts_clustering` and Carrot running, we will have the chance to use the carrot algorithms and visualizations. For example, by adopting *Lingo*, we could obtain some very suggestive visual synthesis for our analysis, which can really help us in refactoring the domain configuration, or in presenting the actual context in which our data exists to the clients. The documents in a cluster are considered to be similar by an emergent theme or topic, connected to the same concepts, it does not matter if they are actually representing an artist or paintings. Imagine the possibility of reviewing your domain with your clients, planning refactorization of facets, or configuring a topic-specific text analysis.

In the following screenshot we can see different kinds of visual representations of document clustering, for example, searching for `oil painting`:

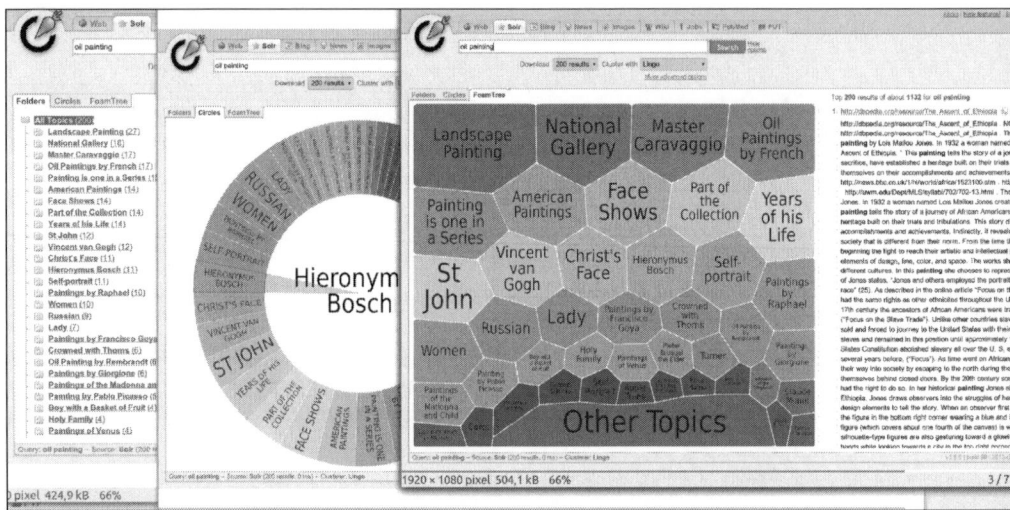

As you can see these kinds of tools can be very useful and can help us to avoid losing time, so I hope you will spend some time going in this direction for your experiments, when you have some more experience in using Solr by itself. The presentation at `http://2011.berlinbuzzwords.de/sites/2011.berlinbuzzwords.de/files/solr-clustering-visualization.pdf` will give you a clearer idea.

Looking from left to right you will probably think about faceting, but remember that in this case the aggregation is done by similarity and adopting specific algorithms for clustering such as Lingo or Suffix Tree, not by simple direct terms matching. This way it's possible to see emerging latent themes, which we can't imagine by simply searching for the same textual content over the data.

Managing index replication

On a more technical side, we need to be able to scale up our indexes when needed (especially if we chose to use a single schema), and we will see that this can be done by using replications by hand, or as a feature of SolrCloud. A replicated index is generally adopted when high traffic on our site will require the capability to serve more contemporary clients. In this case we can define a *master core* and a *slave core*. The master will contain the original version of the index, and the slave will be synchronized on its changes, so that we can produce lots of replicas to serve a huge query traffic. The indexing process should have a noncritical impact on the searching experience, at the cost of some overhead in network activities, which can become intensive.

A typical scenario will require the detailed configurations and tuning, but the main elements will be the definitions of two specific request handlers to let the different Solr cores communicate with each other.

A master core will typically require a definition similar to this:

```
<requestHandler name="/replication" class="solr.ReplicationHandler" >
  <lst name="master">
    <str name="replicateAfter">commit</str>
    <str name="confFiles">schema.xml,mapping-ISOLatin1Accent.txt
       ,protwords.txt,stopwords.txt,synonyms.txt,elevate.xml</str>
  </lst>
</requestHandler>
```

However, a slave core will have to specify the name of the master core to which it is connecting:

```
<requestHandler name="/replication" class="solr.ReplicationHandler" >
  <lst name="slave">
    <str name="masterUrl">http://${MASTER_CORE_URL}
      /${solr.core.name}</str>
    <str name="pollInterval">${POLL_TIME}</str>
  </lst>
</requestHandler>
```

You will find more detailed instructions on how to define and use replicas on the official wiki page:

```
http://wiki.apache.org/solr/SolrReplication
```

Note that this peculiar communication system is hierarchical and exposes *a single point of failure in the master*. If this goes offline the system might suffer from problems. It is a more resilient and self-reconfiguring approach. It is used for SolrCloud, by combining and managing the sharding and replication capability via the **Zookeper** server.

Clustering Solr for distributed search using SolrCloud

Since Solr 4, every Solr instance is also a SolrCloud instance. All the capabilities we need to use are already included, and it's up to us whether to start Solr with Zookeper (and the basic configurations for it) or not. In fact when started with Zookeper, Solr will act as a SolrCloud instance, so that it can create, destroy, split, or replicate shards in a way transparent to us.

Taking a journey from single core to SolrCloud

Starting from a single index on a single core, we saw that we can split a single logical index into multiple indexes by using **multiple cores**. If we see this as a vertical-logical subdivision, as we described earlier talking about *denormalization*, we can also adopt a horizontal subdivision for a logical index, introducing the concept of shards.

But we saw that **sharding** must be done manually, and this usually means using some specific programming in SolrJ or similar libraries. Queries are sent to multiple shards and then the results are assembled, so this is useful when we have to handle very big indexes. Let's say there is a *distributed search* but no distributed indexing; this has to be managed by our custom programs that need to know the specific schema.

Replication is good for managing *distributed indexing* and scales well on increasing traffic requests, but it has to be manually configured and managed, too. Moreover, it introduces some network traffic overhead and delays for synchronization, and it's not so simple to recover after some bad failure.

With SolrCloud we are adopting both sharding and replication, but hiding the complexity so that we can to manage a single logical index that can be composed by multiple cores on different machines. A **collection** is in short a single logical index, which can be composed by many cores on many nodes, obtaining redundancy and a scalable and resilient index. We can of course think about adopting multiple collections that can be managed independently from each other.

Internally, every collection will be divided into logical parts called **slices**. Every slice will have several materialization of its own data (physical copies), which is what we usually call a shard. Finally, there always is a leader shard, from which updates are distributed, and in the same way there will always be some node that acts as a master for others. The concept of nodes here is important because they tell us that this environment does not have a single point of failure, and every node or shard could be promoted when needed if any one node fails, this is why we can define it as a *resilient network*. This way recovery and backup could be done automatically using the shards/replica functions.

The main orchestrators in this network are the Zookeeper companion instances for the active Solr, and they need to be studied specifically to understand their technical configuration details and behavior.

Understanding why we need Zookeeper

Zookeeper is a standalone server that is able to *maintain configuration information and synchronization between distributed services*, by using a shared hierarchical name space of data registers. You can think about these kind of namespaces as analogous to how a filesystem normally manages files. The main difference is that here the namespace is designed to manage shared distributed service endpoints, and let them communicate with each other, possibly sharing their data.

This kind of coordination service can improve availability of the endpoints they manage (they can track problems and eventually perform updates and request balancing), and a series of Zookeeper instances that communicate with each other will effectively design a fault tolerant environment. Internally, some nodes are used as *overseers* for others and, when launching multiple Zookeeper instances, an ensemble of instances is considered to be running if more than half of the server instances are up (this is what is called a *quorum*).

ZooKeeper actually serves as *a repository for cluster states*.

Time for action – testing SolrCloud and Zookeeper locally

Every Solr instance now also includes an embedded Zookeeper instance, so we can start our experimentation with that, and then move to a more robust configuration with an external Zookeeper server.

1. We can start from the default example in the Solr distribution. We can write the following command:

    ```
    >> cd ~/SolrStarterBook/solr/example
    ```

2. Then we can start the first SolrCore instance using the configuration for the `arts` core:

    ```
    >> java -DzkRun -DnumShards=2 -Dbootstrap_confdir=../../solr-app/
    chp07/arts/conf/ -jar start.jar
    ```

3. We can then start two more instances, with a slightly different choice of parameters:

    ```
    >> java -Djetty.port=7777 -DzkHost=localhost:9983 -jar start.jar
    >> java -Djetty.port=8888 -DzkHost=localhost:9983 -jar start.jar
    ```

4. This specific approach involves a central Zookeper as this approach is simpler to use. On a real, distributed system we will probably need to adopt a multiple instance Zookeeper instead.

5. If you post some data to the Solr instance, you will see that the process is transparent. If we want to know from which of the shards a document has been retrieved, we have to use the usual parameter `fl=[shard]`.

What just happened?

The parameter `-DzkRun` is the one that actually starts a Solr instance, requiring to start the internal Zookeeper one. The result is that this instance will now act as SolrCloud one.

In the first example we adopt the configuration for `arts` Solr core using the `-Dbootstrap_confdir` parameters. Remember that your configuration needs to be specified only the first time you connect the instance to Zookeper, in order to publish it on Zookeeper itself. Another option would be using a specific command-line command (refer to `http://wiki.apache.org/solr/SolrCloud#Command_Line_Util`), and if we publish an already published configuration again this will be discarded to load the new one.

The parameter `-DnumShards=2` needs to be specified only at the beginning. If we want to change the number of available shards later, we will have the chance to do it by using some specific collection API:

```
/admin/collections?action=<chosen_action>
```

Here, we can use some self-explicative action, `RELOAD`, `SPLITSHARD`, `DELETESHARD`, `DELETE`, and others. For example, let's try the following command:

```
>> curl -X GET 'http://localhost:8983/solr/admin/collections ?action=CREA
TE&name=newCollection&numShards=3&replicationFactor=4'
```

This could be used to create a new collection. This is only a brief introduction, but you can find some growing documentation at

```
http://wiki.apache.org/solr/SolrCloud#Managing_collections_via_the_
Collections_API
```

You will also find more details on using external Zookeeper, configuring files manually, and so on.

When starting the other two instances, we only needed to choose a different port for every jetty instance (`-Djetty.port=7777`), and finally to point the instance to the same Zookeper running instance (`-DzkHost=localhost:9983`), in our case it started with the first core. Note that we know the port where our Zookeper is running, because when it is started as an embedded component with Solr, it uses a port value equal to `solr_port + 1000` by default. Since we had defined two shards, and started a first core and then two new cores so that we have more running cores than the pre-defined number of shards, the third will be automatically chosen to be used as a replica, using a round-robin selection strategy.

If we want we can verify that by using an almost still evolving web interface:

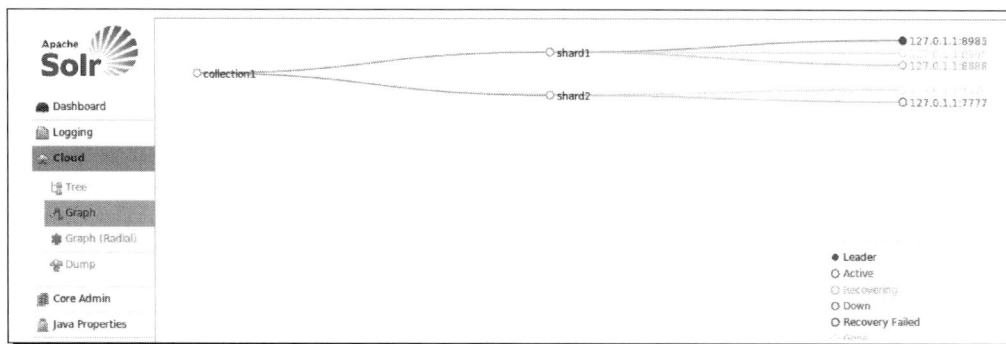

Looking at the suggested configurations for SolrCloud

When using SolrCloud we require a unique ID over multiple shards internally, and a version marker field, in order to be able to manage data and eventually store them pretty much as a NoSQL database. All documents will be available quickly, after a *soft commit*, and can be retrieved in Near Real Time search, so we need to configure some fields and components for this to work properly.

Changing the schema.xml file

We can introduce a _version_ field in our schema, to track changes in a certain document:

```
<field name="_version_" type="long" indexed="true" stored="true"
multiValued="false"/>
```

Changing the solrconfig.xml file

If we want to enable the transaction log, currently used for real-time GET, we can add a configuration, as shown in the following code:

```
<updateLog>
  <str name="dir">${solr.data.dir:}</str>
</updateLog>
[...]
<requestHandler name="/replication" class="solr.ReplicationHandler"
startup="lazy" />
[...]
<requestHandler name="/get" class="solr.RealTimeGetHandler">
  <lst name="defaults">
    <str name="omitHeader">true</str>
  </lst>
</requestHandler>
```

Note that we are already using most of these configurations, so the adoption of SolrCloud should not be too complicated. The /get handler is generally suggested to check if a document exists on one of the shards, but it's not strictly needed, and the /replication handler manages replicated data almost transparently.

Knowing the pros and cons of SolrCloud

Since using SolrCloud involves several different aspects of managing Solr, and requires a deep understanding of how the components work and how to use them effectively, I have collected some clear web resources that I suggest for learning more on the topic and starting your own custom experimentation, when you feel you are ready:

- http://wiki.apache.org/solr/SolrCloud
- https://cwiki.apache.org/confluence/display/ZOOKEEPER/Index
- http://architects.dzone.com/articles/solr-43-shard-splitting-quick
- https://cwiki.apache.org/confluence/display/solr/Shards+and+Indexing+Data+in+SolrCloud
- https://cwiki.apache.org/confluence/display/solr/Getting+Started+with+SolrCloud
- https://cwiki.apache.org/confluence/display/solr/Command+Line+Utilities
- https://cwiki.apache.org/confluence/display/solr/Collections+API
- http://www.youtube.com/watch?v=IJk8Hyo6nv0

Pop quiz

Q1. What is Zookeeper? Why do we have to use it with Solr?

1. Zookeeper is a standalone server that can be used to maintain synchronized configurations between distributed services.
2. Zookeeper is a component of SolrCloud that can be used to maintain synchronized configurations between distributed services.
3. Zookeeper is a standalone server that can be used to synchronize data between distributed Solr instances.

Q2. What are the differences between a distributed search and index replication?

1. A replicated index is a copy of an original index, which can be used as a shard for serving more users at the same time. A distributed search is a search over different shards, generally different Solr instances.

2. A replicated index uses a master and one or more slaves to replicate data of a single index multiple times, providing the capability of serving more users at the same time. A distributed search is a search over different shards, generally different Solr cores.

3. A replicated index is a collection of shards, which are actually replicas of the same original index. A distributed search is a search over different shards.

Q3. Is it possible to use shards over different schema definitions?

1. Yes, we can use shards with different schemas as long as long as their configurations are compatible.

2. No, we cannot use use shards with different schema as we must use the same configuration for every core.

Q4. What is Carrot2 document clustering?

1. Carrot2 is a Solr component that can be used to add a specific similarity algorithm to Solr.

2. Carrot2 is an engine that can be used for document clustering from the Solr results.

3. Carrot2 is a web application that can be used to visualize clusters of Solr documents.

Q5. What differences exists between using multicores and shards?

1. A shard is a single Solr core that can be used inside a distributed search involving all the cores from the same Solr instance (multicore).

2. A shard is a self-sufficient Solr multicore installation, whose cores can be used inside a distributed search, while with multicore we refer to more than a single core inside the same Solr instance.

3. A shard is a self-sufficient Solr core that can be used inside a distributed search, while with multicore we refer to more than a single core inside the same Solr instance.

Summary

In this chapter we have designed a journey from a single core definition to multicore and then to distributed search. We discussed the analysis of multiple entities and how to choose between indexing them using different cores or denormalizing them into one single index.

A single, logical index could give us insights on how to best use our data (we left some suggestions to Carrot2 and similar tools, which we gave a fast introduction), permitting us to "see the full picture" of our domain.

Lastly, a logical index can be managed using SolrCloud; this way we will have it robust and scalable, as it relies on a collection of shards, and it is physically subdivided into many distributed cores.

Introducing these ideas is a further step toward a real system in production, but we need to take care of some fine tuning and customization, as we will see later.

8
Indexing External Data sources

In this chapter, we will have the chance to play with the DataImportHandler facility. We will provide an introduction to the most interesting directions where it's possible to use it.

We will see how it's possible to use a Solr instance to index all different sources without necessarily resorting to a lot of programming, focusing on how to define a simple indexing workflow with XML configuration. This can be interesting; for example, for acquiring data for preliminary prototyping and analysis, in order to provide integrations for existing legacy sites. It can also be used to implement a central service for searching data we want to access over our applications, e-commerce sites, or OPAC.

Stepping further into the real world

Since the beginning of this book, we have decided to focus on making example data available quickly, just to have the opportunity of learning how to manage the basic elements in Solr and how to combine them. Most of the indexing and searching examples have been designed to give an idea about how to do the same in a way agnostic from a specific programming language. We used cURL just to fix the idea, but we could have used other tools as well. However, generally you don't want to expose your Solr data directly. On most of the projects, you will have a Solr machine available for the other components, similar to what we usually have in other services like DBMS, Single Sign-On, and so on.

There are many ways in which Solr can be integrated in your application. It can be used as a remote service that is external to your site or application but not publicly exposed, and this will be the most common use case. It can even be exposed directly by using a ResponseWriter, to provide results in other formats (think about the examples we made using XSLT and RSS). Or else, we can even provide a direct navigation over the data, as for the VelocityResponseWriter. As a last option, you can of course write your own components that can be used on every step in this workflow.

> There is an interesting presentation by *Brian Doll*, describing a case study for e-commerce, in which you will find a lot of important aspects at `http://www.slideshare.net/briandoll/ecommerce-4000378`, for example good language stemmers, faceting, avoiding the one-size-fits-all strategy, and others.

Solr can be used in many ways, and it can be used to speed up the procedure of finding the reference to data records that are stored in many different ways. From this point of view, it can be seen as a basic component for writing your own deduplication and fast master data management processes, obtaining an index which is really decoupled from the actual data. From this perspective, we want to play a little with the "automatic" indexing from external sources, which is provided from `DataImportHandler`. But don't worry, we don't have plans to use Solr as a general purpose tool: we only want to have overview on `DataImportHandler`.

In this scenario, the `DataImportHandler` is one of the most interesting and useful family of components. This component permits us to read data from external data sources, and index them directly and incrementally. From the configuration, we can define how to handle the records of data while reading them, in order to create at runtime a new Solr document for each one and indexing it directly. This is basically an implicit definition of an indexing workflow, and it is designed to be easily chained with the maintenance tool (using an event handler) or called as a scheduled task.

This kind of process will generally start by calling a specific handler, passing to it one of the following possible commands: `full-import`, `delta-import`, `status`, `reload-config`, `abort`. We will see these commands from the web UI interface in a while, but they can be called from the command line as well. In that case, `abort`, `reload-config`, and `status` will help us to monitor the process. With `delta-import`, we will be able to start a new indexing phase for new records. Also, `full-import` will be the most-used command as it will start a complete reading and indexing activity on our data.

The complete import in particular will support extra parameters. Some of them are quite intuitive (`clean`, `commit`, `optimize`, `debug`) and refer to the operations that we were able to perform on other handlers in previous examples. But there is also an interesting entity parameter that offers us a good starting point for learning how the process will work.

The process is described in the following diagram:

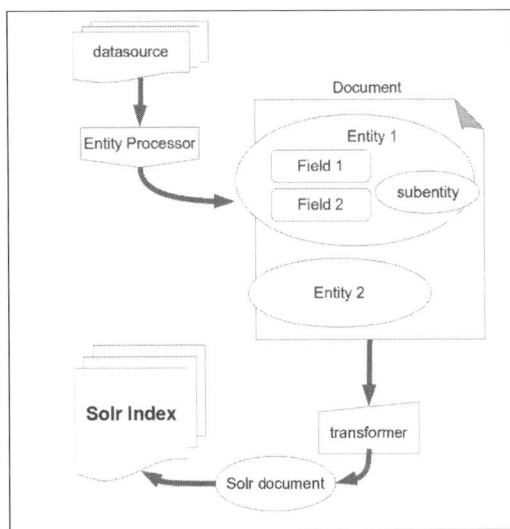

As you can see in the diagram, an entity is basically a collection of fields. We can have more than one entity for the same document, and we can even collect sub-entities. As you can imagine, the role of such entities is to collect fields into a logical container (it's similar to the logical denormalization seen before in *Chapter 7, Working with Multiple Entities, Multicores, and Distributed Search*). This is important when we are posting data on a single index, and we need to construct our document assembling data that can be read from different sources in different ways.

The main element will then be the entity itself. It should have the pk attribute to identify its instances uniquely during the indexing process, a name to be able to reuse its field's value later when needed, and a reference to one or more transformers. These components are useful to manipulate data during the workflow, just before indexing it.

From this point of view, it's simple to imagine that an entity will be always handled by a specific type of processor, to know how to handle a certain specific data type available from the data source connected to the entity. Every processor will emit a specific predefined field for the data it processes, and we can manipulate them before posting them to Solr, using the transformers.

A processor can be designed to handle a stream of data, a single line of data (a record), or collections of data. This turns out to be useful because we can collect, for example, a list of filenames with an entity, and then manipulate the content of a single file with a subentity that will use a specific processor.

When we handle the data emitted from some kind of **Entity Processor**, we have predefined fields. They can be indexed directly into an appropriate Solr schema, or we can manipulate their values and add more customized ones. Note that during prototyping, you can add almost every field, and spend time later to shape the `schema.xml` and `DataImportHandler` configuration in a more specific way.

There are many more interesting details on the `DataImportHandler` in the official wiki page: `http://wiki.apache.org/solr/DataImportHandler`. I encourage you to play with our examples while reading them, in order to become more familiar with the tool. Now, we will have a look at a simple `DataImportHandler` configuration

An initial configuration for a `DataImportHandler` is really simple, although it's intuitive to understand that complex processes on heterogeneous and structured data can be very complex depending on the schema and data manipulations. We will start our example with a simple configuration in order to fix the idea on the basic elements.

In order to define a `schema.xml` file, we don't need a lot. So, I suggest to start with a minimal one (using dynamic fields, mostly). Then, we can define a `/SolrStarterBook/solr-app/chp08/solr.xml` file as usual for handling the examples in this chapter.

What we really need to configure here is a new request handler in `solrconfig.xml` that will trigger the process. This handler will also use a library that we have to import, and most important of all, it will reference one (or more, but keep it simple) external file where we will put all the configuration specific to the `DataImportHandler`:

```
<lib dir="../../../solr/dist/" regex="solr-dataimporthandler-.*\.jar"
/>
<lib dir="${solr.solr.home}/${solr.core.name}/conf/lib/"
regex="sqlite-jdbc-.*\.jar" />
...
<requestHandler name="/dih" class="org.apache.solr.handler.dataimport.
DataImportHandler">
  <lst name="defaults">
    <str name="update.chain">data-extraction</str>
    <str name="config">DIH.xml</str>
  </lst>

...
<updateRequestProcessorChain name="data-extraction">
  <processor class="solr.StatelessScriptUpdateProcessorFactory">
    <str name="script">extract_fields.js</str>
  </processor>
  <processor class="solr.LogUpdateProcessorFactory" />
  <processor class="solr.RunUpdateProcessorFactory" />
</updateRequestProcessorChain>
```

In this example, `DIH.xml` is the name of your specific configuration (you can find it under `/SolrStarterBook/test/chp08/wgarts/conf/DIH.xml`), and you can also define multiple request handlers, as well as add multiple different configurations for the same handler. I suggest you to separate the different configurations for different sources whenever it's possible, but sometimes you need to put all of them at one place. There is no general rule for this, and it really depends on the need.

As we will see, it's possible to define a script inside the `DataImportHandler` configuration file directly. This is useful to do manipulation on the data. However, we can also bind an update chain to the `DataImportHandler` process. In the example, I have created an external `extract_fields.js` script to parse some of the data and save them into specific fields.

By using `<lib dir="${solr.solr.home}/${solr.core.name}/conf/lib/" regex="sqlite-jdbc-.*\.jar" />`, we will be able to add to the Java classpath to a local lib folder, which contains the library that we need to access the specific JDBC driver we will use. This is needed by Solr to be able to load the library and use it. Every JDBC implementation will expose a common standard interface, but we need to download the actual implementations we are going to use. So, it's very common to put here more than once.

Instead, the `${variable}` syntax is used to acquire the data that is already defined at some point in memory. In this case, they simply refer to the current Solr home and core name.

The `${some.variable.name}` format is widely used within many Java libraries and frameworks (it is also supported as a language feature in Scala). It's worth noting that Solr uses the usual convention of variable names divided with points to represent a sort of namespace. For example, by reading `${solr.core.name}` we can understand the meaning of the variable, and we can imagine to find other variables with names, such as `${solr.core.dataDir}`, `${solr.core.config}`, and `${solr.core.schema}` for other core-specific configurations. While the core configurations usually also require the restarting of a core when their values are changed, a change on entity in the DIH context does not require to reload the core.

Collecting example data from the Web Gallery of Art site

At this point, we need sample data to and we need it to be from sources other than the one from where we downloaded data before. In particular, we want to approach using the `DataImportHandler` by one of the most recurring use case: indexing the data that are actually stored on a relational database, such as Oracle, MySql, or Postgres.

In order to have data, and keep the process simple, I decided to download a free copy of the very good art database provided by the project Web Gallery of Art.

> The Web Gallery of Art is a project created by *Emil Krén* and *Daniel Marx*. The site is a kind of virtual museum for European fine arts from 11th to 19th century. You can find details on the project at `http://www.wga.hu`.

The original database is available in various formats, including MySQL; but in order to avoid installing other things and to keep the process simple, I converted it into the SQLite format. You can find the actual SQLite file database in the `SolrStarterBook/resources/db` directory.

> SQLite is a library that implements a self-contained SQL database engine, which is used by browsers such as Firefox or Chrome to save bookmarks and navigation data. We will use a SQLite Java implementation. You can find more information on the project at: `http://www.sqlite.org/`.

As we want to simulate the basic operation of a real-world use case here, I have changed the original database schema slightly, introducing a shallow normalization on the tables. You will find the final tables on the right-hand side of the following screenshot:

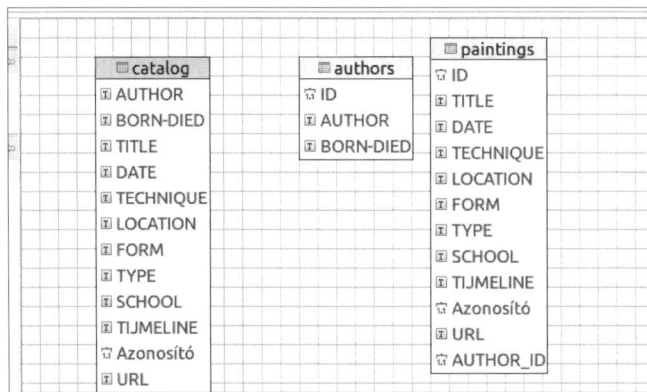

Basically, I have moved the `authors` information to a separate table, introduced an ID for every table in the right as a primary key (this is the commonly used situation), and introduced an `AUTHOR_ID` parameter on the `paintings` table to be able to perform joins between tables. In order to have the chance to play a little with the data, I decided to maintain the original names and values of the columns, so that we can manage normalization or manipulation on both of them directly during the import phase.

These little changes give us the chance to play with more than a single table at once, without introducing too much complexity. But the general approach we use on this is basically the same we can use, for instance, over data from an e-commerce sites (with far more complex schema), such as Magento or Broadleaf, or similar ones.

When using `DataImportHandler` for indexing data on a relational database, we are decoupling the search and navigation capabilities offered by Solr services from the maintenance of the actual data. This is good, because we can still perform the usual CRUD operation on the database, for example, using our CMS or backend and putting in place a parallel service to explore our data, making them easy to search.

An interesting point here is that if the navigation on the site frontend is deeply integrated on Solr services (this is possible when using Drupal, for example) that contain references to content pages, we obtain the chance of using Solr as a sort of "hot caching" the navigation to our data.

A good point to start is the QuickStart at `http://wiki.apache.org/solr/DIHQuickStart`, and we will follow a similar approach to construct our simple example.

Time for action – indexing data from a database (for example, a blog or an e-commerce website)

In this first example, we will use the most basic configuration for managing our example database. In SQL, starting from the two tables, we would write a simple `JOIN` statement similar to the following one:

```
SELECT A.AUTHOR AS artist, A.'BORN-DIED', P.*
FROM authors AS A JOIN paintings AS P ON (A.ID=P.AUTHOR_ID)
WHERE (FORM='painting')
```

Note that we have used the `char` data type to avoid problems with the field originally named `BORN-DIED`.

Once we have defined the SQL query that we want to use, we simply have to use this query from an appropriate `JDBCDataSource` and `SqlEntityprocessor`, which are defined in `DIH.xml`, as follows:

```
<dataConfig>
    <script>... HERE there is javascript code ... </script>

    <dataSource type="JdbcDataSource" driver="org.sqlite.JDBC"
    url="jdbc:sqlite:../../resources/wgarts/db/WebGalleryOfArts.sqlite"
    batchSize="1" />

    <document name="painting_document">
        <entity name="painting" pk="uri" transformer="script:normalize
    ArtistEntity, script:normalizeUri, script:generateId" query="SELECT
    A.AUTHOR AS artist, P.TITLE AS title, A.'BORN-DIED', P.LOCATION AS
    city, P.TYPE AS type, P.URL, P.TECHNIQUE AS subject FROM authors AS A
    JOIN paintings AS P ON (A.ID=P.AUTHOR_ID) WHERE (FORM='painting')">

            <field column="entity_type" template="painting" />
            <field column="entity_source" template="Web Gallery Of Arts" />

        </entity>
    </document>

</dataConfig>
```

As you can see, we have defined a new data source pointing to the file containing the database. Also, we have used our SQL query in the entity acquisition by using the query attributes. The other attributes used in entity configuration will be discussed in a while. Note that we also have a <script> section at the beginning where we can put, for example, customized JavaScript code to manipulate the data:

```
<dataConfig>
  <script><![CDATA[

  function capitalize(word) { … }

  function normalizeArtistEntity(row) { … }

  function normalizeUri(row) { … }

  // initialize a counter
  var id = 1;
  function generateId(row) {
      row.put('id', (id ++).toFixed()); // save the current counter
state in id
      return row;
  }

]]></script>
```

Note that the last function in particular can be used to generate a numeric ID during the import phase, if needed. You will find several similar examples of this technique on the Internet or on the Solr mailing list. I have placed one here just to give you an idea about what we can do.

> In this particular case, the ID variable is defined outside the scope on the function. So, it is handled as a `global` variable, and permits us to save its state between one row indexing and the next. If you have data to be handled during the process, you can consider using this technique. But, beware that using it with complex data structure can give bad performance due to large memory consumption, regardless of the intrinsic, stateless nature of the updating process components.

Once we have our `DataImportHandler` in place, we can start the Solr instance usual using `>> ./start.sh chp08`. We will have a new tab available in the admin web interface to interact with the Data Import Handler, as shown in the following screenshot:

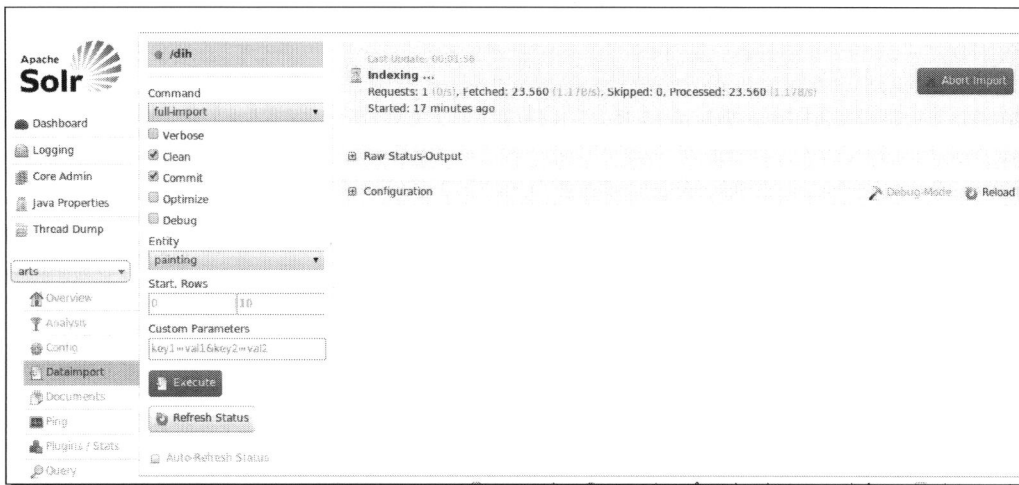

In this way, we can start a new import process by simply clicking the **Execute** button, as well as directly apply other parameters to enable cleaning of existing data, optimization, and so on. Here, the most important attribute is the choice of the import command by `command=full-import`. For example, another very useful choice would be delta import. You can still run almost the same command as usual by using cURL:

```
>> curl -H 'Content-Type:application/json; charset=UTF-8' -X POST
'http://localhost:8983/solr/wgarts/dih?command=full-import&clean=true&com
mit=true&optimize=true&debug=true&verbose=true&entity=painting&wt=json&in
dent=true'
```

Moreover, we need time to have the records correctly loaded. If you have access to the console where Solr is running, you should see the data as it is processed. If we want details to track data while indexing, we can, for example, customize the logger configuration, or even introduce and bind a specific logging component during the import phase. But this isn't important at the moment.

As a side note, we can schedule these automatic indexing jobs by `DataImportHandler`. This can be done by a cronjob (or similar scheduled activities on Windows) that uses direct calls via HTTP (using cURL, Java libraries, or whatever you prefer), or it will require a bit of customization, introducing a new listener in the Solr web application configuration. You will find the procedure details on the `DataImportHandler` wiki page (`http://wiki.apache.org/solr/DataImportHandler#Scheduling`). We prefer to focus on a single simple configuration as we have to understand the main concepts.

What just happened?

In this example, we are using a lot of things. Let's see them one by one in detail then.

First of all, in this case we obviously use a data source specific for our JDBC connection, by using `type="JdbcDataSource"` and `driver="org.sqlite.JDBC"`. The data source is pointed at our database file, with `url="jdbc:sqlite:local-path"` using a relative path. Note that we did not define any username and password pair, because SQLite does not require them; but when you use a common RDBMS, you have to define them by a configuration similar to the following one:

```
<dataSource type="JdbcDataSource" name="paintings" driver="com.mysql.
jdbc.Driver" url="jdbc:mysql://my_host/db_name" user="db_username"
password="db_password"/>
```

Then, we have defined our `painting_document` value, which internally make use of a root entity as a container of fields.

This `painting` entity will emit every field projected into the SQL query (from the SELECT statement, with its original name or alias, if defined). So, we will have a BORN-DIED field, as well as a `city` field in place of LOCATION. In addition to these fields which are bound automatically, we have adopted two fixed-value fields for transcribing information about the type of resource indexed (this is similar to what we have already done in *Chapter 7, Working with Multiple Entities, Multicores, and Distributed Search*, for multiple entities) and the source of this information. For example, by writing `column="entity_source"` and `template="Web Gallery Of Art"`, we are defining a new field named `entity_source` that will contain the text defined "statically" by the `template` attribute. Note that these two fields can contain values generated by manipulating the entity data itself, because they will be created while handling the `painting` entity. This is very useful, because we can perform several different tasks in this way, from simply renaming a field to extracting content with RegEx, and much more. In this particular case, however, we simply want to write a constant value; so the use of template is needed to define the actual data to be inserted in the field.

Furthermore, our `painting` entity can define one or more **transformer**. Transformers are defined in the opposite section, and could be written using JavaScript. We can think about every function defined in the script section as a *callback* to manipulate Java objects directly via a transparent interface, in a similar way as what we already saw when using an update script. For example, the following code:

```
function normalizeUri(row) {
  var text = row.get('URL').toString();
  var uri = text.split('#')[1];
  row.put('uri', uri);
  return row;
}
```

The preceding code has been used to remove the trailing # character in the original URL data, which was (for some reason) originally transcribed in the form, `#http://path-to-something#`.

> We didn't explicitly pass the row parameter to the function in the `transformer="script:normalizeUri"` part since the function is used as a callback. The first parameter will be passed from Solr itself. This particular parameter is a JavaScript wrapper for the `java.util.HashMap` class, which Solr uses internally for managing the actual data for a row. A Java HashMap is a simple collection of key-value pairs. Once we understand this, we can simply use code to extract the data without # and put it into a new field named `uri`. To define a new field, all we need to do here is simply put a new value in the HashMap, associating the key URI to it. When the modified row is returned, it will include the new fields. Of course, every entity will need a `pk` attribute to uniquely identify the record in the index. We can find the unique data in the record, or we can even decide to use our new URI field for that. This should give you an idea on the power of this scripting part. Please refer to the code in detail for a look at how the other example functions are defined to perform minor normalizations.

Once the importing process (which is actually an automatic indexing process) has successfully ended, we can, for example, verify that we have correctly obtained our results by using the following grouping query:

```
>> curl -X GET 'http://localhost:8983/solr/wgarts/select?q=*%3A*&start=0&rows=1&wt=json&fl=title,artist_entity,artist&group=true&group.field=artist_entity&group.limit=-1&group.cache.percent=100&json.nl=map'
```

We will obtain an output similar to one given in the following screenshot:

```
- grouped: {
  - artist_entity: {
      matches: 23560,
    - groups: [
      - {
          groupValue: "nicolaes berchem",
        - doclist: {
            numFound: 22,
            start: 0,
          - docs: [
            - {
              - title: [
                  "Return from the Falcon Hunt"
                ],
                artist_entity: "Nicolaes Berchem",
              - artist: [
                  "BERCHEM, Nicolaes"
                ]
              },
            - {
              - title: [
                  "Rocky Landscape with Antique Ruins"
                ],
                artist_entity: "Nicolaes Berchem",
              - artist: [
                  "BERCHEM, Nicolaes"
```

While asking for grouping, we ask the results to be cached (in this case, we cache every record, 100 percent is defined via `group.cache.percent=100`). We don't want to limit the number of records for a specific group (`group.limit=-1`), but we want to obtain a single group at a time (`rows=1, when using group=on`). If you will handle this data directly via JavaScript, you again have a fast overview on that; and if we imagine multiple entities and data sources, we can even imagine using Solr as a centralized data hub to have a general access over our data reference and a wide overview.

In the previous screenshot, you should notice that we have been able to generate a new `artist_entity` field, which has the same format as in the previous chapters. We will preserve the original AUTHOR field just to see what is happening.

Obviously, you can obtain a detailed and fast view on the data by asking for a facet on `artist_entity` once the data has been correctly imported using the following command:

```
>> curl -X GET 'http://localhost:8983/solr/wgarts/select?q=*:*&start=0&ro
ws=0&wt=json&facet=on&facet.field=artist_entity&json.nl=map'
```

We can also try to make use of joins/shards capabilities (because the schemas are quite the same) between this core and the arts that were defined previously; but this can be done just as an exercise, following the same steps seen in the previous chapter.

Time for action – handling sub-entities (for example, joins on complex data)

In most cases, we will not necessarily find plain records while reading the data from external sources. So, you should be able to define sub-entities by "navigating" some kind of data structure to eventually construct our full Solr document. We can collect fields at the document level, at the entity root level, and at every level on sub-entities, whenever we are able to read the corresponding data. Because relational databases are used in many contexts, this approach is useful in a wide number of scenarios when we have to index the existing data for an e-commerce site, blog, or an application. In these cases in particular, being able to work with a divide-and-conquer approach could be a strong improvement in our way to proceed.

In order to keep things as simple as possible, we can use the same data as the previous example, from another point of view. Initially, we used the SQL JOIN query to return a collection of single plain records, creating a tuple that combines data from two different tables (and you know there can be many more such tuples). A tuple is an ordered list of elements, usually an "abstract" record in SQL. A good, simple (and funny) reference site for SQL statements is: `http://sqlzoo.net/wiki/Main_Page`.

Even if from the SQL point of view we are handling tuples for the actual records, from the DataImportHandler point of view we can simply see them as rows of data. Once it is able to read them, there is not much distinction between them and a line read from a textual file. This idea is simple and yet useful, because even if we are reading content with SQL now, we can apply the same approach to a very different data source, pretty much in the same way as in the following example.

So, another approach could be, reading a row of data from the first table (paintings) and searching for a collection of related row in the second table (authors). This can be done as follows:

```
<document name="paintingBy_author_document">
  <entity name="painting_by_author" pk="uri"
    transformer="script:normalizeUri"
    rootEntity="true"
    query="SELECT * FROM paintings AS P WHERE (P.FORM='painting')">

    <field column="entity_type" template="painting" />
    <field column="entity_source" template="Web Gallery Of Art" />

    <entity name="author" pk="A.ID"
      rootEntity="false"
      transformer="script:normalizeArtistEntity"
      query="SELECT * FROM authors AS A WHERE (A.ID='${painting_by_
author.AUTHOR_ID}')" />

  </entity>
</document>
```

In the code, I have used the selected * statement to improve readability. If you want, you can find the full projections in the configuration for a specific wgarts_sub example core. Note how the transformers are used here on a per-entity basis.

Remember that at the moment, we are not thinking about performance or the best ways to handle this kind of data from a SQL point of view here, we are only exploring possibilities using the same data, introducing sub-entities as an exercise. Our intention is to do a comparison with the previous example.

However, the consideration about performance is not trivial when using sub-entities in particular, especially when we have to manage lots of data and joins.

To get a more specific idea please read: http://wiki.apache.org/solr/DataImportHandlerDeltaQueryViaFullImport.

What just happened?

In this case, we have divided the problem into two parts. Without using the SQL JOIN query, we are designing the reading of data to be indexed in two steps: a main step for the entity `paintings` and a dependent step for the entity `authors`.

Selecting a list of "rows" representing `paintings` is really simple, and it is done as follows:

```
SELECT P.*
FROM paintings AS P WHERE (FORM='painting')
```

After this, all we have to do is look up the data about an `author` related to this particular `painting` using the following code:

```
SELECT * FROM authors AS A WHERE (A.ID='${painting_by_author.AUTHOR_
ID}')
```

Here, we are using an internal binding in the `${entity_name.field_name}` form for selecting the current value of an author ID. Then, we use it as a select criteria on a very specific and fast query.

We have adopted an explicit `rootEntity` parameter here, just to suggest that when you handle two or more entities, you can have situations where you need to read from a `container` entity. This will not be the one in which you are most interested. For example, if you're reading a filesystem, and you are mostly interested in file metadata, you will still need to explore folders as root entities in order to inspect the files contained in each folder.

The transformers are applied here on a per-entity basis, and this is probably slightly more readable.

If you want to have a wider idea on the kind of transformers you can use for our projects, there is a very informative page on wiki that will give us references: `https://cwiki.apache.org/confluence/display/solr/Uploading+Structured+Data+Store+Data+with+the+Data+Import+Handler`.

Time for action – indexing incrementally using delta imports

Once we understand the basic elements for handling entities during the construction of a document structure to be posted to Solr with JDBC, we can, for example, write our own script to manage this kind of operation on a scheduled interval of time (think about scheduled task on a Windows machine or crontab on *nix machines). A scheduled script will use the `command=delta-import` parameter, as given in the following command:

```
>> curl -H 'Content-Type:application/json; charset=UTF-8' -X POST
'http://localhost:8983/solr/wgarts/dih?command=delta-import&commit=true&w
t=json&indent=true'
```

And, it will need the following internal query to resume its activity:

```
<document name="painting_document_delta">
  <entity name="painting_delta" pk="uri" transformer="..."
    query="SELECT * FROM authors AS A JOIN paintings AS P ON (A.ID=P.
AUTHOR_ID) WHERE (P.FORM='painting')"
    deltaImportQuery="SELECT * FROM authors AS A JOIN paintings AS P
ON (A.ID=P.AUTHOR_ID) WHERE (P.FORM='painting' AND P.ID='${dih.delta.
id}')"
    deltaQuery="SELECT P.ID FROM paintings AS P WHERE (last_update
&gt; '${dih.last_index_time}')" >

    <field column="entity_type" template="painting" />
    <field column="entity_source" template="Web Gallery Of Art" />
  </entity>
</document>
```

In this case, to improve readability, we have omitted minor details that have not changed from the previous examples.

What just happened?

This example should be read mostly as a draft. A suggestion on how to add the delta import definition for a JDBC indexing (if you want to look at a complete example, you will find it at `/SolrStarterBook/solr-app/chp08/wgarts_delta`).

The first interesting element here is the `deltaQuery="SELECT P.ID FROM..."` statement by itself. By using this query, we are in fact projecting only the unique ID for the most recent (newly added) resources. Note that we use an internal `${dih.last_index_time}` variable to identify the last index time for a resource. Moreover, the > comparator needs to be written as `&gt;` for compatibility with the XML syntax.

Once we have found a row to be indexed by its own `ID`, a `deltaImportQuery` is finally triggered. Note that this query will generally contain a clause that will use this `ID` value (by selecting only the relative row), or we will index every single row, every time. Note how the `P.ID='${dih.delta.id}'` parameter is used to select rows from the ID that will be emitted from the other time-based query.

When an indexing is performed using the `DataImportHandler`, a properties file will be produced. This is a simple textual file with the name `dih.properties`, which has a simple internal structure similar to the following one:

```
#Mon Sep 01 18:32:11 CEST 2013
f.last_index_time=2013-09-01 19\:24\:38
last_index_time=2013-09-01 19\:32\:03
files.last_index_time=2013-09-01 19\:32\:03
```

Note that this can be manually edited (if needed) to give default values also to the delta import process. It will be overwritten when a new running process will start with the updated values.

Time for action – indexing CSV (for example, open data)

There are times when we can use external CSV files. This is not unusual, because it's very simple and easy to work with Excel or similar spreadsheet tools and save the data on a text-separated format (the most widely used are CSV and TSV). We already saw that Solr supports the indexing of CSV via an update handler, so it's not surprising at all that we could handle some of these files with a `DataImportHandler` processor, as follows:

```
<dataSource name="fds" type="FileDataSource" encoding="UTF-8" />
<document>
  <entity name="files"
    dataSource="null"
    rootEntity="false"
    processor="FileListEntityProcessor"
    baseDir="${solr.solr.home}/../../resources"
    fileName=".*\.csv"
    onError="abort"
    newerThan="${dataimporter.last_index_time}"
    transformer="script:console"
    recursive="true">
  <entity name="csv_file"
    processor="LineEntityProcessor"
    url="${files.fileAbsolutePath}"
    dataSource="fds"
    transformer="RegexTransformer">
  <field column="rawLine"
      regex="^(.*);(.*);(.*)$"
      groupNames="AUTHOR,TITLE,URL" />
    <field column="URL" name="uri"  />
  </entity>
</document>
```

In this case, we have defined a subentity that does all the work, reading from a local file—even if we would have pointed directly to a URL containing the file. With this approach, we will be able to index every new CSV file in a specific folder. This can be useful for some tasks.

What just happened?

The external entity here uses a `FileListEntityProcessor` only to obtain a list of files to be processed (in our specific case, we have a single `/SolrStarterBook/resources/wgarts/csv/catalog.csv` file; but if you want to test the configuration, you can split the file into multiple ones, or simply add a new file). The base folder is relative to the active Solr instance we started, and it will emit a list of filenames ending with the `.csv` suffix. Here, the last import time is crucial when you have to manage multiple imports.

In this case, all the real processing is handled by a `LineEntityProcessor`. This particular processor will read the textual content, emitting a line at a time. So, it's up to us to correctly process the field for each line. In order to maintain readability, I only projected three fields in the previous example; but you will find the complete configuration in the `/SolrStarterBook/solr-app/chp08/csv` directory. A `LineEntityProcessor` always emits a raw line, which contains all the text read for that line. By using a `RegexTransformer`, we can extract specific part of the line to produce new fields.

In the example, we want to have only three fields for each row, separated by `char`; we will eventually assign the correct name to them by the `groupNames` attribute. There is some similarity with the definition of a common `INSERT INTO` syntax for databases. The names of the fields where the current values are to be put should be declared in the exact order, and should be separated by a `,` character. We can read the data in the same way even from the remote sources. (Remember we are using an URL, not a simple file path! So it can either be `file:///some_path` or `http://some_path`.) We can assemble different sources and we can continue using custom JavaScript transformers to fix problems with data.

> As a general recipe, I strongly suggest to adopt the UTF-8 encoding explicitly whenever possible. In contexts such as rapid prototyping, automatic remote open data indexing, or some kind of search over share documents, it would be useful to define a list of paths and links and save it on a textual file. In this way, you can change the external entity and emit a list of resources to be indexed directly by a `LineEntityProcessor`. This can be useful sometimes to move faster, and it's simple to change later to a more appropriate solution.

Once we have seen how to manage an external entity to iterate over a collection of files and emit their list names (or URLs), it's simple to apply the same strategy to different file types, adopting a different processor if necessary.

Time for action – importing Solr XML document files

In the previous chapters of this book, we had the chance to produce and save several XML files containing well-formatted Solr documents. A simple idea would be to configure a `DataImportHandler` to be able to acquire new Solr documents by a specific folder, where we will put them as soon as they are produced.

The basic part of the new configuration will be very similar to the previous one:

```
<dataSource name="fds" encoding="UTF-8" type="FileDataSource" />
<document>
  <entity name="files" processor="FileListEntityProcessor"
    baseDir="${solr.solr.home}/../../resources"
    fileName=".*\.xml">

    <entity pk="uri"
      name="file"
      format="text"
      processor="XPathEntityProcessor"
      url="${files.fileAbsolutePath}"
      useSolrAddSchema="true"
      rootEntity="true"
      dataSource="fds"
      stream="true"
      onError="skip" />

  </entity>
</document>
```

You can find the full configuration at `/SolrStarterBook/solr-app/chp08/solr_docs`.

What just happened?

In this case, we are listing the saved XML files representing Solr documents that were created from our initial DBpedia resources, and then we process every single XML code with a specific `XPathEntityProcessor`. This processor can be used by default to emit an XML result in the Solr format (here, we are also explicitly specifying this option by using `useSolrAddSchema="true"`; but it's not mandatory as it is the default). Because we adopted this default format, we really don't have to specify lot of things. For example, we can skip files that cause an error (`onError="skip"`), every resource handled by this processor will coincide to a root entity (`rootEntity="true"`). Most important of all, we adopted the `stream="true"` parameter in order to achieve a minor impact on performance, because the XML files can be too resource intensive to be loaded fully into memory by using `XPathEntityProcessor` with XML

Once we understand how the `XPathEntityProcessor` works in practice, it's also simple to use it on a very wide variety of XML files. Let's look at how to index the dataset dump of Wikipedia. This is described in the official wiki section at: `http://wiki.apache.org/solr/DataImportHandler#Example:_Indexing_wikipedia`. This example will require some time due to the huge amount of data; but if you follow the examples, you should be able to apply it to your own experiments. So, I suggest you to play with it as the next step.

Just to give you an idea, a similar extraction of data can also be performed directly on the RDF/XML files we previously downloaded from DBpedia. A simple skeleton of a configuration for the root entity could be similar to the following code:

```
<entity name="file"
  processor="XPathEntityProcessor"
  pk="uri"
  dataSource="files"
  stream="true"
  forEach="/RDF/Description"
  onError="skip"
  rootEntity="true"
  url="${files.fileAbsolutePath}"
  xsl="xslt/post.xsl"
  transformer="script:console" >

  <field column="artist" xpath="/RDF/Description/title"
commonField="true" />
  <field column="subject" xpath="/RDF/Description/subject"
commonField="true" />
  <field column="uri" xpath="/RDF/Description/title"
commonField="true" />
  <field column="title" xpath="/RDF/Description/title" />
</entity>
```

As you can see, it's simple to iterate over a list of root elements in the file (for example on all the /RDF/Description elements), specifying a forEach parameter. Then, we can project a value for every field by simply pointing it with its own XPath expression. What is interesting here is that we are currently not using the explicit form /rdf:RDF/rdf:Description, including prefixes, because they are not required here. Moreover, even if the forEach parameter is used to acquire the list of root elements, the XPath expression used for fields are not relative and there is some minor limitation. For example, abbreviation via the // characters should not be used. Also, note that this usage of the XPathProcessor needs well-formed XML data. This is not true while indexing over RDF/XML serialization (for example in our case, there are many problems in the files downloaded from DBpedia) or even on simple HTML that can be written violating the requirements for XML. In these cases, you should write your own code or adopt a custom script to index your data (as we already do for ours), normalize the data from the scripting counterpart when possible, or finally, you can still use the DataImportHandler after introducing a custom components to sanitize the data.

Importing data from another Solr instance

As we saw, using a standard Solr XML structure allows us to index them with `DataImportHandler` without problems. A similar and even more direct approach can be used, if needed, for "importing" data from another Solr instance. For example, if we would like to import documents from the cities core, we can do it using the following code:

```
<dataconfig>
  <document>
    <entity name="city" processor="SolrEntityProcessor" query="*:*"
url="http://localhost:8983/solr/cities" />
  </document>
</dataconfig>
```

As far as I know, this is not very widely used; but it is however useful, simple to adopt, and good to know in advance when needed.

Indexing emails

Indexing emails can be as simple as adopting a configuration similar to the following one:

```
<document>
  <entity
    name="emails"
    processor="MailEntityProcessor"
    user="username@mail_provider.com"
    password="password"
    host="imap.gmail.com"
    protocol="imaps"
    recurse="true"
    folders="INBOX,SENT"
  transformer="script:generateId" />
</document>
```

In this way, we can construct a simple assisted search (even with faceting!) that can really help us to manage mail conversations and attachments. As far as I know, there isn't any specific `CalendarEntityProcessor`, and writing this can be a good exercise for starting the acquisition of knowledge needed to write customized components.

Time for action – indexing rich documents (for example, PDF)

So, here we are. We have seen many simple, yet different ways to index documents in Solr; starting from the initial examples (based on direct indexing on PDF, using a Tika extraction), followed by a "manual" indexing using cURL and HTTP (and this is the most widely used case), and finally adopting one or more specific `DataImportHandler` configurations. At this point, we can close this circle by seeing how to index rich documents (PDF in particular, but also others) by using Tika again for metadata and text extraction, but this time with a `DataImportHandler` processor.

We will define a new core in `/SolrStarterBook/solr-app/chp08/tika`, which will be almost identical to the previous one. First of all, we have to verify that the required libraries are correctly added in our `solrconfig.xml` configuration file:

```
<lib dir="../../../solr/dist/" regex="solr-dataimporthandler-.*\.jar"
/>
<lib dir="../../../solr/contrib/extraction/lib" />
<lib dir="../../../solr/dist/" regex="solr-cell-\d.*\.jar" />A
```

Once the imports are corrected, we have to configure a binary data source for the import handler. We will handle the binary files with a specific `TikaEntityProcessor` as follows:

```
<dataSource name="bin" type="BinFileDataSource" />
<document>
  <entity name="files" dataSource="null"
    rootEntity="false"
    processor="FileListEntityProcessor"
    baseDir="${solr.solr.home}/../../resources/arts_pdf"
    fileName=".*"
    onError="skip"
    transformer="script:console"
    recursive="true">
    <field column="fileAbsolutePath" name="path" />
    <entity pk="uri" name="file"
      dataSource="bin"
      processor="TikaEntityProcessor"
      url="${files.fileAbsolutePath}"
      format="text"
      rootEntity="true"
      onError="skip">
      <field column="Author" name="author" meta="true" />
      <field column="title" name="title" meta="true" />
      <field column="text" name="text" />
      <field column="fileSize" name="size" />
      <field column="fileLastModified" name="lastmodified" />
```

```
        </entity>
      </entity>
    </document>
```

In the example, we are using some common fields; but obviously we can use every single metadata field emitted by the Tika processor. If you are not familiar with Tika, you can still define a script transformer and start printing all the fields emitted, to decide what you want and whether you need to manipulate the values during the indexing phase.

What just happened?

This processor uses Tika to extract common metadata (based on dublin core and others) from rich documents. We will obtain very commonly used metadata with Tika, depending on the type of binary file indexed. A MIDI file can offer musical notations and lyrics, an image can contain its own EXIF data, and a PDF file will have at least an author, title, and a raw, unstructured, unparsed plain text. The latter will be always emitted by a specific text field.

Using a `format="text"` parameter is the default parameter, and it will produce a plain text containing all the content for an MS Word or PDF file. Beware that this can produce a very dirty file, so sometimes it can be better to obtain a `format="xml"` version of the same data in order to be able to handle the XML data produced with an `XPathProcessor` too.

Adding more consideration about tuning

Using `DataImportHandler` is usually a good chance to make considerations about performance and tuning of a Solr installation. For example, while indexing we can suffer through problems that are mostly dependent on memory usage (of both the index and the documents to be posted), merge time, and optimization time.

These kinds of problems can be reduced by using the `omitNorms="true"` parameter and studying a good value for the `mergeFactor` parameter, both in `schema.xml`. Merging is critical because it introduces an overhead, and it's easy to consider the same problem with optimization.

A good list of the factors in which we are interested for understanding the performance can be assembled from the following two wiki pages:

+ `http://wiki.apache.org/solr/SolrPerformanceFactors`
+ `http://wiki.apache.org/solr/SolrPerformanceProblems`

Critical elements can be assumed to be on an extensive use of faceting, lot of sort parameters, and the memory related to a huge index or very big documents to be indexed.

Understanding Java Virtual Machine, threads, and Solr

Solr runs on a **Java Virtual Machine** (**JVM**), and its own performance relies on a good configuration on that, based on things such as memory, encoding, and threads management.

In order to manage memory allocation correctly, one of the best approaches is using tools like jconsole that are connected to a running JVM. It gives us very detailed information about the usage of memory and—most important of all—on the minimum requirement for it. Identifying good values for that is a very common problem indeed.

To avoid problems with memory consumption and free memory available during runtime, we can easily pass a specific parameter to the JVM while starting Solr. For example:

```
>> java -Xms512M -Xmx1024M -XX:ThreadStackSize=128 -jar start.jar
```

This command can be used to tell the virtual machine to adopt a heap size of 512 MB, and the maximum available memory for the JVM. `-XX:ThreadStackSize` or `-Xss` can be used instead to manage the memory allocated for local resources of the threads in memory.

> Reading from articles at `http://www.vogella.com/articles/JavaPerformance/article.html` makes it clear that another critical element is based on garbage collector policies. If you can choose between more than one JVM implementation, consider reading about what kind of garbage collector strategy is used. If you are a programmer, try to write code that is stateless and as concurrent as possible. This is because allocating and releasing memory for new objects is more garbage-collector friendly than acting from time to time to big referenced objects.

I found an improvement in performance with the adoption of an actor system, such as AKKA that supports both Java and Scala, for writing concurrent code to post new data on Solr. This avoids typical synchronization problems that are faced by the data isolation when using actors.

Choosing the correct directory for implementation

Ideally, we can imagine Solr to handle all documents in memory. Even if this kind of implementation does exist (`solr.RAMDirectoryFactory`), it is only useful for testing purposes as it is volatile by nature and it does not scale at all! What we have really adopted in our previous examples are disk-based implementations, in which a binary format is used to fast access the records on disk without the need to having them already in memory all the times. In this scenario, there are two crucial points of possible failures: the need for caching to improve performance, and the underlying filesystem where we are actually writing our own data. We have adopted `solr.MMapDirectoryFactory` for most as it designed to work on 64-bit systems and internally uses an I/O cache capability by the virtual machine, so it's either fast or works well on multithreads. This implementation replaced the previous local implementations that had problems with lots of threads (`solr.SimpleFSDirectoryFactory`) and are very slow on Microsoft platforms (`solr.NIOFSDirectoryFactory`).

If you are unsure about what implementation to adopt, you can always use the default on `solr.StandardDirectoryFactory`, as described in `http://wiki.apache.org/solr/SolrCaching`.

From a distributed and real-time point of view, things are evolving fast. At the moment of writing this book, we have a `solr.NRTCachingDirectoryFactory` at our disposal, which is designed to expand the capability of a `MMapDirectoryFactory` in the direction of near real-time search by storing part of the data into an in-memory, transparent cache.

> For reading about near, real-time search, I would suggest you to start from the CAP theorem at `http://en.wikipedia.org/wiki/CAP_theorem`, which is used for designing the strategy behind many current NoSQL and distributed filesystem products.

A simple workaround of these problems is to adopt solrcloud, and spread a large index over several shards, so that every single instance will suffer minor heap problems. Other experiments were done in the past on storing indexes on a database backend, but they intrinsically produce bad performance, as far as I know. In the past few years, there have been many experiments on using distributed filesystems or even NoSQL storage. So, we can expect really good improvements in the future.

Adopting Solr cache

Solr provides three levels of caching management: Filter, Document, and Query cache. You should probably notice that what is really missed here is a Field level; it does exist, but it is an internal caching level managed directly from Lucene. So, we cannot handle it directly, unless we want to provide our custom implementation.

However, most of the caching needed at the Field level are really manageable from the document. This component will manage a cache of documents and their stored fields. You don't really need to cache only indexed fields, as they are already used to construct the index and caching them makes no sense.

A typical example configuration for a Filter cache is, for example:

```
<filterCache    class="solr.LRUCache"
        initialSize="4096" size="16384"
        autowarmCount="4096"/>
```

The other cache type will be very similar, and they always include a minimum allocation and a dynamic max value. The class used here depends on the chosen strategy for caching, and lastly the autowarm parameter is really important to load at the start along with other common values, reducing the need to reload them later.

The Filter cache is instead more focused on caching the mostly used filters combinations and the most recurring terms from faceting.

The Query cache is probably the most intuitive, and it is similar to what we expect. It simply provides caching for results of queries.

If you want to know more on caching visit http://wiki.apache.org/solr/SolrCaching.

Time for action – indexing artist data from Tate Gallery and DBpedia

Finally, we can create an example involving more than a single data source. We will use the Open Data of the well-known Tate Gallery (http://www.tate.org.uk/), recently released with GitHub in different formats (https://github.com/tategallery/collection).

1. The first thing we will need at the start is the CSV file containing metadata about the artists in the repository: https://github.com/tategallery/collection/blob/master/artist_data.csv.

2. We will augment those metadata with information from DBpedia. We will use just the essentials to keep the example simple; but you can easily add more fields for an exercise. We will define a new Tate core (in /SolrStarterBook/solr-app/chp08/) using the same configuration from the previous examples for the schema.xml and solrconfig.xml files.

3. In solrconfig.xml, we can add the usual import using one of the following configurations:

    ```
    <lib dir="../../../solr/dist/" regex="solr-dataimporthandler-.*\.
    jar" />
    <lib dir="${SOLR_DIST}/../dist/" regex="solr-
    dataimporthandler-.*\.jar" />
    ```

4. Then, we can consider adding a propertyWriter configuration to customize the format used to save the last indexing time.

    ```
    <propertyWriter  type="SimplePropertiesWriter"
        dateFormat="yyyy-MM-dd HH:mm:ss" locale="en_US"
        directory="data" filename="dih_tate.properties" />
    ```

5. The last step will be writing the specific DIH.xml file for this example:

    ```
    <dataConfig>

    <script><![CDATA[
    function fixCSV(row) {
      var line_fixed = row.get('rawLine')
        .replaceAll(",\\s+",":::::").replaceAll(",",";")
        .replaceAll(":::::",",").replaceAll("\"(.*?)\"","$1");
    ```

```
    row.put('rawLine_fixed', line_fixed);
    java.lang.System.out.println("#### FIXED:\n"+line_fixed+"\n\n");
    return row;
}
function console(row) {
    java.lang.System.out.println("#### ROWS:\n"+row.keySet()+"\
n\n");
    return row;
}
var id = 1;
function GenerateId(row) {
    row.put('id', (id ++).toFixed());
    return row;
}
]]></script>

    <dataSource
      name="source_url" type="URLDataSource"
      baseUrl="https://raw.github.com"
      encoding="UTF-8"
      connectionTimeout="5000" readTimeout="10000" />

    <document>

    <entity
      name="artist"
      processor="LineEntityProcessor"
      url="/tategallery/collection/master/artist_data.csv"
      stream="true"
      dataSource="source_url"
      onError="skip"
      newerThan="${dataimporter.last_index_time}"
      transformer="TemplateTransformer, script:fixCSV,
RegexTransformer, script:console">

      <field column="rawLine_fixed"
      regex="^(.*);(.*);(.*);(.*);(.*);(.*);(.*);(.*);(.*)$"
         groupNames="id,name,gender, dates, yearOfBirth,
yearOfDeath, placeOfBirth, placeOfDeath,url" />

        <field column="url" name="uri" />
        <field column="doc_type" template="artist" />

        <entity name="dbpedia_lookup"
                processor="XPathEntityProcessor"
                stream="true"
                forEach="/ArrayOfResult/Result"
                onError="skip"
```

```
                    rootEntity="true"
                    url="http://lookup.dbpedia.org/api/search.asmx/Keywo
        rdSearch?QueryString=${artist.name}"
                    transformer="script:console" >

              <field column="dbpedia_uri"
                xpath="/ArrayOfResult/Result/URI"
                commonField="true" />
              <field column="dbpedia_description"
                xpath="/ArrayOfResult/Result/Description"
                commonField="true" />
              <field column="doc_type" template="dbpedia_lookup" />

          </entity>

        </entity>

      </document>

    </dataConfig>
```

6. Once the core configuration is ready, we can start the data import process directly from the web interface, as in the previous examples. The process will index the metadata for every artist, adding information from DBpedia when they can be retrieved. Looking at the upper part of the following screenshot we can see how the original data looks, and in the lower part we can see how the data will be expanded for this simple example.

In my case, the full import requires about 10 minutes, but this time can vary depending on your computer and network.

What just happened?

First of all, we will define as usual the import of the library JAR needed. In this case, I will write two different configurations that can be used for this. The `${SOLR_DIST}` variable, in particular, acts as the placeholder for the value of a corresponding environment variable passed during the Solr startup just as in Java `DSOLR_DIST=$SOLR_DIST -Dsolr.solr.home=/path/to/solr/home/ -jar start.jar`.

The `propertyWriter` configuration is useful because it can be used to customize the format of the temporal mark saved for tracking the last index/update operation. These customizations permit us to define a specific date format of our choice (but I suggest you to adopt the standard format, `yyyy-MM-dd HH:mm:ss` unless you have very specific motivation), and change the data directory where to update the property file, or simply the name of this file.

As we already saw, the example includes a script part where the JavaScript syntax is encapsulated using the CDATA part in order to avoid breaking the XML validity. In the scripts, we can sanitize the format of a single CSV row; while the other functions are similar to previous examples.

This example will use two entities: the first representing metadata for a resource from the Tate source, the second representing data from DBpedia about a specific resource. While we read data from the first entity, we will be able to look up on DBpedia and finally construct a single Solr document. From this point of view, the entity `artist` is the primary entity in this example. We will start by reading the CSV file from an `URLDataSource` data source, then we will index one artist at a time, using a `LineEntityProcessor`. Note that the data is not stored on the local machine. Using different transformers, we will fix the data format (saving the results in `rawLine_fixed`), and finally split the single `rawLine_fixed` parameter into multiple fields. During the indexing phase, it's possible to take the `${artist.name}` parameter emitted by the first entity and use the value for a lookup on the DBpedia API. If a corresponding page is found, we will use XPath to extract data and add it to our original document. At the end of this process, we will be able to intercept user queries containing terms that are not in the original metadata, because we would have indexed our examples on the fields added from DBpedia too.

Using DataImportHandler

I suggest you to read the following articles that would help you to have a broader idea of the adoptions of the `DataImportHandler` and the related components for real-world situations:

- Refer to the article at `http://solr.pl/en/2010/10/11/data-import-handler-%E2%80%93-how-to-import-data-from-sql-databases-part-1/`
- Refer to the article at `http://docs.lucidworks.com/display/lweug/Indexing+Binary+Data+Stored+in+a+Database`

♦ Refer to the article at `http://searchhub.org/2013/06/27/poor-mans-entity-extraction-with-solr/`

Pop quiz

Q1. What is the `DataImportHandler`?

1. The DIH is a library of components which can be used to index data from external data sources.

2. The DIH is a component which can be used to index data from external data sources.

3. The DIH is a library of components which can be used to index data from external Solr installation.

Q2. Is DIH a way to replace a direct HTTP posting of documents?

1. Yes, the `DataImportHandler` is used to index documents without using the HTTP posting.

2. No, as the `DataImportHandler` internally posts the data via HTTP posting.

Q3. What is the relationship between entities in DIH and a Solr index?

1. An entity in DIH is used as a collection of fields. These fields can be indexed on a compatible Solr schema. The Solr schema must explicitly define the entities handled by DIH.

2. An entity in DIH is the collection of fields defined by the corresponding Solr schema for a core.

3. An entity in DIH is used as a collection of fields. These fields can be indexed on a compatible Solr schema. However the Solr schema does not explicitly define the entities handled by DIH.

Q4. What are the data formats emitted by a DIH processor?

1. Every DIH emits the same standard Solr format.

2. Every DIH emits a single row which is internally handled as an HashMap, where the key/value pairs represent the fields used in the specific core.

3. Every DIH emits a stream of rows, one by one, which is internally handled as an HashMap, where the key/value pairs represent the fields used in the specific core.

Q5. Does the DIH provide an internal way to schedule tasks?

1. No, at the moment it should be programmed with a specific component, or using a schedule tool invoking the delta-import command.

2. Yes, using the delta-import command it's possible to also provide the time for the next start of the indexing process.

Summary

In this chapter we had the chance to play with the `DataImportHandler`, which is a powerful facility that is designed to configure an indexing workflow from external sources of Solr, without using external programming. In most cases, these techniques will not. However, replace the need for programming our own components or our specific workflow, but should be read more as a skeleton in which we can put our own custom configurations or components for handling our data.

We saw how DIH helps us to decouple an indexing process from external sources, such as files, mail, database, and even other Solr installations. Finally, we reviewed some of the concerns regarding performance that are often encountered while indexing large amounts of data with `DataImportHandler`.

9
Introducing Customizations

In this chapter, we will introduce paths for customizations.

First of all, we will see how to handle the Solr core configurations in a more flexible way, so that it is compatible with the new standard that will become mandatory from Version 5.

Then, we will focus on the language analysis, starting from the adoption of a widely used stemmer, and moving to the creation of a very simple named Entity Recognizer. This process will give us the possibility to introduce a quick and easy way to create new plugins. We will use th=e Scala language for this because of its simplicity, and we will create the base for a new ResponseWriter. Then, it's up to you to complete its development.

Looking at the Solr customizations

This is the last chapter, and will be a little different from the previous ones, because it will involve writing code for some of our examples.

Once we learn how to manage the basic components and typical configurations for common Solr usage, it's important to have an idea of where to start for specific customizations—even if it's obvious that in most cases we will not need them at all.

The following will be the main topics:

- **Detecting and managing language**: We will start with what we call an advanced configuration, more than an actual customization which includes language recognition and managing multiple languages. I decided to put this argument in this chapter because the configurations that depend on language require specific analysis, testing, and libraries. So, we will introduce some of the libraries that can be used for this task; but our examples will only be a beginning.

- In order to test language analysis chains, we will see that it's possible to test the components in a more precise way by using units test. For this purpose, we will use a specific Solr testing library and the Scala language, because it's concise and simple to use here.

- The choice of the Scala language could seem a bit risky, but the motivations are simple. If you already have experience with Java, you should find the examples very concise and simple to read. If not, it' a good point from which to start, since it can be used as Java without too much boilerplate code. With this approach in mind, we can introduce the basic structural elements for writing new plugins using Java or Scala. We do this by looking at the methods inherited from the most common interfaces. Writing new plugins will require the knowledge of how a plugin structure is made, and what are the basic phases of a plugin lifecycle.

The code we will write and analyze should be considered only as a start. You need to know a lot more things and I hope you'll find our first experiment a good way to move further with more specific and deeper explorations.

Adding some more details to the core discovery

Previously, we have introduced the `solr.xml` configuration syntax as fast as we could. Since the current syntax will be adopted as mandatory from Solr Version 5.0, it's important to look at the Solr reference for acquiring knowledge on other details from `https://cwiki.apache.org/confluence/display/solr/Format+of+solr.xml`. The structure will now include configurations of shards and nodes, as shown in the following example code:

```
<solr>
  <solrcloud>
      <str name="host">127.0.0.1</str>
      <int name="hostPort">${hostPort:8983}</int>
      <str name="hostContext">${hostContext:solr}</str>
      <int name="zkClientTimeout">${solr.zkclienttimeout:30000}</int>
      <str name="shareSchema">${shareSchema:false}</str>
      <str name="genericCoreNodeNames">${genericCoreNodeNames:true}</str>
      <str name="zkHost">${zkHost:}</str>
  </solrcloud>
```

```
<shardHandlerFactory name="shardHandlerFactory" class="HttpShardHa
ndlerFactory">
    <int name="socketTimeout">${socketTimeout:120000}</int>
    <int name="connTimeout">${connTimeout:15000}</int>
</shardHandlerFactory>
<logging>
    <str name="class">${loggingClass:}</str>
    <str name="enabled">${loggingEnabled:}</str>
    <watcher>
      <int name="size">${loggingSize:}</int>
      <int name="threshold">${loggingThreshold:}</int>
    </watcher>
</logging>
</solr>
```

In the examples for this chapter, we have added some of these configurations with predefined values just to use them as a template. We can easily recognize the options to be used for configuring logging and the component that will be used as a factory for managing shards. The configurations can be written as usual by using the `core.properties` file.

Please remember that the presence of the `<solrcloud>` element is needed but that doesn't mean that the current instance is running in the SolrCloud mode. To start the instance in the SolrCloud mode, we need to specify the `-DzkHost` and `-DzkRun` parameters at startup, or add the corresponding configuration in the `<solrcloud>` element, as done in some of the previous examples.

Playing with specific languages

One of the most recurring and important use cases while adopting Solr or similar technologies is the ability to tune our language analysis components over one or more specific languages. Even if this may seem simple from a beginner's point of view, it introduces some complexity. In a real world scenario, we probably have to manage several different languages, each of them with its own specific configuration. This process of obtaining a good working configuration can consume a considerable amount of time, so you shouldn't underestimate that. Start with as simple configuration as possible, then take time to elaborate upon one aspect at a time, as we normally do. The first step in this path will be, needless to say, the identification of the language itself. Then, we could start adopting a very simple stemmer, just to give an idea on a general case.

Time for action – detecting language with Tika and LangDetect

It's frequently the case that you need to index more than a single language. We might have different language versions for the same document, or else multivalued fields that contain different languages.

1. The Tika library (used in previous chapters with the SolrCell component) can also help with multilingual content. Another good option is to use the LangDetect library, as stated in the wiki: `https://cwiki.apache.org/confluence/display/solr/Detecting+Languages+During+Indexing`. This library is very precise, and seems to be a bit more precise than using Tika, for this specific task.

   > However, we can adopt the corresponding Tika component `TikaLanguageIdentifierUpdateProcessorFactory`, which supports compatibility of the same parameters.

2. Looking at our first example of this chapter (`/SolrStarterBook/solr-app/chp09/arts_lang/solrconfig.xml`), the configuration will require the addition of the following code:

```
<updateRequestProcessorChain name="langid">
   <processor class="org.apache.solr.update.processor.
LangDetectLanguageIdentifierUpdateProcessorFactory">
      <lst name="defaults">
        <str name="langid.fl">fullText,abstract,title,comment</str>
        <str name="langid.langField">languages</str>
        <str name="langid.fallback">en</str>
        <float name="langid.threshold">0.85</float>
      </lst>
   </processor>
   <processor class="solr.LogUpdateProcessorFactory" />
   <processor class="solr.RunUpdateProcessorFactory" />
</updateRequestProcessorChain>
```

3. This processor will then be chained on an update handler in the usual way, as seen before.

4. Once we have copied a `schema.xml` file from the previous chapters, we will add a new `core.properties` file. And then, we will start the core by using `/SolrStarterBook/test/chp09/arts_lang/start.sh`. We can easily test if the processor is working using the following command:

```
>> curl -X POST 'http://localhost:8983/solr/arts_lang/
update?commit=true&wt=json' -H "Content-Type: text/xml" -d'@
example.post.xml'
```

5. Here, the XML Solr document file posted is an example file located in the same test directory.

What just happened?

The example is really simple and self explanatory. We can use the `lang.fl=fullText,abstract,etc` parameter to provide a list of fields that can be used for language detection. In order to avoid false identifications, it's preferable to adopt fields with text that are not too short. In our case, to state that our documents are written in English, the document returned in our queries will include a `languages=en` field. This is detected by the tool by using the `fullText` or `abstract` field.

The `langid.langField=languages` parameter is used to create a new field named `languages`, which will be a multivalued field in our case as a document can contain data from different languages.

This is an important aspect to be handled. We can provide different language-oriented analysis on a per-field basis. We can adopt a convention for managing the alternate version of a same field. If we have an abstract field for every language, we can, for example, manage an `abstract_it` field with its own configuration (in this case, with some language-specific tuning for the Italian language). You should not miss the connection between adopting such a naming convention and introducing at runtime (indexing time) a field for tracking the detected language. In this way, it is simple and up to us to trigger some field transformation and decide by scripting what will be the correct field configuration to be adopted for the indexing.

We can provide a `langid.fallback=en` parameter to treat the data as English by default (when we are not able or just don't need to detect the language), and a `langid.threshold=0.85` parameter to assign a threshold that we consider good to be a precision value.

Introducing stemming for query expansion

We have already adopted some file-based synonym query expansion. We can now adopt a stemmer-based approach, which is useful to add another level of flexibility, to intercept a certain amount of variance on user queries and needs.

> We call stemming the process by which we map the words derived from different forms of a certain original form to the same stem (or base, or root form). Words that share the same stem can be seen as a different surface for the same root, and they can be used as synonyms. This is useful to expand query adopting terms that are probably related because they have a similar form, for example, indexing for "painting" can produce the stem "paint" so that we are able to expand the query with results from the adoptions of terms "painter" or "painted". You should keep in mind that different languages may require quite different approaches, algorithms, and tools. If you want to read about stemming, I suggest you to start reading from the related section from the almost classical information retrieval book: `http://nlp.stanford.edu/IR-book/html/htmledition/stemming-and-lemmatization-1.html`.

The **stemming** algorithms are not trivial, as natural languages can be very different from each other in terms of morphology and the forms the words can assume. Imagine how the German words are composed and how they use suffixes, or think about the genre declination in different languages, or the difficulties in hadling a language that is not European-centric with an English-by-default approach. Handling these kinds of very specific configurations will be (maybe not surprisingly) one of the tasks that will engage us very soon to some more advanced topics that we are not able to cover here in detail.

However, there are a lot of resource on the Web on this. These algorithms are still evolving by adopting different approaches—from statistic based to rule based, and many more. Moreover, in the "big data" era they have improved a lot due to the huge quantity of data that was freely available to perform testing and tuning up models. Most of these tools exist in libraries for **Natural Language Processing** (**NLP**), which can also provide features such as tokenization, language detection, POS tagging (Part Of Speech annotation, useful for deeper analysis of the text that goes in the direction of handling semantics), entity recognition, and even more advanced features.

A vast list of some interesting tools in the NLP field can be found as usual on Wikipedia: `http://en.wikipedia.org/wiki/List_of_natural_language_processing_toolkits#Natural_language_processing_toolkits`.

You must not have missed the fact that many of these features are being integrated with the Solr workflow itself in some way, as an external tool or even plugins or internal components. So, I'll suggest you to subscribe to the developer's mailing list to follow any updates.

Time for action – adopting a stemmer

What we need to do now is configure a stemmer for our language. We will adopt an English one to see how to proceed. You can use the following simple configuration as a starting point for future and more advanced improvements.

1. We can, for example, define a new field for our `arts_lang` core; or simply modify the existing `text_general` field we designed before as follows:

```
<fieldType name="text_general" class="solr.TextField">
  <analyzer>
    <charFilter class="solr.MappingCharFilterFactory"
mapping="mapping-ISOLatin1Accent.txt" />
    <tokenizer class="solr.WhitespaceTokenizerFactory" />
    <filter class="solr.WordDelimiterFilterFactory"
generateWordParts="1" generateNumberParts="1" catenateWords="0"
catenateNumbers="1" catenateAll="0" splitOnCaseChange="1"
preserveOriginal="0" stemEnglishPossessive="1" />
    <filter class="solr.StopFilterFactory" words="stopwords.txt"
ignoreCase="true" />
    <filter class="solr.KeywordRepeatFilterFactory" />
    <filter class="solr.PorterStemFilterFactory" />
    <filter class="solr.RemoveDuplicatesTokenFilterFactory" />
    <filter class="solr.LowerCaseFilterFactory" />
    <filter class="solr.SynonymFilterFactory" synonyms="synonims.
txt" ignoreCase="true" expand="false" />
  </analyzer>
</fieldType>
```

> Note how we are using a combination of token filters. Once we have normalized the problems with accents and split a sentence into a sequence of words by splitting on whitespaces, we need to adopt the `WordDelimiterFilter` if we want to perform stemming on each individual term as well. Note that example such as "painting portraits" will be stemmed as "paint" for the first term and "portrait" for the second. So, the collection of stems will probably be the same as for the phrase "portrait of a painter". What I am suggesting here is that we are only playing with the expansion of the form of every single term, we did not make any assumption on the meaning of the terms expanded by the same stem.

What just happened?

The goal is to index both the stemmed and unstemmed terms at the same position. We generally adopt a `KeywordRepeatFilterFactory` that will emit a copy for every keyword, so that one of them can be reduced to its stem later and then indexed too. To generate a stem for a certain term, a component will often need some model that has been previously trained on a large set of data. In our case, we have decided to start with the simple `PorterStemmer` class. It does not need external files to be handled for the model counterpart as it already supports rules for English-only stemming. So, we will be warned that this may not work as expected if we plan to use it on a different language. When a `KeywordRepeatFilterFactory` is used before the actual stemmer filter factory, we generally put after it a `RemoveDuplicateTokenFactory` to remove the duplicates emitted when the original term does not produce any new stem.

There are a lot of alternate stemmers that are already provided with Solr for your use. They are either designed for a specific language, such as the `ItalianLightStemFilterFactory`, or to internally switch between different models, for example: `<filter class="solr.SnowballPorterFilterFactory" language="Italian"/>`.

You will find a list of available stemmers at the following wiki page: `http://wiki.apache.org/solr/LanguageAnalysis`.

Testing language analysis with JUnit and Scala

Suppose that at a certain point we need to develop a component on our own, or integrate existing components into some standard analyzer chain. If you and your team have some interest in this, a good step with which to start is to be able to perform local unit testing. This will help you to see how a tool will perform, before we put it into the entire workflow.

I think that the Scala language is a good option because it has powerful syntactic features. It is compatible with Java, and I think it is also very compact and simple to read—at least while writing simple code.

For example, if you consider the following code snippet:

```
import org.apache.lucene.analysis.BaseTokenStreamTestCase.
assertAnalyzesTo
[...]
class CustomItalianAnalyzer extends Analyzer {
  override def createComponents(fieldName: String, reader: Reader) = {
    val tokenizer = new WhitespaceTokenizer(Version.LUCENE_45, reader)
    val filter1 = new ItalianLightStemFilter(tokenizer)
    val filter2 = new LowerCaseFilter(Version.LUCENE_45, filter1)
    val filter3 = new CapitalizationFilter(filter2)
    return new TokenStreamComponents(tokenizer, filter3)
```

```
    }
  }
  @Test
  def testCustomAnalyzer() = {
    val customAnalyzer = new CustomItalianAnalyzer()
    assertAnalyzesTo(customAnalyzer, "questa è una frase di esempio",
  List("Quest", "È", "Una", "Frase", "Di", "Esemp").toArray)
  }
```

You should be able to recognize the involved elements even if you are not familiar with programming. Note how the unit testing permits us to focus on simple examples that will be used as reference. We can write as many test examples as we want, just to be sure that our combination of components is working correctly. The preceding Scala code snippet, when every object handled is used as an input for the sibling, is more or less equivalent to the following XML configuration:

```
<fieldType name="myField" class="myPackage.CustomItalianAnalyzer">
  <analyzer>
    <tokenizer class="solr.WhitespaceTokenizerFactory" />
    <filter class="solr.ItalianLightStemFilterFactory" />
    <filter class="solr.LowerCaseFilterFactory" />
    <filter class="solr.CapitalizationFilter" />
  </analyzer>
</fieldType>
```

It should help us to understand what happens. You will find some examples of this testing at /SolrStarterBook/projects/solr-maven/solr-plugins-scala/src/test/scala/testschema/TestAnalyzers.scala. Here, the class BaseTokenStreamTestCase, which is included in the solr-test-framework.jar package already available in the Solr standard distribution, plays a major role, because it provides facility methods that helps us by simplifying the task.

Writing new Solr plugins

It's not difficult to write new Solr Plugins, because the Solr internal workflow is well designed. From Solr 4, we have access to many more aspects of the data—from the execution of a query to the storing and indexing of the counterparts to the final response.

The main problem is very often in understanding quickly how to proceed, which interface and classes are needed for our purposes, how to test our code, and so on. The obvious first step is following the instructions on the wiki: http://wiki.apache.org/solr/SolrPlugins.

However, I suggest that you subscribe to the official mailing list (http://lucene.apache.org/solr/discussion.html) in order to follow interesting technical discussions, ask suggestions or help for your problems.

Introducing Solr plugin structure and lifecycle

There are many types of Solr plugins that can be written and inserted at different stages in the internal workflow. The previous example suggests that every plugin will have to implement certain predefined methods to communicate with the engine. For example, a StopWordFilter class would need to find the txt file where we have put our stop list, and then implement a ResourceLoaderAware interface to delegate the resolution and handling of the resource on disk to the core; or a new searcher can implement a SolrCoreAware interface to be able to capture core-specific information.

Implementing interfaces for obtaining information

We can implement the ResourceLoaderAware interface to directly manage resources. The classes implementing this interface are as follows:

- TokenFilterFactory
- TokenizerFactory
- FieldType

If a new component needs to have access to other component's or configuration's references for its core, it should implement the SolrCoreAware interface. The classes implementing this interface are as follows:

- SolrRequestHandler
- QueryResponseWriter
- SearchComponent

As you can see here, the Aware suffix is almost self explanatory; and as you can imagine, a class may want to implement both the interfaces.

Following an example plugin lifecycle

In this context, two methods play a major role: an init() method to handle general parameters, and an inform() method that will handle a different type of object, depending on the Aware interface implemented.

A typical lifecycle of these components will be defined in a few steps. It is shown in the following diagram:

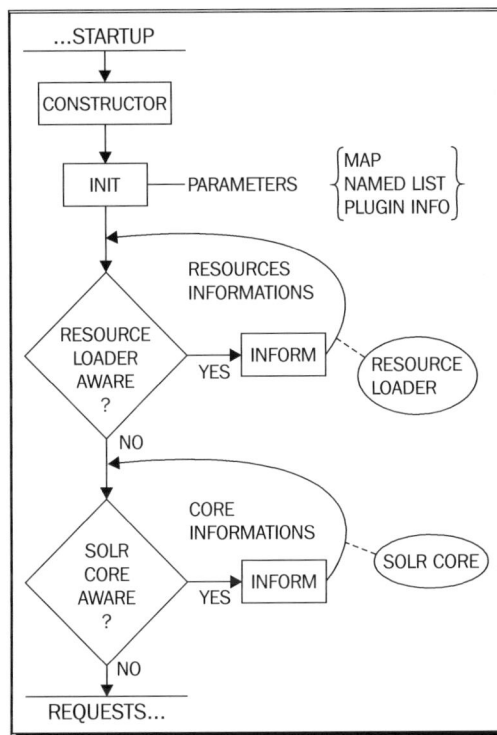

Let's read the sequence given in the preceding diagram in order:

1. The Solr instance is started.

2. The component constructor method is called.

3. An `init()` method is called to inject values via its arguments. The parameters accepted here will be of one of the following types such as `Map`, `NamedList`, and `PluginInfo`. The `NamedList` parameter is a collection designed to be similar to the `Map` parameter, but it contains repeatable keys.

4. All the classes implementing `ResourceLoaderAware` call `inform(ResourceLoader)` to obtain the information needed.

5. At last, and yet before the first request, after all the plugins have been registered, all the `SolrCoreAware` plugins call `inform(SolrCore)` to obtain the core-specific configurations.

6. Solr starts processing incoming requests.

You will find more references at the wiki page: `http://wiki.apache.org/solr/SolrPlugins`. However, starting from this simple schema, it's not too much complex to have an idea on how to proceed for our code. So let's look at some example.

Time for action – writing a new ResponseWriter plugin with the Thymeleaf library

There are many options for new customizations, depending on your use cases, and the continuous evolution of the framework is still simplifying things and making room for new improvements. For example, I feel that it is interesting to adapt the very flexible Thymeleaf template system to play with Solr as a `ResponseWriter`.

> Thymeleaf is a Java XML/XHTML/HTML5 template engine. It can serve XHTML/HTML5 in web applications or process any XML file: `http://www.thymeleaf.org/`.

1. A basic outline of the source should be similar to the following code:

```
class ThymeleafResponseWriter extends QueryResponseWriter {

    override def getContentType(request: SolrQueryRequest, response:
SolrQueryResponse) = "text/html"
    override def init(namedList: NamedList[_]) = logger.
debug("THYMELEAF PARAMETERS: {}", namedList.toString())

    override def write(writer: Writer, request: SolrQueryRequest,
response: SolrQueryResponse) = {

      val sb: StringBuffer = new StringBuffer

      val templateDir = new File(request.getCore().getDataDir() +
"/../conf/thymeleaf").getCanonicalPath()
      val template = new File(templateDir, "home.html").
getAbsolutePath()

      val now = new SimpleDateFormat("dd MMMM YYYY - HH:mm").
format(new Date())
      val resultContext = response.getValues().get("response").
asInstanceOf[ResultContext]
      val doclist: SolrDocumentList = SolrPluginUtils.
docListToSolrDocumentList(
        resultContext.docs, request.getSearcher(),
        response.getReturnFields().getLuceneFieldNames(), null
      )
```

```
    // inject new objects into the Thymeleaf context, to make them
available in the template
      val ctx = new Context()
      ctx.setVariable("today", now)
      ctx.setVariable("response", response)
      ctx.setVariable("resultContext", resultContext)
      ctx.setVariable("request", request)
      ctx.setVariable("core", request.getCore())
      ctx.setVariable("docs", doclist)
          val templateEngine = new TemplateEngine()
      val resolver = new FileTemplateResolver()
      resolver.setCharacterEncoding("UTF-8")
      templateEngine.setTemplateResolver(resolver)
      templateEngine.initialize()
          val result = templateEngine.process(template, ctx)

    sb.append(new String(result.getBytes())
    writer.write(sb.toString())
  }


 }
```

2. The choice of Thymeleaf is driven by the simplicity of its template system. We can write a template in plain real HTML5, and we can modify the template without restarting Solr once the writer is up. The aim is to play with a simple example that can live on its own and can be improved in the direction of a real embedded near-template system (such as the existing `VelocityResponseWriter`), but introducing some more fun and simplicity.

3. To give you an idea of the results, look at the following simple HTML snippet, which also includes a little JavaScript code:

```
<h1 th:text="${'Solr Core: '+core.getCoreDescriptor().
getName()}">CORE NAME</h1>
<section id="documents" th:each="doc : ${docs}">
   <article class="document">
     <header><h2 th:text="*{doc.get('title')}">A TITLE for the
DOC</h2></header>
     <div class="content" th:text="*{doc.get('abstract')}">LOREM
IPSUM..</div>
   </article>
</section>

<script type="text/javascript" th:inline="text">
/*<![CDATA[*/
// you can post-process view data here :-)
```

```
$(function(){
  var c = $(core_name)
  c.html(c.html().replace('_', ' '))
});
/*]]>*/
</script>
```

> The example still contains too much code in the template
> counterpart. But I tried to find a good balance between simplicity
> and readability; so, please feel free if you want to improve it, or even
> completely rewrite it in a more appropriate way.

4. You will find the example in the `/SolrStarterBook/solr-app/chp09/arts_`
   `thymeleaf` directory, including libraries and more detailed configurations.
   For example, adding the new response writer is as simple as adding in
   `solrconfig.xml` as follows:

```
<queryResponseWriter name="thymeleaf"
  class="it.seralf.solrbook.writers.thymeleaf.
ThymeleafResponseWriter">
  <str name="content-type">text/html; charset=UTF-8</str>
  <str name="template">home.html</str>
</queryResponseWriter>
```

5. Once the configuration is ready, our new core can be started in the usual way. If we
   put the URL `http://localhost:8983/solr/arts_thymeleaf/select?q=a`
   `rtist:*&wt=thymeleaf&indent=true` in the browser, we will obtain an output
   similar to the one in the following screenshot:

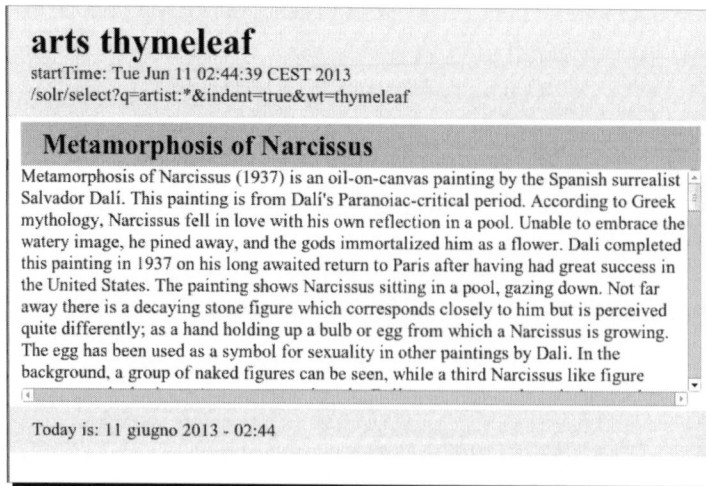

arts thymeleaf

startTime: Tue Jun 11 02:44:39 CEST 2013
/solr/select?q=artist:*&indent=true&wt=thymeleaf

Metamorphosis of Narcissus

Metamorphosis of Narcissus (1937) is an oil-on-canvas painting by the Spanish surrealist
Salvador Dalí. This painting is from Dalí's Paranoiac-critical period. According to Greek
mythology, Narcissus fell in love with his own reflection in a pool. Unable to embrace the
watery image, he pined away, and the gods immortalized him as a flower. Dali completed
this painting in 1937 on his long awaited return to Paris after having had great success in
the United States. The painting shows Narcissus sitting in a pool, gazing down. Not far
away there is a decaying stone figure which corresponds closely to him but is perceived
quite differently; as a hand holding up a bulb or egg from which a Narcissus is growing.
The egg has been used as a symbol for sexuality in other paintings by Dali. In the
background, a group of naked figures can be seen, while a third Narcissus like figure

Today is: 11 giugno 2013 - 02:44

I know that this is not exactly pretty, and it lacks so much information that it seems broken. The point is that this is not broken, and it is instead the product of our very first simple exploration in writing a working (let's say it's almost working) custom component. You can use it as a playground for experimentations, and easily extend it by working on the HTML template directly to add more features. All you have to do is read a little about writing attributes with Thymeleaf.

What just happened?

The class inherits the contract of a `QueryResponseWriter` class, so we have to override the `getContentType` and `init` methods. The first is trivial; the second is not really used here, but it's interesting to track the parameters received by a `NamedList` instance.

The entire logic lies in the `write` method. The signature is similar to a standard service method for a Servlet. So, we have a request and a response wrapper object—in this case, a `SolrQueryRequest` and a `SolrQueryResponse` in particular.

From the request, we can obtain a reference to the currently used parameters and the core itself. This is useful to find resources (for example, the HTML template files) by using a relative path. But, the same approach can be used with every configuration and internal objects that is handled by a core reference.

From the response, we can obtain a reference to the results of our query, such as the list of documents and number of facets. We can handle all the things we generally see with an XML or JSON serialization, the main difference will be in the names and in the hierarchy. So, we will have to study a little, and we cannot expect to find an exact match with the XML serialization. For example, the best way is to open the Java API for Solr and explore what we can do by using them, for example for a result context at: `http://lucene.apache.org/solr/4_5_0/solr-core/index.html?org/apache/solr/response/ResultContext.html`. Note that if there exists an object of the `ResultContext` type that encapsulates the query and document list objects, we also need to create a Thymeleaf context. This will be the object where we will inject all the data that we will be able to manage from the HTML counterpart.

> If you look at the HTML template, Thymeleaf permits us to write valid HTML5 templates and construct the page as we want—even using Lorem-Ipsum and similar placeholder text when needed. At runtime, the processor will take the directive we placed on the tags by using the Thymeleaf dialect (`http://www.thymeleaf.org/doc/html/Using-Thymeleaf.html`) to substitute the placeholder with the actual data. What I like in this approach is that once the skeleton is created for our plugin, the HTML views are editable without recompilation; they are parsed at runtime on the server.

If we want to play with this almost *hello world* example, we can simply request by using the following command:

```
>> curl -X 'http://localhost:8983/solr/arts_thymeleaf/
select?q=*:*&wt=thymeleaf'
```

In this way, we are directly exposing the Solr API and providing a new simple HTML5 rendering of the data. This is not exactly what we want to do on a production environment; but this can be useful for prototyping, for fast presentations of basic features, and even for creating specific views for monitoring or exploration of data on the internal network.

Moreover, we are writing the code in a very similar way then and if we are handling HTML with JavaScript at the client side, with improvements on performance (all the logic is at the server and the client will receive only the HTML part), and the assumption to have a well formed, validated HTML code. I feel that this approach is easy to understand for a beginner, although it contains a robust way to proceed, which can be used later in more advanced contexts, without too much boilerplate code.

The data injection is simple, because HTML attributes are used to define rules and placeholders for the data. It will then be syntactically compliant to HTML5. For example, to inject all the titles using some `<section>` elements, all we have to do is iterate over the collection of documents `<section id="documents" th:each="doc : ${docs}">` and read the specific data for every document with something similar to: `<h2 th:text="*{doc.get('title')}">some-dummy-text</h2>`. At runtime, the text will be overwritten by the actual one; and we can associate the Thymeleaf rules to the elements we want, in order to obtain a natural mapping. In this way, your team can be easily involved in prototyping from the earlier stages, because the designer can work on valid HTML templates (using their own editor) that are loosely coupled to the software internals as well.

Using Maven for development

If you want to look at the code and modify it for starting your own implementation, you can look at the code in `/SolrStarterBook/projects/solr-maven/solr-plugins-scala`.

> Maven is one of the best known solutions for automating the build process and to resolve dependencies at the moment. It can be used with Java and any other JVM language. We can have a module containing a self-running Solr installation to test the software components we are developing in another module. This approach is well covered in the excellent proof of concept by *Petri Kainulainen* at `http://www.petrikainulainen.net/programming/maven/running-solr-with-maven/`. The examples provided are inspired by it and adapted to our needs. If you are not yet familiar with Maven, please start by reading how to install it: `http://maven.apache.org/guides/getting-started/maven-in-five-minutes.html`.

The Solr-Maven folder contains a Maven project for our code, organized for convenience in separated modules. In particular, the parent project includes the following modules:

* `solr-maven/webapp`: This is the module for running a Solr instance with Maven
* `solr-maven/solr-plugins-java`: This is a module containing example Java code
* `solr-maven/solr-plugins-scala`: This is a module containing example Scala code

We can have a Solr instance running using a pair of Maven commands.

In order to build an entire Maven project (also installing copies of an artifact into the local repository for our dependencies), the following command is used vey commonly:

```
>> mvn package install
```

In our case, we execute this command from the parent folder. But, we can also execute it only for a certain module from its own folder. Another useful option is adding the clean directive on the Maven command, so that every artifact will be deleted and rebuilt from scratch. This can be useful during development.

In order to start the Solr instance included in the `webapp` module, we can also use the following command from the `webapp` module folder:

```
>> mvn jetty:run -Dsolr.solr.home=solr-app
```

In the preceding command, `solr-app` will be the directory containing the configuration to be used (in this case, a relative path inside the project). Feel free to use the provided examples as a base for your own experimentations.

Time for action – integrating Stanford NER for Named Entity extraction

Another good place to start writing custom code can be thinking about the integration of a Named Entity Recognizer. For this task, we can adopt the well-known Stanford NER (http://nlp.stanford.edu/software/CRF-NER.shtml). We need to write code to wrap the functionality of this library, and decide it will run at what stage in the internal workflow.

> A simple and working idea on how to handle this library with Scala can be found in a good example by *Gary Sieling* at http://www.garysieling.com/blog/entity-recognition-with-scala-and-stanford-nlp-named-entity-recognizer.

One good choice is to implement it as an update processor or as a language analyzer, and then use it as well as the other standard components.

1. First of all, let's write a simple test case in Scala, inspired by the default behavior of the NER (note that it loads a model from an external file):

```
@Test
def testNERFilterNoXML() = {
  val tokenizer_stream = new KeywordAnalyzer().tokenStream("TEST_
FIELD",
    new StringReader("Leonardo da Vinci was the italian painter
who painted the Mona Lisa."))
  assertTokenStreamContents(new NERFilter(tokenizer_stream, false,
"ner/english.all.3class.distsim.crf.ser.gz"),
    List("Leonardo/PERSON da/PERSON Vinci/PERSON was/O the/O
italian/O painter/O who/O painted/O the/O Mona/PERSON Lisa/
PERSON./O").toArray)
  }
```

2. The actual plugin will require some attention, but it's not as complex as we may expect:

```
final class NERFilterFactory(args: Map[String, String]) extends
TokenFilterFactory(args) with ResourceLoaderAware {
  val useXML: Boolean = getBoolean(args, "useXMLAnnotations",
false)
  val model: String = new File(this.require(args, "model")).
getCanonicalPath()
  override def create(input: TokenStream): TokenStream = {
    new NERFilter(input, useXML, model)
  }
```

```scala
  override def inform(loader: ResourceLoader) = { // TODO }
}

final class NERFilter(input: TokenStream, useXML: Boolean,
classifierModel: String) extends TokenFilter(input) {
  val ner = new NER(classifierModel)
  this.clearAttributes()
  override final def incrementToken(): Boolean = {
    if (input.incrementToken()) {
      val term = input.getAttribute(classOf[CharTermAttribute])
      val text = term.buffer().toList.mkString("").trim
      term.setEmpty()
      val annotatedText = ner.getAnnotatedText(text, useXML)
      term.append(annotatedText)
      true
    } else { false }
  }
}
```

3. While developing a new plugin, it should be made available to the Solr instance we'd like to use for testing. This can be done in the following ways:

   ❑ Place the JAR files in the lib directory of the `instanceDir` object of the current SolrCore, which is used for test.

   ❑ Write a lib directive in `solrconfig.xml`, as we already did for Tika or SolrCell earlier.

   ❑ Using Maven or similar tools for testing. In this case, the tool will assemble your WAR file directly with the new JAR file, or give you the chance to manage the classpath.

4. After we finish developing and testing our new plugin, we can load it to our Solr core by adding the following lines to `solrconfig.xml`:

```xml
<lib dir="${solr.core.instanceDir}/lib/" regex="solrbook-
components-scala.jar" />
<lib dir="${solr.core.instanceDir}/lib/" regex="scala-.*\.jar" />
<lib dir="${solr.core.instanceDir}/lib/" regex="stanford-
corenlp-.*\.jar" />
```

5. In this case, `solrbook-components-scala.jar` is the compiled library containing our new custom components, and then we will also add the Scala library and the Stanford core. Then, our `schema.xml` file will be updated as follows:

```xml
<fieldType name="text_annotated" class="solr.TextField">
  <analyzer>
    <tokenizer class="solr.KeywordTokenizerFactory" />
```

```
    <filter class="it.seralf.solrbook.filters.ner.
NERFilterFactory"
        useXMLAnnotations="false" model="${solr.core.instanceDir}
conf/ner/english.all.3class.distsim.crf.ser.gz" />
    </analyzer>
</fieldType>
[...]
<field name="abstract" type="text_annotated" indexed="true"
stored="true" multiValued="false" />
```

6. And the last thing to do is perform a query to see how the data returned will be annotated, as the Unit Test suggests. You will find the complete code for this at /SolrStarterBook/projects/solr-maven/solr-plugins-scala.

What just happened?

This is a simple query that will return an annotated version of the original text data. So, if we index on the text Leonardo da Vinci was the italian painter who painted the Mona Lisa., we will obtain the resultant data as an alternate, which is an annotated version of the same data in XML: <PERSON>Leonardo da Vinci</PERSON> was the italian painter who painted the <PERSON>Mona Lisa</PERSON>. or as a plain annotated text file: Leonardo/PERSON da/PERSON Vinci/PERSON was/O the/O italian/O painter/O who/O painted/O the/O Mona/PERSON Lisa/PERSON./O. The annotated text will be a bit less readable for us, but this way it's easy to recognize the entities.

> Apache UIMA is a powerful framework providing not only NER components, but also annotations based on rules, dictionaries, and part of speech tagging. The adoption of UIMA requires to go far beyond the scope of this book, but you can find a simple trace of configuration at /SolrStarterBook/solr-app/chp09/arts_uima. You can use this draft to start your experiments with this framework. Follow the instructions provided on the official wiki: http://wiki.apache.org/solr/SolrUIMA.

The BaseTokenStreamTestCase plays a central role here, because it provides facility methods to simplify testing. Looking at the example, we will see that we have adopted a KeywordAnalyzer class to emit a phrase without splitting it on terms. We can then pass its output to our new NERFilter, and then verify whether the original phrase has been correctly annotated as we expected.

The most interesting part is on the actual code for `NERFilter`. The class will be a subclass of `TokenFilter` (extends `TokenFilter`), so that it can be used inside a normal chain of analysis. In order for this to work, we generally need to create a specific implementation of the `incrementToken()` method where we perform our analysis. In our case, we will simply put all the logic instantiating the NER class wrapper, and then execute an entire phrase annotation. Remember this code is just an example. It is not meant to be fully functional. However, you will find the complete source (including the source for NER wrapper) in the `it.seralf.solrbook.filters.ner` package in the `/SolrStarterBook/projects/solr-maven/solr-plugins-scala` project.

Once we have written our filter, we have to make it available through a specific `NERFilterFactory` class (a subclass of `TokenFilterFactory`). The `create()` method of this class will take a `TokenStream` object as input, and will also emit the output as a `TokenStream`. As you can see, we need to pass a couple of configurations to the filter (one of them being the name of the file from which to load the model). The parameters will be available as an `args` map for our factory. A typical implementation will also implement the `ResourceLoaderAware` interface to load the resources by the internal components.

When all seems to work correctly we can finally put our new component into a Solr core. You'll find `/SolrStarterBook/solr-app/chp09/arts_ner`, including a lib folder that will contain the JAR files for our plugins and the Standford libraries. Note that we decided to write our draft with the Scala language. So, in order to obtain a reference to the standard library of the language, we can also simply put the Scala core libraries in the same directory (if you have not yet put it on the classpath earlier).

Remember we can put our JAR files into a lib directory local to the Solr core, or into a lib directory shared between Solr cores, or anywhere else on the filesystem. The choice really depends on how we'd like to manage our configurations, because it's possible to use any of the options seen before to point a relative or absolute path to a lib directory containing third-party JAR files from a `solrconfig.xml` or a `solr.xml` file, or even by adding it to classpath from the command line.

Pointing ideas for Solr's customizations

The first thing to remember while thinking about Solr customization is the most obvious one. We have to ask ourselves what we really need, and if this is really not yet covered by some existing (sometimes not yet well documented) components. I know that from a beginner's point of view, reading about too complex components may seem contradictory; but I feel that after reaching the end of the book, you should have a last chance to look at different concepts and components in perspective:

- Low-level customization involves writing new components such as `Analyzers`, `Tokenizers`, `TokenFilters`, `FieldTypes` for handling Terms, Fields, and Language Analysis.

◆ In this context, we can also override the default similarity implementation `<similarity class="my.package.CustomSimilarity"/>`.

◆ The codec choice is strictly related to the Terms internal format. From Lucene 4, it is possible to adopt different codecs (for example, the `SimpleTextCodec` used for some examples). It's even possible to write our own examples when needed. In the same way, we can change the `directoryFactory` used, for example, introducing an HDFS compliant one: `<directoryFactory name="DirectoryFactory" class="solr.HdfsDirectoryFactory">`, or we can adopt different SolrCache strategies.

◆ From Solr 4 onwards, it's also possible to provide preanalyzed fields: `http://wiki.apache.org/solr/PreAnalyzedField`. These particular fields are useful in the direction of a NoSQL usage of Solr, since they act as a common tokenized field on certain terms. They also give the option of storing data directly into the Solr index without analyzing it, for example, in the JSON format. On the other hand, there are chances to save field values on some external files as well: `http://docs.lucidworks.com/display/solr/Working+with+External+Files+and+Pr ocesses`. In both the cases, searching on these fields is not supported for obvious reasons. But these implementations can be extended to store more structured data.

◆ While handling queries, we can implement a new `ValueSourceParser` to expand the set of available functions queries with new, customized ones: `<valueSourceParser name="a-new-function" class="some.package. CustomValueSourceParser" />`. We can even change the query parsing by itself by using subclasses of `QparserPlugin`: `<queryParser name="a-new-queryparser" class="some.package.CustomQueryParserPlugin" />`. In the latter case, we have the chance to use the brand new parser as usual, with the adoption of a parameter `qt` or by a specific configuration in `solrconfig.xml`.

In this list, there are elements that you should now be able to recognize; and others that require some more study of Solr and its internals. The `UpdateHandler` and `DataImportHandler` are the most interesting ones for customizations, because they offer access to the indexing workflow. In addition to these, we can use some specific `SolrEventListener` to trigger customized actions or command-line tools when a certain event occurs (for example a document is deleted or updated).

In order to define the logic for every request, we can create a new request handler, as we already saw `<requestHandler name="a-new-handler" class="some.package. CustomHandler">` that can re-use new `SearchComponent`.

Finally, a useful possibility is to define a different formatting for outputting the results of a certain query: `<queryResponseWriter name="a-new-responseWriter" class="some.package.CustomResponseWriter" />`.

Remember that these are only some of the possibilities in the path for customizations. I hope that this recap will be useful to you to reorder your ideas and decide where you want to move next with your experimentations and studies, prototyping the frontend with an embedded Solr using `VelocityResponseWriter`. There is also a good `VelocityResponseWriter` plugin, with which you can play. It is available with the standard example. Please refer to `http://wiki.apache.org/solr/VelocityResponseWriter` for an introduction on that.

We did not use it in detail as this requires knowledge about a specific dialect in order to be used. But it is interesting to look at the following component source in detail because it internally uses classes such as `QueryResponse`:

```
SolrResponse rsp = new QueryResponse();
NamedList<Object> parsedResponse = BinaryResponseWriter.getParsedResponse(request, response);
try {
  rsp.setResponse(parsedResponse);

  // page only injected if QueryResponse works
  context.put("page", new PageTool(request, response));  // page tool only makes sense for a SearchHandler request... *sigh*
} catch (ClassCastException e) {
  // known edge case where QueryResponse's extraction assumes "response" is a SolrDocumentList
  // (AnalysisRequestHandler emits a "response")
  e.printStackTrace();
  rsp = new SolrResponseBase();
  rsp.setResponse(parsedResponse);
}
context.put("response", rsp);

// Velocity context tools - TODO: make these pluggable
context.put("esc", new EscapeTool());
context.put("date", new ComparisonDateTool());
context.put("list", new ListTool());
context.put("math", new MathTool());
context.put("number", new NumberTool());
context.put("sort", new SortTool());

context.put("engine", engine);  // for $engine.resourceExists(...)
```

This class is related to an "embedded" Solr instance. Indeed it exists as an `EmbeddedSolr` wrapper object too: `http://wiki.apache.org/solr/Solrj#EmbeddedSolrServer`. As we said in the beginning of this book, we focused on using Solr as a standalone application; but it can easily be used as a library embedded into other Java (or JVM) applications. In order to do this it's necessary to adopt a convenient named called SolrJ, which contains some useful classes to handle a remote, local, or even an embedded instance of Solr. The point here is that, from the SolrJ perspective, we are interacting with Solr as a client. And if you think about the fact that the `QueryResponse` class that is used as a wrapper in the `VelocityResponseWriter` class is available in this library, the distinction between a client library and a facility component becomes very fuzzy. We will have a chance to introduce the existing clients for Solr in the appendix of this book, where we will be reading about more specific Solr customizations.

When you'll want to work on your own customizations, there are many resources that can be used as a reference. I suggest that you start with the following list:

- **Solr Reference Guide**: This is the official reference guide, recently donated to the the community by Lucid Works: `https://cwiki.apache.org/confluence/display/solr/Apache+Solr+Reference+Guide`.

- **Writing new plugins**: Starting from the official wiki page, it's possible to look for the usage of Unit Test and Mock objects at `http://wiki.apache.org/solr/SolrPlugins#Building_Plugins`.

- **A WikipediaTokenizer**: This is available at `http://lucene.apache.org/core/4_5_0/analyzers-common/org/apache/lucene/analysis/wikipedia/WikipediaTokenizer.html`.

- **Third-party components**: There are also many third-party components that can adopt very different approaches, and can be integrated with Solr if/when needed. A good option is, for example, the stemmer based on the WordNet dictionary at `http://tipsandtricks.runicsoft.com/Other/JavaStemmer.html`.

> Wordnet is a lexical dictionary for English, which aims to collect (almost) all English words and group them by their stem: `http://wordnet.princeton.edu/wordnet/`.

- **Similarity** algorithm based on singular value decompositions is available at `http://www.ling.ohio-state.edu/~kbaker/pubs/Singular_Value_Decomposition_Tutorial.pdf`.

- **Text categorization with Solr**: `http://raimonb.wordpress.com/2013/01/02/text-categorization-with-k-nearest-neighbors-using-lucene/`.

- **NLP with UIMA and Solr**: `http://www.slideshare.net/teofili/natural-language-search-in-solr`.

- **Sentiment Analysis and Visualization using UIMA and Solr**: `http://ceur-ws.org/Vol-1038/paper_5.pdf`.

This is obviously just a small selection, but I hope they can give you some suggestions to move further with the introduction of natural language capabilities, the improvement of language analysis, and the integration of information retrieval tools.

If and when you'll develop new components, please remember to share them with the community if possible.

Pop quiz

Q1. What is a stem?

1. A stem is a synonym for a certain word.

2. A stem is a Term which can be used as a root for constructing compound words.

3. A stem is the base root for a group of words.

Q2. What is a Named Entity Recognizer?

1. It is a component designed to recognize/annotate textual entities.

2. It is a component designed to give a name to textual entities.

3. It is a component designed to recognize the correct name of a textual entity.

Q3. What are the purposes of the `ResourceLoadedAware` and `SolrCoreAware` interfaces?

1. They can be implemented from the components that need to load the resources and specific cores.

2. They can be implemented from the components that need to obtain references to the resources and core configurations.

3. They can be implemented from the components to write new resources to the disk and change the core configuration values.

Q4. What is the correct order in which plugins are evaluated?

1. First the classes implementing `ResourceLoaderAware`, and then the classes implementing `SolrCoreAware`.

2. The order is not relevant.

3. First the classes implementing `SolrCoreAware`, and then the classes implementing `ResourceLoaderAware`.

Summary

The main topic in this chapter is the customization of Solr. This goes from the adoption of language specific configurations to identifying what are the most commonly used tools for expanding queries by using some techniques derived from natural language processing, linguistic, or information retrieval.

Even if we did not go in detail, it's important to design the scenario and the options for our hypothetical Solr customizations.

And I hope this will all inspire you and let you begin your journey into some of the advanced topics, such as NLP and semantic search, which we can only suggest here.

Solr Clients and Integrations

While using Solr, at some point you will need to interact with it from your application. Now, since Solr is by itself a web application that exposes services in a REST fashion, we can ideally write code to interact with it using the language we prefer. The most used transport formats for sending the document to be indexed or to retrieve results are XML and JSON. But there are some others, such as the JavaBin format, which may be used for direct marshalling of Java objects, and it can be faster in some cases.

Introducing SolrJ – an embedded or remote Solr client using the Java (JVM) API

If you navigate to `/SolrStarterBook/projects/client-example`, you'll find some essential examples that should help you understand how to interact with Solr by using your own JVM language. If you use one of the supported languages on the JVM, you can use the SolrJ library API to interact with Solr locally or remotely without too much effort (details of the SolrJ version used in this book with the Solr 4.5 version can be found at `http://lucene.apache.org/solr/4_5_0/solr-solrj/index.html`). From this perspective, adopting languages such as Groovy or Scala gives us some syntactic advanced support that can really simplify the interactions, or using JavaScript on the server side can be more comfortable for people already working on the Web.

Let's see some examples of this, starting from Java.

Time for action – playing with an embedded Solr instance

I assume that we already have an instance of our arts core running. You can use the instance defined in *Chapter 7, Working with Multiple Entities, Multicores, and Distributed Search*, or you can start from the basic schema in `/SolrStarterBook/solr-app/appendixes/arts` and run it in the usual way.

1. But say we don't want to use an external Solr application, and simply want to put the core Solr functionality inside an existing Java application. In this case, we will use an embedded Solr, which means we are actually using the Solr API directly as a framework, without passing through its services. It will be up to us to start a core with the correct configuration, post or query data, optimize the core, or release it when the application shuts down. As you can imagine, this is a very particular use case, and I expect you to not do this in most of the cases, but only in some very specific scenarios (for example, if we need to create a single web application, or a desktop one, including Solr capabilities as well).

2. A really basic example can be similar to the following one:

```
System.setProperty("solr.solr.home", "solr-home");
CoreContainer container = new CoreContainer();
container.load();
EmbeddedSolrServer server = new EmbeddedSolrServer(container,
"arts");

// delete all documents
server.deleteByQuery("*:*");

Artist doc = new Artist("http://TEST/Leonardo_da_Vinci","Leonardo
Da Vinci", "Vinci", "Florence");
server.addBean(doc);

server.commit();

QueryResponse response = server.query(new SolrQuery("leonardo"),
METHOD.GET);

for (SolrDocument d : response.getResults()) {
  for (String field : d.getFieldNames()) {
    System.out.printf("%s = %s\n", field, d.getFieldValue(field));
  }
}

server.shutdown();
```

3. Here, we start a server with a specific configuration and then index a specific custom data type. As we are writing code in Java, we can also use one of the most adopted Java conventions for describing our data and creating a Java bean, which represents an instance on our domain (in this case, only few fields are used for readability, just to give an idea).

```
public class Artist {
  @Field
  final URI uri;
  @Field
  final String artist;
  @Field("city")
  final String[] cities;

  public Artist(final String uri, final String artist, final
String... cities) {
    this.uri = URI.create(uri);
    this.artist = artist;
    this.cities = cities;
  }
}
```

Note that the Solr API provides us with some Java annotations to be used on beans that simplify both the process of indexing data and returning it from a query. Obviously, the example is designed only to give you a skeleton for starting your own experimentation. If you study the API, you'll find several other useful methods that you can use for your convenience.

What just happened?

The base for interacting with Solr from the Java code is obtaining a valid server instance. In this first case, we are using an `EmbeddedSolrServer` instance, so we also need to load the configuration and start the server if not already started. Our server instance, in particular, can be seen as a wrapper for core functionalities. We have to expect it to expose methods for indexing, searching, and removing SolrDocuments.

The first step will be instantiating a `CoreContainer` instance. This will be the object that will actually load and parse our configuration from the filesystem. In this case, we have adopted as little code as possible, so we have defined a default `solr.solr.home` location by overwriting a system property. This helps us to avoid passing too many parameters and focus on more interesting steps. The `load()` method here is used not only to load the configurations in memory, but also to actually start a multicore server instance on our configurations.

The second step will be the instantiation of the server instance by itself. This is created, starting from the container (imagine it handling our `solr.xml` file) and providing the name of the specific core configuration we want to access.

If we are able to use JavaBeans for transporting data inside our application, for example, by assembling data from a query on a database, we can index them using the `server.addBean()` method that will internally look for annotations, parsing the field with an appropriate type if possible.

The server instance also exposes methods to delete documents (we use it to clear the current index for repeating our tests), trigger a commit when needed, and shut down the Solr instance when the application ends.

Constructing a basic query is simple, and we can easily obtain a collection of results using the `getResults()` method of a `QueryResponse` object. Note that this object is the same one that was seen before when we briefly inspected the `VelocityResponseWriter` code, and the method used to inspect looks similar to the one we used from JavaScript in the update chain. You won't miss the `METHOD.GET` value passed to the `QueryResponse` object, suggesting that queries are treated the same way by an embedded or by an external server instance.

Choosing between an embedded or remote Solr instance

While using SolrJ, we can basically use the same API over an embedded or remote instance. The choice mainly depends on our needs, usage, and of course the environment and runtime we have. We should consider the following:

- **EmbeddedSolrServer**: This denotes in-process access to Solr or to a similar JVM as Solr. This approach may provide performance improvement in a few scenarios (`http://wiki.apache.org/solr/Solrj#EmbeddedSolrServer`).

- **CommonsHttpSolrServer**: This can be used to access a remote Solr server. In this case, an important factor we also need to consider is the latency between the client and the remote instance, which usually occurs with HTTP.

- **StreamingHttpSolrServer**: This may provide some improvement in the performance factor.

Let's see another example to clarify this, while also looking at an `HTTPSolrServer` instance.

Time for action – playing with an external HttpSolrServer

An `EmbeddedSolrServer` instance can be substituted for by other server wrapper types, for example, an `HttpSolrServer` instance, which exposes the same basic API and differs only in the way it is instantiated.

Once we adopt an `HttpSolrServer` instance, we can send our data to an external remote Solr instance via HTTP. This is the most common way to communicate with Solr via a Java interface, whether they are on the same machine or not, because it permits us to decouple the client from the server (for example, they will not necessarily share the same system resource).

```java
HttpSolrServer server = new HttpSolrServer("http://localhost:8983/
solr/arts");

// construct a generic SolrDocument
SolrInputDocument doc = new SolrInputDocument();
doc.addField("uri", "http://TEST/Leonardo_da_Vinci");
doc.addField("artist", "Leonardo Da Vinci");
doc.addField("city", "Vinci");
doc.addField("note", "document updated");
server.add(doc);

server.commit();

// constructing a query with fluent api...
SolrQuery solrQuery = new SolrQuery()
  .setQuery("vermeer~0.5")
  .setFacet(true).setFacetMinCount(1).setFacetLimit(8)
  .addFacetField("museum_entity").addFacetField("city")
  .setHighlight(true).setHighlightSnippets(3)
  .setParam("hl.fl", "artist");

// ... and seeing how our query is actually made
System.out.printf("QUERY: %s/%s\n\n", server.getBaseURL(), solrQuery);

// executing the query
QueryResponse rsp = server.query(solrQuery);

// retrieving the collection of documents
  System.out.println("#### DOCs");
for (SolrDocument d : rsp.getResults()) {j
  System.out.println(d);
```

```
}

// retrieving the collection of facets
System.out.println("#### facets");
for (FacetField e : rsp.getLimitingFacets()) {
  System.out.println(e);
}

// retrieving the collection of highligths
System.out.println("#### highligths");
for (Entry<?,?> e : rsp.getHighlighting().entrySet()) {
  System.out.println(e);
}

server.shutdown();
```

As you can see in the preceding code, the results are available in sections, one for every section that we already know from its XML representation. Some generic document collection results, faceting results, highlighting results, and others are made available by a specific method and collection.

What just happened?

We first created an `HttpSolrServer` object that will be used as a bridge to encapsulate the interaction with a remote Solr application instance. Once created, we interacted directly with this object as if it was a reference to a local instance.

We can construct a generic `SolrInputDocument` instance to send to the server the data to be indexed. We have already seen this class in action while playing with the updating chain, and this approach is much more general than using a Java bean, as it's not being shaped over a particular domain class. It represents only a generic fluid container for metadata. Note how its consistency with the schema is verified only when the object will be received and handled by an actual remote Solr core.

In this second example, the query is constructed by chaining the method calls that are designed to be easily used by adopting this Fluent API, which is simple to read.

If we print the `solrQuery` object that is yet to be constructed, it's easy to find out that it is indeed equivalent to the following query:

```
>> curl -X GET 'http://localhost:8983/solr/arts/q=vermeer%7E0.5&facet
=true&facet.mincount=1&facet.limit=8&facet.field=museum_entity&facet.
field=city&hl=true&hl.snippets=3&hl.fl=artist'
```

It's easy to figure out how to construct the object in the reverse direction, by taking a query we have already tested with cURL and deconstructing it on a chain of method calls.

Note how the results are wrapped for convenience into independent collections. For example, for obtaining a faceting results collection, we need to use the `getLimitingFacets()` method on the `QueryResponse` object, and then we will be able to iterate over the collection.

The collections used here could be Lists, Maps, or NamedLists in certain cases. In every case, they will be iterable or will expose an iterator in order to simplify our needs for consuming their data, even on a streaming scenario where a huge quantity of results are returned.

Time for action – using Bean Scripting Framework and JavaScript

At this point, it should be clear that it's simple to index data with the Java API (we simply have to call the methods `.add()` and `.addBean()` on a server instance), thereby making querying flexible, and we can use some different wrappers of a SolrServer instance that are functionally equivalent.

This is not the end of the story, however, as it's possible to use the SolrJ library's APIs in JavaScript by using the **Bean Scripting Framework (BSF)**, which is an Apache library designed to integrate scripting languages' code into a Java application. Note that there are other languages supported by BSF, such as Groovy or Clojure, and the same approach used here with JavaScript can be adopted for one of those. For a complete list of the languages supported by BSF, please refer to: `http://commons.apache.org/proper/commons-bsf/index.html`. If you are curious about the current support for an external scripting language in the standard Java distribution, please refer to: `http://download.java.net/jdk8/docs/technotes/guides/scripting/prog_guide/api.html`.

1. For example, to use JavaScript to index a document, you will need to write some snippet of code similar to the following one (I left only the essential parts):

```
importClass(org.apache.solr.client.solrj.impl.HttpSolrServer)
importClass(org.apache.solr.common.SolrInputDocument)

var url = "http://localhost:8983/solr/arts"
var server = new HttpSolrServer( url );

var doc = new SolrInputDocument()
...
doc.addField("note", "TEST document added to the index by
javascript")

server.add(doc)

server.commit()
```

2. If we want to save this code in a file named `example.js` under the `scripts/javascript/` folder of our client's example project, we only need to write the following three-lined Java class to execute it:

```
String myScript = new Scanner(new FileInputStream("scripts/
javascript/example.js")).useDelimiter("\\Z").next();
BSFManager manager = new BSFManager();
manager.eval("javascript", "example.js", 0, 0, myScript);
```

3. All you have to do is prepare a code similar to the previous one, and you can write code to communicate to a remote Solr server. You will need to have an appropriate interpreter library available for the BSF; for example, I added Rhino in my dependencies.

In a really similar way, we can also handle Groovy, JRuby, Jython, or other languages.

What just happened?

Starting from the end, you can easily recognize the declaration of the interpreter to be used with the BSF manager. We loaded the content of the file as a common string, and then let the BSF transparently execute it.

If you look at the JavaScript code, it's almost identical to what we would have written in Java. There are very minor syntactical differences, such as the use of a specific function for the imports or for the `var` declaration of variables, but the APIs called are the same.

Jahia CMS

Jahia (`http://www.jahia.com`) is an open source **Content Management System (CMS)**, which exposes the Restful API and uses Solr as an internal search framework. The Jahia content platform (`http://www.jahia.com/tech/jahia-content-platform`) supports development of apps and includes a workflow engine based on rules with the support of Drools. The platform also has multiscripting support to enable the development of templates using different languages or frameworks such as PHP, Freemarker, JavaScript, and others.

Magnolia CMS

Another good open source CMS on the Java platform is Magnolia (`http://www.magnolia-cms.com/`). This CMS supports management of different configurations and revisions, inline editing, development of apps, support for user-generated content, and concurrent collaboration editing. It also has facility classes for JBPM workflow integration and writing of code with Groovy.

In this case, the Solr integration is enabled by a module (`http://wiki.magnolia-cms.com/display/WIKI/Magnolia+Apache+Solr+integration`) that adds not only full-text search but also spellchecking and access-controlled search based on metadata. Magnolia also extends these features with article categorizations, support for Dublin core metadata, and **Digital Asset Management** (**DAM**) capabilities as well as a standard **Content Management Interoperability Services** (**CMIS**) interface at `http://www.magnolia-cms.com/product/features/digital-asset-management.html`.

Alfresco DMS and CMS

Alfresco is an open source **Document Management System** (**DMS**) that also offers modules for CMS, CMIS integration, team collaboration, design of document workflow with activities, office, or GoogleDocs integration, multiscripting, and much more. For a complete list of features, you can refer to the official site: `http://www.alfresco.com/`.

The Solr integration module is based on an internal local Solr web application (`http://wiki.alfresco.com/wiki/Alfresco_And_SOLR#Configuring_the_Solr_web_app`), which is fully functional and integrated with Alfresco's advanced structured content handling with metadata **Catalog and Archive Support** (**CAS**).

Liferay

Liferay is an open source web portal (`http://www.liferay.com/products/liferay-portal/features/portal`) based on a **service oriented architecture**. The platform is open source, and it is possible to write new components, modules, and portlets on top of the existing services. There is already a CMS module, and the Solr integration is provided as an app (`http://www.liferay.com/it/marketplace/-/mp/application/15193648`), which, once installed, is accessible as a Liferay service.

Broadleaf

Broadleaf is an open source, e-commerce CMS that is built on top of a technology stack that includes Spring, Maven, Google web toolkit, and Thymeleaf for writing the templates easily. Solr is integrated not only to provide full-text searches over the description of articles, but also an easy customization of per-category facets.

You can find more information on the official site: `http://www.broadleafcommerce.org/`.

Apache Jena

Apache Jena (`http://jena.apache.org/`) is an open source Java framework for handling RDF data and building linked data and semantic web applications. It provides integrations with other frameworks and triple stores, and it is internally divided in modules for storing data (TDB triple store), exposing the SPARQL end point (ARQ and Fuseki), and parsing RDF or OWL. There also exists an Solr integration for full-text search into the SPARQL queries at `http://jena.apache.org/documentation/query/text-query.html`.

Solr Groovy or the Grails plugin

Solr can be easily handled by Groovy, and there also exists a Grails plugin (`http://www.grails.org/plugin/solr`) built on top of the SolrJ library, and it is installable directly from the Grails command line.

Solr scala

With the Scala language, it is possible to use the SolrJ library directly, and there also exist some different third-party implementations, such as the solr-scala-client (`https://github.com/takezoe/solr-scala-client`) or the excellent Solr DSL for the spray.io web framework (`http://bathtor.github.io/spray-solr/api/index.html#spray.solr.package`) that exposes the Solr service as an actor-based asynchronous service with the Akka framework (`http://akka.io/`). Note how it is possible to access this actor-based, full-text service from any web framework based on Akka.

Spring data

If you use the popular spring framework (or the project built on top of spring, as some of the previous ones) you should look at the spring-data module. A good place to start using it could be the excellent tutorial by *Petri Kainulainen* at `http://www.petrikainulainen.net/programming/solr/spring-data-solr-tutorial-configuration/`. This library greatly simplifies the interaction with NoSQL databases and MapReduce frameworks, and offers a simple object-oriented access on relational databases, integrating Solr capabilities on the mapped object.

You can find a more detailed description of all the possible integrations supported on this site: `http://projects.spring.io/spring-data/`.

Writing Solr clients and integrations outside JVM

Writing code using a language supported by some interpreter that runs on the virtual machine simplifies things, as we can re-use the existing Java API directly. Most of the clients are written using "external" languages that then need to construct some wrapping layer over the HTTP protocol. This is interesting because the general approach is to try to reproduce the internal structure of the response, adding some object-oriented design and some facility class or syntactic sugar, when the language permits it. A practical example would be consuming JSON output.

The first place to start if you want to write your own client for interacting with Solr is generally writing some code to send parametric queries and consume results in XML or JSON. Constructing a request generally requires some simple composition of strings (for creating the correct URL request format) and some function calls to perform the HTTP request in itself. Consuming results can be simplified using some XML parser or DOM implementation for handling results, which is generally available for most programming languages. However, most of the languages are nowadays also offering support for a kind of direct binding to JSON due to its diffusion and simplicity.

For example, let's look at the following simple skeleton example in PHP:

```
$url = "http://localhost:8983/solr/paintings/select?q=*:*&rows=0&facet=on
&facet.field="+field_name+"&wt=json&json.nl=map";
$content = file_get_contents($url);
if($content) $result = json_decode($content,true);
// handle results as an array...
```

In JavaScript, using jQuery style for simplicity, the preceding code looks as follows:

```
var url = "http://localhost:8983/solr/paintings/select?q=*:*&rows=0&facet
=on&facet.field="+field_name+"&wt=json&json.nl=map";
$.getJSON(url, function(data) {
  var facets = data.facet_counts.facet_fields[field_name];
  for(f in facets){
    // handle facet f
  }
});
```

Note how both these snippets construct the URL with string concatenation, and in both cases the JSON result can be parsed directly as a structured object that is generally an associative array (the specific type will depend on the language used), which is similar to the `NamedList` object in the Solr API. Approximately the same can be easily done in Groovy, Scala, Python, or the language that you prefer by using a third-party implementation of JSON at `http://www.json.org/`.

On the other hand, the XML format will probably remain the best choice if you need validation over a schema, or, for example, if you want to continue using libraries that already support it for the persistence layer.

> Also note how the JavaBin serialization can be an interesting alternative format. This is intuitively useful while using a Java (or JVM compliant, via BSF) client, but there can be alternative implementations written directly using other languages to marshal the objects.
>
> A brief introduction to the JavaBin marshalling is found on wiki: `http://wiki.apache.org/solr/javabin`, that also contains a two-liner example in Java.

The existing third-party clients for Solr, however, encapsulate the HTTP level as well as the parsing of a JSON or XML result. This way, they can offer a more appropriate object-oriented design to expose a simplifier and natural access to data.

JavaScript

The most interesting language to start with while searching for a Solr client is probably JavaScript, as it permits us to consume the Solr services directly into some kind of HTML visualization, if we need it. It is useful on the server side too if you plan to use server-side JavaScript interpreters, for example, Node.js. We already saw how it is possible to use JavaScript to consume a Solr Java object internally in an update workflow, or externally by calling the code from Java. And if we plan to use JavaScript to directly parse the XML or JSON results of some query and to construct queries too, we can do both from the client and the server side in pretty much the same way as with every service exposed on the Web, for example, the Twitter API.

Taking a glance at ajax-solr, solrstrap, facetview, and jcloud

If you look for some more structured libraries built on top of JavaScript, and are aware of the Solr services format, you can take a look at facetviews by Open Knowledge foundation (`http://okfnlabs.org/facetview/`) that supports both Solr and ElasticSearch, and ajax-solr by Evolving Web (`https://github.com/evolvingweb/ajax-solr`). The latter is the most known and mature HTML/JavaScript frontend for Solr, and I strongly suggest you have a look at it for your prototypes. You can easily start following the very good tutorial (`https://github.com/evolvingweb/ajax-solr/wiki/reuters-tutorial`) that will help you construct the same interface you can see in the demo (`http://evolvingweb.github.io/ajax-solr/examples/reuters/index.html`). The entire library is conceived to help you construct a Solr frontend with HTML and JavaScript, but you can, of course, use only the JavaScript part, if you plan to use it only for parsing data from / and to Solr. I have not done any tests of this, but it can be a good experimentation to do on the server side, for example, with node.js.

I have created a simple frontend for our own application that you can find in the `/SolrStarterBook/test/chp06/html` folder, just to give you a simple and (I hope) useful starting point. In the same directory, you will find a basic Solrstrap interface. **jcloud** is not directly designed for Solr, but I found it useful to create a funny tag cloud on the facets provided by Solr. The number of hits can be used to generate variance in the color and size of a term, for example, as in the following example named `wordcloud.html`:

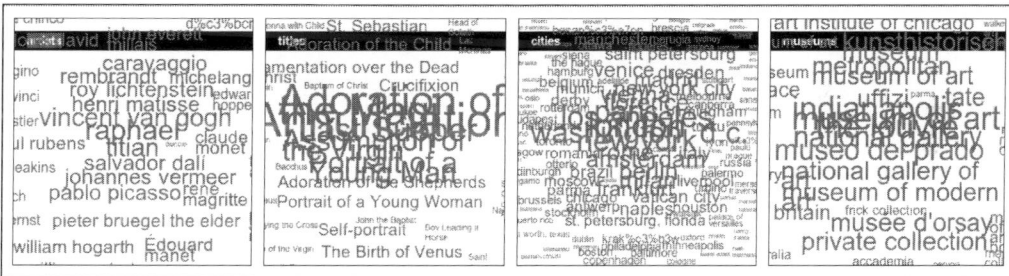

The core code for the example in the preceding screenshot by an essential custom JavaScript that uses the jcloud and jQuery libraries is as follows:

```
function view(field_name, min, limit, invert){
  var url = "http://localhost:8983/solr/arts/select?q=*:*...&wt=json";
  $.getJSON(url, function(data) {
  var facets = data.facet_counts.facet_fields[field_name];
    var words = [];
  for(f in facets){
    search_link = "http://.../arts/select?q="+field_
name+":"+f+"&wt=json";
    w = {
```

```
        text: normalize(f),
        weight: Math.log(facets[f]*0.01),
        html: {title: "search for \""+f+"\" ("+facets[f]+" documents)"},
        link: search_link
      },
      words.push(w);
    }
    $("#"+field_name).jQCloud(words);
  });
  }
  view("artist_entity", 3, 100);
  ...
```

Note how the last line is simply a parameter call to the `view()` function. This function is internally and conceptually very similar to the structures of the code suggested before for handling facets. For every field used as a facet, the HTML part is prepared and then added to the corresponding box.

As you can imagine, the placeholder on which the data will be injected by the library is really simple:

```
<section id="artist_entity" class="wordcloud"><h1>artists</h1></
section>
```

The idea behind many JavaScript libraries is to add the data formatted by a specific template with asynchronous calls at runtime.

Solrstrap is a recent project, and aims to provide an automatic creation of faceting, built on top of an HTML5 one-page template with Boostrap, so that you only have to configure a few parameters in the companion JavaScript file. I have created a small, two-minute `solrstrap.html` example if you want to look at the code. The example will let you navigate through the data that is similar to the one shown in the following screenshot:

Looking at the following snippet of code, you will get an idea on the kind of configurations needed at the beginning of the JavaScript code:

```
var SERVERROOT = 'http://localhost:8983/solr/paintings/select/';
var HITTITLE = 'title';
```

```
var HITBODY = 'abstract';
var HITSPERPAGE = 20;
var FACETS = ['artist_entity','city_entity','museum_entity'];
...
var FACETS_TITLES = {'topics': 'subjects', 'city_entity':'cities',
'museum_entity':'museums', 'artist_entity':'artists'};
```

For the HTML part, we will look at how the facets column template is created:

```
<script type="text/x-handlebars-template" id="nav-template">
  <div class="facet">
    <span class="nav-title" data-facetname="{{title}}">{{facet_
displayname title}}</span><br>
    {{#each navs}}
      <a href='#' title='{{@key}} ({{this}})'>{{@key}}</a>
({{this}})<br/>
    {{/each}}
  </div>
</script>
```

Also note how the code extracted from the HTML view is actually produced by a template written in JavaScript, so that it needs some reading before using it.

And finally, **ajax-solr** is the most structured library and has a modular design. There exists a main module that acts as an observer for Solr results, and you can plug into it some other specific module (they are called Widgets, thinking in the HTML direction) for handling suggestions while typing based on prefixed facets query, geospatial filters, or again, paged results.

We already saw what a simple example would look like. The following screenshot depicts it:

This library will require more working on the code in order to customize the behavior of different modules. The HTML placeholders will be very simple as usual:

```
<div class="tagcloud" id="artist_entity"></div>
```

A simplified version of the custom code required to use the different modules is similar to the following code:

```
// require.config(...);
var Manager = new AjaxSolr.Manager({
  solrUrl : 'http://localhost:8983/solr/arts/'
});
Manager.addWidget(new AjaxSolr.ResultWidget({
id : 'result',
  target : '#docs'
}));

var fields = [ 'museum_entity', 'artist_entity', 'city_entity' ];
for ( var i = 0, l = fields.length; i < l; i++) {
  Manager.addWidget(new AjaxSolr.TagcloudWidget({
    id : fields[i],
    target : '#' + fields[i],
    field : fields[i]
  }));
}

Manager.init();
Manager.store.addByValue('q', '*:*');
var params = {
  facet : true,
  'facet.field' : [ 'museum_entity', 'artist_entity',    'city_entity'
],
  'facet.limit' : 20,
  'facet.mincount' : 1,
  'f.city_entity.facet.limit' : 10,
  'json.nl' : 'map'
};
for (var name in params) {
  Manager.store.addByValue(name, params[name]);
}
Manager.doRequest();
```

As you can see in the preceding code, the main observer is the `Manager` object, which handles the current state of the navigation/search actions. The manager will store the parameters used inside a specific object (`Manager.store`), and will have methods for initializing and performing the query (`Manager.init()`, `Manager.doRequest()`). All the modules are handled by a specific widget, for example the `TagCloudWidget` object is registered for every field used as a facet. All the modules will be registered in the `Manager` object itself. In the example, we saw the `TagCloudWidget` and the `ResultWidget` classes, but there are others as well that are omitted for simplicity. The `include` statements for the various modules are handled in this case by the RequireJS library.

All these libraries adopt the jQuery convention, so it's really easy to bind their behavior to their HTML counterpart elements.

Ruby

Solr provides a Ruby response format: `http://wiki.apache.org/solr/Ruby%20 Response%20Format`. This is an extension of the JSON output, which is slightly adapted to be parsed correctly from Ruby.

However, if you want to use a more object-oriented client, there are some different options, and the most interesting one is probably Sunspot (`http://sunspot.github.io/`) which extends the Rsolr library with a DSL for handling Solr objects and services.

Sunspot permits you to index a Solr document with an ActiveRecords standard approach, and it's easy to plug it into an ORM system that is not even based on a database (for example, it can be used with filesystem objects with little code).

Python

As for Ruby, there exists a Solr Python response, which is designed by extending the default JSON format: `http://wiki.apache.org/solr/SolPython`.

Sunburnt (`http://opensource.timetric.com/sunburnt/index.html`) is a good option if you want all the basic functionalities, and you can install it directly, for example, by using pip.

C# and .NET

If you want to connect with Solr from a .NET application, you can look at SolrNET `https://github.com/mausch/SolrNet`. This library offers schema validation and a Fluent API that is easy to start from.

There is also a sample web application (`https://github.com/mausch/SolrNet/blob/master/Documentation/Sample-application.md`) that can be used as a starting reference for understanding how to use the basic features.

PHP

PHP is one of the most widely adopted languages for web development, and there exist several applications for frontends and CMS, as well as several popular web frameworks built with it. Solr has a PHP response format that exposes results in the usual serialization format that PHP uses for arrays, simplifying the parsing of the results.

There is also an available PECL module: `http://php.net/manual/en/book.solr.php`, which can be easily adopted in any site or web application development to communicate to an existing Solr instance. This module is an object-oriented library that is designed to map most of the Solr concepts as well as the independent, third-party library Solarium (`http://www.solarium-project.org/`).

Drupal

Drupal is a widely adopted open search CMS built with a modular, power platform that permits content-type creation and management. It has been adopted for building some of the biggest portals on the Web, such as The Examiner (`http://www.examiner.com/`) or the White House (`http://www.whitehouse.gov/`) sites. When the existing Apache Solr plugin (`https://drupal.org/project/apachesolr`) is enabled and correctly configured, it is possible to search over the contents and use faceted search with taxonomies.

There is also a Search API Solr search module (`https://drupal.org/project/search_api_solr`), which actually shares default `schema.xml` or `solrconfig.xml` files with ApacheSolr. Since Drupal 8, it's possible to merge the two approaches into a single effort.

WordPress

If you are using WordPress (`http://wordpress.org/`) for building your site, or if you are using it as a CMS for adopting a combination of modules, you should know that it is possible to replace the internal default search with an advanced search module (`http://wordpress.org/plugins/advanced-search-by-my-solr-server/`) that is able to communicate with an existing Solr instance.

Magento e-commerce

Magento is a very popular e-commerce platform (`http://www.magentocommerce.com/`), built in PHP on top of the excellent Zend framework. It exists in different editions, from open source to commercial, and it offers a module for Solr that can be easily configured (`http://www.magentocommerce.com/knowledge-base/entry/how-to-use-the-solr-search-engine-with-magento-enterprise-edition`) to add full-text and faceted navigation over the products catalog.

Platforms for analyzing, manipulating, and enhancing text

There are also a few platforms that should be cited in this list, as they are designed to use Solr for document indexing, rich full-text search, or as a step in the content-enhancement process. It is important to notice that the internal workflow that we have seen in action in the update chain is one of the most discussed features for future improvements. In particular, there exist some different hypotheses for improving the update chain (`http://www.slideshare.net/janhoy/improving-the-solr-update-chain`), adopting a configurable and general-purpose document-processing pipeline.

Hydra

Hydra is a document-processing pipeline (`http://findwise.github.io/Hydra/`), and is useful for improving the quality of the data extracted from free text, and then to send it to Solr.

UIMA

Apache's **Unstructured Information Management applications** (**UIMA**), `http://uima.apache.org/`) is a framework for information-extraction from text, providing capabilities for language detection, sentence segmentation, part of speech tagging, Named Entity extraction, and more. We already know that UIMA can be integrated into an update processor chain in Solr, but it's also possible to move in the opposite direction, by integrating Solr as a UIMA CAS component (`http://uima.apache.org/sandbox.html#solrcas.consumer`).

Apache Stanbol

Apache Stanbol is a platform designed to provide a set of components for semantic content management (`http://stanbol.apache.org/`). The platform offers content enhancement for textual content, reasoning over the augmented semantic contents, manipulation of knowledge models, and persistence of the augmented data.

A typical scenario would involve, for example, the indexing of a controlled vocabulary or authority file, the creation of a Solr index that can be plugged as one of the platform processors into an internal enhancement chain, and exposing the annotations of recognized, named entities by a specific RESTful service.

One of the main objectives of Stanbol services is providing semantic enhancements by recognizing and annotating the named entities for CMS contents. For example, WordLift (`http://wordlift.it/`) is a WordPress plugin that can be used within a common WordPress installation, helping us to add annotations for connecting our contents on the linked data cloud.

Carrot2

Carrot2 (`http://project.carrot2.org/`) is a document-clustering platform. It provides the Java API for embedding the engine into a Java application, a server that exposes REST services, and a standalone web application. We have yet used the latter for a visual exploration of the Solr results cluster. This can also be very useful for analyzing our data collection and identifying critical aspects that may require some different configuration.

VuFind

Vufind (`http://vufind.org/downloads.php`) is an open platform for **OPAC (Online Public Access Catalog)**, which internally includes an Solr local installation (SolrMARC, with support for MARC and OAI formats), while the web interface is mostly written in PHP.

If you are interested in handling OPAC or a similar use case, there is an old but interesting case study: `http://infomotions.com/blog/2009/01/fun-with-webservicesolr-part-i-of-iii/` that explains how to use an OAI metadata harvester and index the metadata on Solr using Perl. I also suggest reading the very interesting *How to Implement A Virtual Booksheld with Solr*, by *Naomi Dushay* and *Jessie Keck* (`http://www.stanford.edu/~ndushay/code4lib2010/stanford_virtual_shelf.pdf`).

Pop quiz

Q1. How can we write custom client code to talk to Solr?

1.   We can write a new library with almost all the languages, wrapping the HTTP calls

2.   We can use the SolrJ library, using Java or another JVM-supported language

3.   We cannot use external libraries to communicate with Solr

Q2. What are the differences between an embedded Solr instance and a remote one?

1.   If using SolrJ we can use the same API in both cases

2.   A remote Solr instance needs to use external libraries to talk to the Solr instance on which the data is stored

3.   An embedded Solr instance wraps the reference to a core on the same virtual machine, while the HTTP instance wraps a core on a remote virtual machine, hiding the HTTP calls

Q3. Using the Bean Scripting Framework from Apache we can use the SolrJ library with other programming languages. Is that true?

1.   Yes, we can write our client with every language, using SolrJ and BSF

2.   Yes, we can write our client using SolrJ, BSF, and every language which is supported on BSF

3.   No, while we can write custom code to communicate with Solr via HTTP with every language, BSF currently supports only JavaScript

Summary

This chapter is a gentle introduction to clients and integrations with Solr. Instead of looking in detail at each of the many existing projects, we simply cite only some of the most used solutions. This list should not be considered complete, as there exist many other libraries and projects.

Starting from the idea collected for performing queries with cURL, and again using the same API introduced for the examples in *Chapter 9, Introducing Customizations*, we saw how to start writing custom code for our clients.

We also cited some different libraries for specific tasks or languages that can be useful for you to save time.

Pop Quiz Answers

Chapter 1, Getting Ready with the Essentials

Pop quiz

Q1	1	True
	2	False: While Solr can be integrated with Nutch or other similar tools for web crawling, it does not provide direct site indexing by itself at the moment. It is possible to use the DataImportHandler facility to obtain a limited capability of indexing remote URL, however.
	3	True
Q2	1	True: This query will return a list of documents matching all the fields on all the terms.
	2	False: This query will return a list of documents matching all the fields named 'documents', on all the terms. Note that a 'documents' fields does not exists in our example.
	3	False: This query will search over all the fields for matching on the term 'all'. Note that you cannot use a "match-all" approach on fields, while providing a value for term matching, or you will obtain an error.
Q3	1	False: Solr can be deployed as a WAR inside other standard JEE container, even if Jetty is the suggested container.
	2	False: See the previous answer.
	3	True: Solr is deployed as a standard Java web Application, by publishing its expanded webroot directory, or by zipping it into a WAR file. The suggested method for a Solr installation is, however, to use the standard Jetty container, and configure it directly.

Q4	1	False: cURL can be used also to send data over HTTP, not only to receive data.
	2	True: cURL can be used to send and receive data over HTTP, using standard HTTP methods and also always receiving responses from the remote server.
	3	False: cURL can not only be used for sending data but also to receive data.
Q5	1	True
	2	False: While it's possible to index database data with Solr, it will expose data on a new service, without a direct interference with the original database.
	3	True: Solr can be used as a remote service, it can be wrapped with SolrJ for remote querying, and it can also be used as an embedded Framework, using SolrJ.

Chapter 2, Indexing with Local PDF Files

Pop quiz

Q1	1	False
	2	False
	3	True
Q2	1	False: You can, for example, put values from an administrative metadata in a stored field in order to have them saved and returned in the results, without actually the need to perform searches on them.
	2	True: This is the reason why we decide to use an indexed field.
	3	False: A field must be stored to be returned in the results.
Q3	1	False: This query will simply delete every document.
	2	False: The syntax is not correct.
	3	True: This is the correct syntax.
Q4	1	False: This particular codec only partially uses binary format, and it exposes most of the data in plain text.
	2	True: Looking at the plain text structure saved, we can recognize the internal structure of an inverted index, and make an idea of how it's made.
	3	True: The values are saved as plain text, so they are easy to read.

Q5	1	False: The files saved reflects the changes in the index.
	2	False: What we mean to be "a word" can be composed by one or more tokens, depending on the chosen text analysis chain. Every token will be saved as a single term.
	3	True: Every term will be saved and updated with its reference.
Q6	1	True: The number of segments should vary depending on the action you do on the index. Note that in some circumstances, imagine for example you ask to clean an already empty index, the number of segments will not vary at all, but if you look at the time of last modification, you'll easily see that the files are updated as well.
	2	False: Even while cleaning an index, not all segments files are deleted: there will be always at least one file which represents a created index.
	3	False: See the previous answers. Furthermore, the core/data folder can contain other files needed for specific components, such as compiled dictionary for spell checking.
Q7	1	True
	2	True
	3	False: It is partially true, as we can use DataImportHandler and connect it to a specific handler, but we will change the configuration for the DataImportHandler itself, and not for an update handler.
Q8	1	True
	2	False: We can use the Tika configurations.
	3	False: We can change the configurations, but we can also send the added metadata by appending a parameter in the URL.

Chapter 3, Indexing Example Data from DBpedia – Paintings

Pop quiz

Q1	1	False: It can be used when one needs to post a large amount of documents, but it's not a method for posting, it's a method to trigger commits.
	2	True: It an be used to trigger a commit after a certain number of documents have been posted to Solr.
	3	True: It can be used to trigger a commit after a certain time has passed.

Q2	1	False
	2	True
	3	True
Q3	1	False
	2	False
	3	True
Q4	1	False
	2	False
	3	True

Chapter 4, Searching the Example Data

Pop quiz

Q1	1	True
	2	False: Rows represents the number of rows to return, so as `start` is the first index, then `start+rows` is the last.
	3	False
Q2	1	True
	2	False: Wildcard searches are designed for searching over incomplete words.
	3	False: As the names says, phrase search is designed to work with sequences of words.
Q3	1	True
	2	False
Q4	1	False
	2	False
	3	True
Q5	1	True: While designed to work mostly with misspelled terms, fuzzy search uses the concept of distance. By this metrics there can be case where incomplete terms are matched, it depends on the confidence value.
	2	True: This is the common method for this kind of queries.
	3	False: However, it can be true, if we consider the particular case of a single term phrase query.

Q6	1	True: By this way we can search for an exact sequence of words or subsequences, with proximity searches.
	2	True: This is true, but there can be also other cases. For example it's possible to use phrase query for proximity search.
	3	False: This is only partially true, as multiple words can be searched also without using the double quotes. With double quotes the entire words' sequence is tested for a match.

Chapter 5, Extending Search

Pop quiz

Q1	1	False
	2	True
	3	False
Q2	1	False
	2	True
	3	False
Q3	1	True
	2	True
	3	False: While it's true that there are specific parameters, the standard Lucene parameters are used in a more, less restrictive and more flexible way.
Q4	1	False: Pseudo-fields does not represent any actual field.
	2	True: Pseudo-fields syntax can be used to calculate a single value with a specific function, at runtime.
	3	True: Pseudo-field syntax can be used at runtime to represent a single value.
Q5	1	True: It's possible to boost the score of a document, obtaining it on top of the results list.
	2	False: While it's possible to construct similar user interfaces, Solr does not provide this feature at the moment.
	3	False: The document does not change with boosting, and boosting can be easily changed for a specific query execution.

Chapter 6, Using Faceted Search – from Searching to Finding

Pop quiz

Q1	1	False
	2	False
	3	True
Q2	1	False: But partially true, as when exposing the `subject_entity` field as a facet, we can recognize a facet for 'adoration of the magi', including the number of related documents.
	2	False: Using directly a value for matching a facet is not allowed.
	3	True: When we want to use a partial match on the value, for a facet, we can use the `facet.prefix`.
Q3	1	False
	2	False
	3	True
Q4	1	False: This is partially true, but we have to define more precisely what we mean by document similarity.
	2	False: This is again imprecise, as the concept of similar terms should be defined over a specific context.
	3	True
Q5	1	False
	2	True
	3	True

Chapter 7, Working with Multiple Entities, Multicores, and Distributed Search

Pop quiz

Q1	1	True
	2	False: While it can be used with Solr, ZooKepeer is not a component of Solr.
	3	False: Zookeeper does not provide data synchronization; it only synchronize configurations.
Q2	1	False: Two shards does not necessarily contains the same values
	2	True
	3	False
Q3	1	True
	2	False
Q4	1	False
	2	True
	3	True: While this is not exactly true, as Carrot2 is not a visualization tool but a clustering, it provides also some good visualizations.
Q5	1	False
	2	False
	3	True

Chapter 8, Indexing External Data sources

Pop quiz

Q1	1	True
	2	False: The DataImportHandler includes more than one single component.
	3	False: This is possible, but it's only one of the possible options.
Q2	1	True
	2	False

Q3	1	False: The schema does not necessarily define all the fields.
	2	False: This is not entirely true, as we can also index fields which are not explicitly defined in the schema, using dynamic fields.
	3	True
Q4	1	False: This is partially true, if we consider that a Map is used, but false if we think about the fields emitted and the type of different data they will contain.
	2	False: The rows are handled one by one, but there can be more than one.
	3	True
Q5	1	True
	2	False

Chapter 9, Introducing Customizations

Pop quiz

Q1	1	False
	2	False: This is only partially true in a certain specific case. As a general case a stem is used only on simple, not compound words.
	3	True
Q2	1	True
	2	False
	3	False: Note that the most simpler NER will recognize entities by exact match, but we can define our own strategy to obtain a more flexible recognition, for example querying on a suggester with some confidence.
Q3	1	False: The interfaces does not provide in itself any way to load resources or core instances.
	2	True
	3	False: The main focus is on obtaining results, but we can also write a new component which writes new values.
Q4	1	True
	2	False
	3	False

Appendix, Solr Clients and Integrations

Pop quiz

Q1	1	True
	2	True
	3	False
Q2	1	True: This will let us use for example a local instance for faster prototypes, and then create a well configured instance to be used remotely.
	2	False: This is not correct, since SolrJ it's all we need to talk to a remote Solr instance. However, SolrJ internally uses the Apache HTTPClient library for a transparent HTTP support.
	3	True
Q3	1	False: Not every language is supported by BSF, thus breaking the compatibility with SolrJ.
	2	True
	3	False: There are many other languages supported. However, this is currently true for the default Java Scripting Engine implementation and Apache BSF is the de facto standard at the moment.

Index

D

E

F

G

geolocalization
about 134
providing 134, 135
repository of cities, creating 135-137
spatial search 137
getLimitingFacets() method 271
getResults() method 268
Google Maps API 135
Guardian
URL 20

H

hierarchical facet (pivot)
using 169, 170
HTTP parameters
testing, on browsers 89
Hydra
about 283
URL 283

I

IndexBasedSpellChecker 143
index prototype, creating from PDF
about 42
core, testing 44
fulltext field, defining 45
schema.xml file, defining with only dynamic
fields 42
simple solrconfig.xml file, writing with update
handler 43, 44
text, extracting from PDF using cURL 48
text, extracting from PDF using Tika 46
Information architecture (IA) 155
inform() method 248
Instagram
URL 20
installation, Java 12
installation, Solr 12, 13
inverted index
about 52
optimization affects 53
structure 52

J

Jahia CMS
about 272
URL 272
Java
downloading 12
installing 12
JavaBin marshalling
reference link 276
Java installation
working with 11
JavaScript
about 276
ajax-solr library 277
facetview 277
jcloud library 277
solrstrap library 277
Java Virtual Machine (JVM) 12
jcloud 277
jqcloud
URL 153
Json
about 68
URL 68
JSON
URL 276
JTS (Java Topology Suite) libraries 138

K

KeywordTorkenizer 76

L

langid.langField=languages parameter 243
language analysis
testing, with JUnit and Scala 246, 247
languages
detecting, with Tika and LangDetect 242, 243
legacy solr.xml format
example document, defining 34, 35
example document, indexing with cURL 35-37
new core, starting 32
simple schema.xml file, writing 29, 30
simple solrconfig.xml file, writing 28, 29

[PACKT] PUBLISHING open source*
community experience distilled

Thank you for buying
Apache Solr Beginner's Guide

About Packt Publishing

Packt, pronounced 'packed', published its first book "*Mastering phpMyAdmin for Effective MySQL Management*" in April 2004 and subsequently continued to specialize in publishing highly focused books on specific technologies and solutions.

Our books and publications share the experiences of your fellow IT professionals in adapting and customizing today's systems, applications, and frameworks. Our solution based books give you the knowledge and power to customize the software and technologies you're using to get the job done. Packt books are more specific and less general than the IT books you have seen in the past. Our unique business model allows us to bring you more focused information, giving you more of what you need to know, and less of what you don't.

Packt is a modern, yet unique publishing company, which focuses on producing quality, cutting-edge books for communities of developers, administrators, and newbies alike. For more information, please visit our website: www.packtpub.com.

About Packt Open Source

In 2010, Packt launched two new brands, Packt Open Source and Packt Enterprise, in order to continue its focus on specialization. This book is part of the Packt Open Source brand, home to books published on software built around Open Source licences, and offering information to anybody from advanced developers to budding web designers. The Open Source brand also runs Packt's Open Source Royalty Scheme, by which Packt gives a royalty to each Open Source project about whose software a book is sold.

Writing for Packt

We welcome all inquiries from people who are interested in authoring. Book proposals should be sent to author@packtpub.com. If your book idea is still at an early stage and you would like to discuss it first before writing a formal book proposal, contact us; one of our commissioning editors will get in touch with you.

We're not just looking for published authors; if you have strong technical skills but no writing experience, our experienced editors can help you develop a writing career, or simply get some additional reward for your expertise.

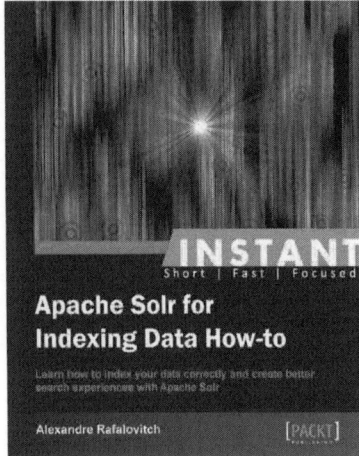

Instant Apache Solr for Indexing Data How-to

ISBN: 978-1-78216-484-5   Paperback: 90 pages

Learn how to index your data correctly and create better search experiences with Apache Solr

1. Learn something new in an Instant! A short, fast, focused guide delivering immediate results

2. Take the most basic schema and extend it to support multi-lingual, multi-field searches

3. Make Solr pull data from a variety of existing sources

4. Discover different pathways to acquire and normalize data and content

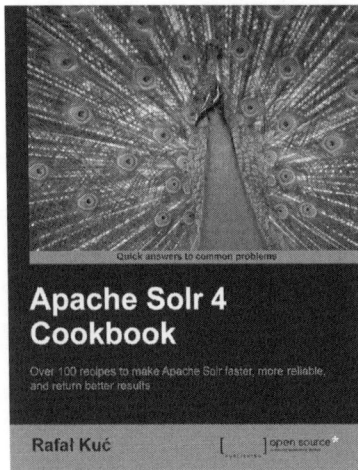

Apache Solr 4 Cookbook

ISBN: 978-1-78216-132-5   Paperback: 328 pages

Over 100 recipes to make Apache Solr faster, more reliable, and return better results

1. Learn how to make Apache Solr search faster, more complete, and comprehensively scalable

2. Solve performance, setup, configuration, analysis, and query problems in no time

3. Get to grips with, and master, the new exciting features of Apache Solr 4

Please check **www.PacktPub.com** for information on our titles

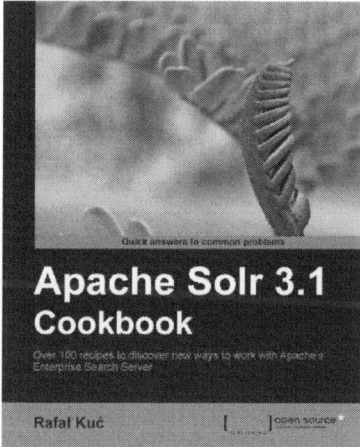

Apache Solr 3.1 Cookbook

ISBN: 978-1-84951-218-3   Paperback: 300 pages

Over 100 recipes to discover new ways to work with Apache's Enterprise Search Server

1. Improve the way in which you work with Apache Solr to make your search engine quicker and more effective

2. Deal with performance, setup, and configuration problems in no time

3. Discover little-known Solr functionalities and create your own modules to customize Solr to your company's needs

4. Part of Packt's Cookbook series; each chapter covers a different aspect of working with Solr

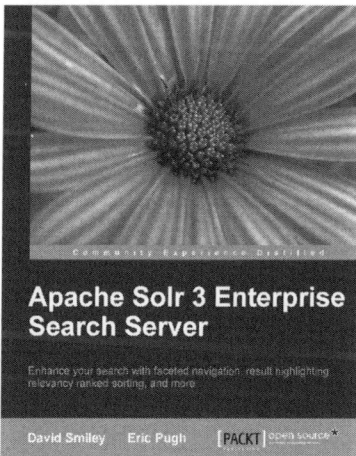

Apache Solr 3 Enterprise Search Server

ISBN: 978-1-849516-06-8   Paperback: 418 pages

Enhance your search with faceted navigation, result highlighting, relevancy ranked sorting, and more

1. Comprehensive information on Apache Solr 3 with examples and tips so you can focus on the important parts

2. Integration examples with databases, web-crawlers, XSLT, Java & embedded-Solr, PHP & Drupal, JavaScript, Ruby frameworks

3. Advice on data modeling, deployment considerations to include security, logging, and monitoring, and advice on scaling Solr and measuring performance

Please check **www.PacktPub.com** for information on our titles

Printed in Poland
by Amazon Fulfillment
Poland Sp. z o.o., Wrocław